SHAKESPEARE AND SEXUALITY

This volume draws together ten essays of interest to students, scholars and Shakespeare enthusiasts which use a variety of approaches and materials to explore the significance of sexuality in Shakespeare's work. Some consider the erotic effect of Shakespeare's language in his use of metaphor and the transgressive riddle and pun. Others are concerned with expressions of desire (male, female, inter-racial, homosexual and heterosexual) in performance as well as text. A radical re-reading of Shakespeare's Sonnets shifts the sexual focus from a male lover to a black woman. The essays, many of which are reprinted from *Shakespeare Survey*, are introduced by Ann Thompson's freshly considered survey of the topic in recent criticism, and conclude with a new account by Celia Daileader of nudity in Shakespeare films.

CATHERINE M. S. ALEXANDER is Lecturer in Shakespeare Studies, Shakespeare Centre, Stratford-upon-Avon and Research Fellow, University of Birmingham. She has written on eighteenth-century appropriations of Shakespeare and is the co-editor with Stanley Wells of *Shakespeare and Race* (Cambridge, 2000).

STANLEY WELLS is Emeritus Professor, University of Birmingham and Chairman of the Shakespeare Birthplace Trust. He is General Editor of the Oxford Shakespeare, co-author of *William Shakespeare: A Textual Companion* (1987), author of *Shakespeare: A Dramatic Life* (1995), co-editor with Catherine M. S. Alexander of *Shakespeare and Race* (Cambridge, 2000) and co-editor with Margreta de Grazia of *The Cambridge Companion to Shakespeare* (Cambridge, 2001).

SHAKESPEARE AND SEXUALITY

EDITED BY
CATHERINE M. S. ALEXANDER
STANLEY WELLS

CAMBRIDGE
UNIVERSITY PRESS

PUBLISHED BY THE PRESS SYNDICATE OF THE UNIVERSITY OF CAMBRIDGE
The Pitt Building, Trumpington Street, Cambridge, United Kingdom

CAMBRIDGE UNIVERSITY PRESS
The Edinburgh Building, Cambridge CB2 2RU, UK
40 West 20th Street, New York, NY 10011-4211, USA
10 Stamford Road, Oakleigh, VIC 3166, Australia
Ruiz de Alarcón 13, 28014 Madrid, Spain
Dock House, The Waterfront, Cape Town 8001, South Africa

http://www.cambridge.org

First published 2001

Printed in the United Kingdom at the University Press, Cambridge

Typeface Baskerville Monotype 11/12.5 pt.   *System* LaTeX 2ε   [TB]

A catalogue record for this book is available from the British Library.

Library of Congress Cataloguing in Publication data
Alexander, Catherine M. S.
Shakespeare and sexuality / Catherine M. S. Alexander, Stanley Wells.
p.   cm.
Includes bibliographical references and index.
ISBN 0 521 80031 5 (hardback) – ISBN 0 521 80475 2 (paperback)
1. Shakespeare, William, 1564–1616 – Views on sex.   2. Sex in literature.
I. Wells, Stanley W., 1930–   II. Title.
PR3069.S45 A44   2001   822.3'3 – dc21   2001025709

ISBN 0 521 80031 5 hardback
ISBN 0 521 80475 2 paperback

Contents

Contributors   *page* vii
Editors' note   ix

1   Shakespeare and sexuality   1
      Ann Thompson

2   Language and sexuality in Shakespeare   14
      William C. Carroll

3   Death and desire in Romeo and Juliet   35
      Lloyd Davis

4   The legacy of Juliet's desire in comedies of the early 1600s   52
      Mary Bly

5   Love in Venice   72
      Catherine Belsey

6   Male sexuality and misogyny   92
      Michael Hattaway

7   Consummation, custom and law in All's Well That
      Ends Well   116
      Subha Mukherji

8   The scandal of Shakespeare's Sonnets   146
      Margreta de Grazia

9   Representing sexuality in Shakespeare's plays   168
      John Russell Brown

10   Nude Shakespeare in film and nineties popular feminism   183
      Celia R. Daileader

Index   201

Contributors

CATHERINE BELSEY, University of Wales

MARY BLY, Fordham University, New York

JOHN RUSSELL BROWN, Middlesex University

WILLIAM C. CARROLL, Boston University

CELIA R. DAILEADER, University of Alabama

LLOYD DAVIS, University of Queensland

MARGRETA DE GRAZIA, University of Pennsylvania

MICHAEL HATTAWAY, University of Sheffield

SUBHA MUKHERJI, University of Leeds

ANN THOMPSON, King's College London

Editors' note

Shakespeare and Sexuality draws together ten important essays, written over the last decade, that use a variety of approaches and materials to explore the significance of sexuality in Shakespeare's work. The chapter by Celia R. Daileader has been specially commissioned, John Russell Brown's piece is reprinted from *New Theatre Quarterly*, and the remainder are reprinted from volumes of *Shakespeare Survey*. Some consider the erotic effect of Shakespeare's language in his use of metaphor and the transgressive riddle and pun. Others are concerned with expressions of desire (male, female, inter-racial, homosexual and heterosexual) in performance as well as text, and a radical re-reading of Shakespeare's Sonnets shifts the sexual focus from a male lover to a black woman.

Elizabethan legal and social history, sexual politics, and writing in a range of genres are used to inform the contemporary settings of the plays and the depiction – and often danger – of desire. Gender-generated theory and criticism interprets subsequent performance on stage and film.

An overview of the trends of the study of Shakespeare and Sexuality is provided in Ann Thompson's introductory essay on the current state of research and scholarship.

CATHERINE M. S. ALEXANDER
STANLEY WELLS

Shakespeare and sexuality

Ann Thompson

Sexuality must not be thought of as a kind of natural given which
power tries to hold in check, or as an obscure domain which knowledge tries gradually to uncover. It is the name that can be given to a
historical construct: not a furtive reality that is difficult to grasp, but
a great surface network in which the stimulation of bodies, the in-
tensification of pleasures, the incitement to discourse, the formation
of special knowledges, the strengthening of controls and resistances,
are linked to one another, in accordance with a few major strategies
of knowledge and power.

The history of sexuality supposes two ruptures if one tries to center
it on mechanisms of repression. The first, occurring in the course of
the seventeenth century, was characterized by the advent of the great
prohibitions, the exclusive promotion of adult marital sexuality, the
imperatives of decency, the obligatory concealment of the body,
the reduction to silence and mandatory reticences of language. The
second, a twentieth-century phenomenon, was really less a rupture
than an inflexion of the curve: this was the moment when the mechanisms of repression were seen as beginning to loosen their grip; one
passed from insistent sexual taboos to a relative tolerance with regard to prenuptial or extra-marital relations; the disqualification of
'perverts' diminished, their condemnation by law was in part eliminated; a good many of the taboos that weighed on the sexuality of
children were lifted.

Michel Foucault, The History of Sexuality, volume I (1976),
translated by Robert Hurley (Penguin, 1990),
pp. 105–6 and p. 115.

'Sexuality' is a fashionable and controversial topic today, not just in literary studies but throughout the whole range of the humanities and
social and behavioural sciences. It is both a new topic and an interdi-
sciplinary one. This is explicitly recognized by the University of Chicago
Press which publishes a periodical called the *Journal of the History of Sexuality*, which claims to cover relevant areas 'from incest to infanticide,

from breast-feeding and women's sexuality to female prostitution, from
pornography to reproductive politics, and from the first homosexual
rights movement to AIDS'. Advertising for the journal stresses the
marked increase in scholarship in the history of sexuality in the past
decade, and points out that publications have been widely scattered
across traditional subject boundaries in social, political and cultural studies. It is evident from the list of topics cited that this explosion of interest relates to the coming together of three current modes of academic
discourse: feminism, post-Freudian psychoanalysis, and homosexual or
gay studies. A modest amount of time spent browsing in any bookstore,
library or even publisher's catalogue will demonstrate how much work
is being done in all of these fields.

   In *Making Sex: Body and Gender from the Greeks to Freud*, Thomas Laqueur
claims that 'Sometime in the eighteenth century, sex as we know it was
invented',[1] but he argues that this 'invention' depended on the cultural
reorientation that went on during the Renaissance period when there
occurred a shift in perception from a one-sex model of humanity to
a two-sex model: that is, instead of seeing the female body as a lesser
(inverted) version of the male body, people began to see it as its incom-
mensurable opposite. The early modern period does seem to feature
heavily in histories of sexuality. As my second quotation from Foucault
suggests, our twentieth-century focus on sexuality can perhaps be seen
as a result of the loosening of the mechanisms of repression, while our
interest in the seventeenth century can be seen as an attempt to inves-
tigate the supposed point of the imposition of those mechanisms. The
strong influence of Foucault on literary critics (especially new historicists)
has made it seem inevitable that the debate about sexuality is conducted
primarily in terms of knowledge and power; despite Laqueur's investigation of the history of the disappearing female orgasm, it seems almost
quaint these days to associate sexuality with pleasure.

   Shakespeare studies have of course been affected by these debates.
'Shakespeare and Sexuality' was the topic of the twenty-fifth Interna-
tional Shakespeare conference at Stratford-upon-Avon in August 1992,
and this volume includes several of the papers delivered at the conference. It also includes relevant essays from other volumes of *Shakespeare
Survey* and other periodicals and two specially commissioned essays. A
great deal of further work in this area has been published since 1992
and it is not practicable to attempt a complete retrospect of such scholarship; rather, I propose to draw out what seem to me to be a number
of key concerns of the past two decades under some fairly broad general

headings: 'Feminism', 'Men in Feminism and Gay Studies', 'The Boy Actor and Performance Studies' and 'Language'.

FEMINISM

In the preface to *Making Sex* Thomas Laqueur says that he could not have written the book 'without the intellectual revolution wrought by feminism since World War II and especially during the last twenty years'. Certainly in Shakespeare studies there can be no doubt that feminist criticism has been enormously influential in putting issues of sexuality and sexual difference on to the critical agenda. In his 1991 annotated bibliography of *Shakespeare and Feminist Criticism*, Philip C. Kolin covers four hundred and thirty-nine items from the publication of Juliet Dusinberre's *Shakespeare and the Nature of Women* in 1975 to his cut-off point in 1988.[2] While all these books and essays could be seen to relate to the question of sexuality in the broadest sense, Kolin lists just thirty-eight items under 'sexuality (female)' in his subject index and eighteen under 'sexuality (male)', of which only thirteen are different from those listed under 'sexuality (female)'. A quite surprisingly high proportion of these, in fact about half, authored by both men and women, deal with the topic of male anxiety about female sexuality. Other topics which recur, but less frequently, are sexual stereotyping, sexuality (and sexism) in the reproduction and reading of Shakespeare, and ambivalence about male sexuality and the issue of homoeroticism.

The focus on male anxiety testifies to the prevalence of psychoanalytical approaches, especially in feminist criticism from North America. A strong tradition can be traced from *Representing Shakespeare: New Psychoanalytic Essays* edited by Murray M. Schwartz and Coppélia Kahn in 1980[3] through Kahn's own *Man's Estate: Masculine Identity in Shakespeare*,[4] Majorie Garber's *Coming of Age in Shakespeare*,[5] David Sundelson's *Shakespeare's Restoration of the Father*[6] and Kay Stockholder's *Dream Works: Lovers and Families in Shakespeare's Plays*[7] to Janet Adelman's *Suffocating Mothers*[8] and Valerie Traub's *Desire and Anxiety: Circulations of Sexuality in Shakespearean Drama*[9] (both published in 1992). At times earlier contributions to this approach have been attacked for exhibiting an ahistorical essentialism (see, for example, Kathleen McLuskie's essay 'The Patriarchal Bard: Feminist Criticism and Shakespeare: *King Lear* and *Measure for Measure*'),[10] but it has provided us with many valuable insights into Shakespeare's treatment of infantile sexuality, female relationships, the formation of sexual identity, male bonding, misogyny, the fear of cuckoldry and other related issues.

The subtitle of Valerie Traub's book, *Circulations of Sexuality in Shakespearean Drama*, is, as she explains, a deliberate allusion to Stephen Greenblatt's *Shakespearean Negotiations* which was subtitled *The Circulation of Social Energy in Renaissance England*.[11] Greenblatt's work in that book as well as in his earlier *Renaissance Self-Fashioning*[12] has been an important influence on all critics who have examined the issue of individual identity in the early modern period, but there has been some tension between feminist critics and new historicist critics with the former accusing the latter of treating issues of sexuality almost entirely in terms of power to the exclusion of gender: see Lynda E. Boose, 'The Family in Shakespeare Studies; or – Studies in the Family of Shakespeareans; or – The Politics of Politics',[13] Carol Thomas Neely, 'Constructing the Subject: Feminist Practice and the New Renaissance Discourses'[14] and my own 'Are There Any Women in *King Lear*?'[15] In this respect, the work of Michel Foucault, in *The History of Sexuality* and especially in *Discipline and Punish: The Birth of the Prison*,[16] has perhaps had an overly negative effect on our definitions of early modern sexuality. At the same time one should in fairness record that feminists have been accused of introducing a new kind of Puritanism into the discourse of sexuality.

Feminist critics have often objected to negative views of Shakespeare's female characters. They have argued that the plays are less sexist than the theatrical and critical traditions which continually reproduce them. Barbara Mowat pointed out in 1977 the discrepancy between Shakespeare's women and the way they are perceived by male characters,[17] and other feminist critics have shown that male directors and critics are all too likely to agree with male characters – to take as it were Hamlet's view of Gertrude rather than Shakespeare's. Irene Dash has used stage history to demonstrate, in *Wooing, Wedding and Power: Women in Shakespeare's Plays*,[18] how regularly women's roles have been distorted and limited in productions, often with the effect of reducing a robust interest in sexuality to the more coy attitudes thought of as feminine by later ages. As long ago as 1957 Carolyn Heilbrun argued that Gertrude had been misunderstood and wrongly condemned by male critics;[19] Linda T. Fitz explored a similar phenomenon in 'Egyptian Queens and Male Reviewers: Sexist Attitudes in *Antony and Cleopatra*',[20] and Jacqueline Rose has argued in 'Sexuality in the Reading of Shakespeare: *Hamlet* and *Measure for Measure*' that the 'problems' in those plays relate to the sexual anxieties of male critics and their determination to hold female desire responsible for any breakdown in moral or aesthetic order.[21]

Paradoxically, as Celia R. Daileader notes in her essay in this volume, 'Shakespeare needs feminism'[22]: despite attacks on 'the patriarchal bard' and revelations of the comparative misogyny of early modern culture, female readers and audience members as well as feminist students and critics have shown no desire to write him off; rather they have contributed to and enjoyed a lively and very much ongoing debate. Many of the most significant essays of the last twenty years have been collected in anthologies such as *Shakespeare and Gender* edited by Deborah H. Barker and Ivo Kamps[23] and *Shakespeare, Feminism and Gender* edited by Kate Chedgzoy.[24] Recent books have included the genre-based studies in Routledge's 'Feminist Readings of Shakespeare' series (I should declare an interest as General Editor of this series). Volumes published so far are Philippa Berry's *Shakespeare's Feminine Endings: Disfiguring Death in the Tragedies*,[25] Coppélia Kahn's *Roman Shakespeare: Warriors, Wounds and Women*[26] and Jean E. Howard and Phyllis Rackin's *Engendering a Nation: A Feminist Account of Shakespeare's English Histories*.[27] All these books make use of current debates about gender and sexuality while displaying a scholarly awareness of the social and historical contexts of Shakespeare's work. Such a dual focus is also evident in Catherine Belsey's *Shakespeare and the Loss of Eden*,[28] whose subtitle, 'The Construction of Family Values in Early Modern Culture', hints at the book's slightly ironic take on how we re-read the past.

Men in feminism and gay studies

There has clearly been a male response to feminist criticism in the publication of a number of books dealing directly with men's relationship to it: see for example *Men in Feminism* edited by Alice Jardine and Paul Smith[29] and *Engendering Men: The Question of Male Feminist Criticism* edited by Joseph Boone and Michael Cadden.[30] The work of many male critics is listed in Kolin's annotated bibliography of *Shakespeare and Feminist Criticism* though not all of them would necessarily describe themselves as feminists. One critic who has explicitly engaged with what it means to write as a male feminist is Peter Erickson whose *Patriarchal Structures in Shakespeare's Drama* provides a clear and at times grim analysis of the sexual politics of the plays.[31] In his recent *Rewriting Shakespeare, Rewriting Ourselves* Erickson discusses in an afterword his own project which 'involves undoing the automatic, apparently given, equation between Shakespeare as white male author and myself as white male critic'.[32] In his essay in this volume, Michael Hattaway addresses his own discomfort in being a man 'reading as a woman' and attempting to analyse misogyny in Shakespearian texts.[33]

At the same time, there has been a growing interest in the history and construction of homosexuality and lesbianism. Did they even exist in the modern sense in the Renaissance period? The issue has been explored by James M. Saslow in 'Homosexuality in the Renaissance: Behavior, Identity, and Artistic Expression'[34] and by Alan Bray in *Homosexuality in Renaissance England*.[35] Literary scholars have also been contributing to this debate: Eve Kosofsky Sedgwick's *Between Men: English Literature and Male Homosocial Desire*[36] invigorated discussion by distinguishing between homosociality and homosexuality and locating male homoerotic desire in the specific social context of patriarchal heterosexuality. She discussed Shakespeare's *Sonnets* which are an inevitable focus of attention in this context, despite Margreta de Grazia's brave attempt in her paper in this volume to locate the 'scandal' elsewhere.[37] While the eighteenth century did its best to eliminate the tricky question of Shakespeare's own sexuality altogether, a twentieth-century scholar like Joseph Pequigney in *Such is My Love: A Study of Shakespeare's Sonnets* tries to put it back, claiming a specifically homosexual identity for the author and deploring the way that most commentators neglect or dispose of the issue.[38] Such an identity today (or, more precisely, such an implied commitment to specific erotic practices) is of course overshadowed by the history of AIDS which makes the association between desire and death grimly literal.

Other related areas of debate have been the differences between Marlowe and Shakespeare in this respect (see Marilyn J. Thorssen, 'Varieties of Amorous Experience: Homosexual and Heterosexual Relationships in Marlowe and Shakespeare',[39] and Joseph A. Porter, 'Marlowe, Shakespeare, and the Canonization of Heterosexuality'[40]), and the question of homoeroticism in *The Merchant of Venice* where the Antonio/Bassanio/Portia triangle has been read as a struggle between homosexual and heterosexual love (see Seymour Kleinberg '*The Merchant of Venice*: The Homosexual as Anti-Semite in Nascent Capitalism',[41] Keith Geary, 'The Nature of Portia's Victory: Turning to Men in *The Merchant of Venice*'[42] and Karen Newman, 'Portia's Ring: Unruly Women and Structures of Exchange in *The Merchant of Venice*'.[43]) Catherine Belsey's essay in this volume puts this debate into the context of the perceived distance between early modern culture and our own over the meaning of sexuality, noting how difficult it is for us to determine the meaning of terms like 'love' and 'desire' in relation to either heterosexual or homosexual relationships.[44]

There has been far less written about lesbianism, though Valerie Traub has explored the question of homoerotic desire from a lesbian angle, especially in her chapters on 'Desire and the Differences it Makes' and 'The Homoerotics of Shakespearean Comedy' in *Desire and Anxiety*.[45] Making use of feminist film criticism on the 'male gaze' and the positioning of the audience in relation to screen representations, she argues eloquently for an eroticism which does not flow directly from gender identity and is not limited to the binary homosexual/heterosexual opposition. (See also her more recent essay on 'The (In)Significance of "Lesbian" Desire in Early Modern England'.[46])

Recent contributions to the area of gay studies include Kate Chedgzoy's *Shakespeare's Queer Children*,[47] which sees Shakespeare as an enabling and empowering force for a range of 'other' voices, including those of Oscar Wilde and Derek Jarman. Jeffrey Masten's *Textual Intercourse*[48] explores the homoerotics of collaborative authorship in the drama of Shakespeare's time, and the anthology *Queering the Renaissance*[49] edited by Jonathan Goldberg provides a wider context for homosexual, homoerotic and homosocial phenomena.

THE BOY ACTOR AND PERFORMANCE STUDIES

Male homosexual desire in the Renaissance period is often represented as something which involves an age difference if not a sex difference: it is seen as the desire of adult men for 'boys', and the use of such terms for the younger partner as 'ganymede', 'catamite' and 'ingle' all testify to this. The boy actor of women's parts has been the focus of considerable interest to gay critics as well as to feminist critics in recent years. At the same time a more general interest in transvestism as a widespread social phenomenon not exclusive to the Renaissance is shown in two recent books by prominent Shakespearian critics: Marjorie Garber's *Vested Interests: Cross-Dressing and Cultural Anxiety*,[50] and Jonathan Dollimore's *Sexual Dissidence: Augustine to Wilde, Freud to Foucault*,[51] which has a chapter on 'Cross-Dressing in Early Modern England'. In fact we still know extraordinarily little about the actual performers, their lives and careers, but we can argue, both from the texts themselves and from secondary material (notably the attacks on the immorality of the stage), that this particular dramatic convention gave rise to a number of debates about sexual identity, sexual difference and sexual transgression.

Several scholars working in this area have discussed cross-dressing as a real-life social phenomenon in Renaissance England as well as a theatrical practice. They have investigated the social and religious background and the possible relationships between women wearing men's clothes on the streets and men wearing women's clothes on the stage. Such work includes Juliet Dusinberre's section on 'Disguise and the Boy Actor' in chapter 4 of *Shakespeare and the Nature of Women*,[52] Lisa Jardine's chapter on 'Female Roles and Elizabethan Eroticism' in *Still Harping on Daughters*,[53] Mary Beth Rose's essay on 'Women in Men's Clothing: Apparel and Social Stability in *The Roaring Girl*',[54] Laura Levine's 'Men in Women's Clothing: Anti-theatricality and Effeminization from 1579 to 1642',[55] Jonathan Dollimore's 'Subjectivity, Sexuality and Transgression',[56] Stephen Orgel's 'Nobody's Perfect: Or Why Did the English Renaissance Stage Take Boys for Women?'[57] and Jean E. Howard's 'Crossdressing, the Theatre, and Gender Struggle in Early Modern England'.[58]

Others have concentrated more specifically on the immediate dramatic effects of the convention: such work includes Paula S. Berggren's 'The Woman's Part: Female Sexuality as Power in Shakespeare's Plays',[59] Kathleen McLuskie's 'The Act, the Role, and the Actor: Boy Actresses on the Elizabethan Stage',[60] Mary Free's 'Shakespeare's Comedic Heroines: Protofeminists or Conformers to Patriarchy?',[61] Matthew H. Wikander's ' "As secret as maidenhead": The Profession of the Boy-Actress in *Twelfth Night*',[62] Phyllis Rackin's 'Androgyny, Mimesis, and the Marriage of the Boy Heroine on the English Renaissance Stage'[63] and Lorraine Helms's 'Playing the Woman's Part: Feminist Criticism and Shakespearean Performance'.[64]

A central issue of debate about the boy actor has been over whether the convention empowers women, by allowing female characters to adopt freedoms denied them in a patriarchal culture, or whether in the end the disguises serve only to reaffirm the sexual hierarchy. On the more positive side, critics such as Dusinberre, Berggren, and Rackin (as well as Catherine Belsey in 'Disrupting Gender Difference: Meaning and Gender in the Comedies'[65]) see at least the possibility for an escape from the constraints of femininity, an opening up of rigid gender distinctions, a playfulness with ideas of androgyny. On the negative side, critics such as Free and Howard reject the view of Shakespeare's heroines as proto-feminists and argue that cross-dressing on the stage was not in fact a strong site of resistance to traditional assumptions about gender. In this context, more than one critic has contrasted Shakespeare's use of the boy-disguised-as-a-girl-disguised-as-a-boy in *As You Like It* and *Twelfth Night*, usually arguing that Rosalind is empowered by her disguise while

Viola is trapped by hers: see Nancy K. Hales' 'Sexual Disguise in *As You Like It* and *Twelfth Night*'[66] and Valerie Traub's chapter on 'The Homo-erotics of Shakespearean Comedy' in *Desire and Anxiety*'.[67] Peter Erickson on the other hand has interpreted both the ending and the epilogue in *As You Like It* as means of containing and even eliminating female power.[68]

The mid-1990s saw the appearance of some major studies in this field, notably Michael Shapiro's *Gender in Play on the Shakespearean Stage*,[69] Laura Levine's *Men in Women's Clothing* (a book incorporating her earlier essay,[70]) and Stephen Orgel's *Impersonations: The Performance of Gender in Shakespeare's England*.[71]

More generally, studies of Shakespeare's plays in performance, on stage and increasingly on film, are directly addressing issues of sexuality, as is evident in the essays by Celia R. Daileader and John Russell Brown in this volume.[72] Recent collections of essays such as *Shakespeare, Theory and Performance* edited by James C. Bulman[73] and *Shakespeare the Movie* edited by Lynda E. Boose and Richard Burt[74] contain several relevant contributions, and there has been a focus on the sexual politics of particular companies and productions in books like Elizabeth Schafer's *Ms-Directing Shakespeare*[75] and Penny Gay's *As She Likes It: Shakespeare's Unruly Women*.[76]

LANGUAGE

If sexuality is socially constructed, it is also, and necessarily on the English Renaissance stage, verbally constructed. Language itself, as feminist linguistics has shown, is far from being gender-neutral. Male/female stereotypes are built into everyday language use as well as into more elaborated literary contexts. In *Literary Fat Ladies: Rhetoric, Gender, Property*[77] Patricia Parker explores the sexual politics of Shakespeare's plays through an analysis of their rhetorical structures, arguing that the 'women are words, men deeds' cliché gave rise to an anxiety about effeminization associated with linguistic excess or 'fatness': Hamlet associates impotence with talking like a drab. Specific tropes such as *hysteron proteron*, *dilation* and *delation*, are seen as moulding the gender hierarchy in *King Lear* and the destruction of Desdemona in *Othello* respectively. Women's supposed lack of verbal self-control is associated with other kinds of 'fluency' or 'leakiness' by Gail Kern Paster in 'Leaky Vessels: The Incontinent Women of City Comedy'.[78]

Men arguably control language, in the plays as in real life. In "The Blazon of Sweet Beauty's Best": Shakespeare's *Lucrece*', Nancy Vickers shows how female characters such as Lucrece, Desdemona and Innogen can become victims of the *blazon*, the elaborated verbal description of a woman's beauty, a trope which originates in the male imagination and functions in situations of male rivalry.[79] To somewhat similar effect, though in relation to a very different text, Carol Cook claims in 'The Sign and Semblance of Her Honor: Reading Gender Difference in *Much Ado About Nothing*' that 'what is at stake is a masculine prerogative in language, which the play itself sustains'.[80] The contest in 'phallic wit' between Beatrice and Benedick contributes in the end to the survival of the masculine ethos. Women can play with words but men own them.

Some critics have been more optimistic about the possibility of a more positive feminine use of language. Deborah T. Curren-Aquino argues in 'Toward a Star that Danced: Woman as Survivor in Shakespeare's Early Comedies' that the women in these plays have more adaptable verbal skills than the men.[81] Taking a comparable line on Isabella and Helena in 'Speaking Sensibly: Feminine Rhetoric in *Measure for Measure* and *All's Well That Ends Well*', Christy Desmet nevertheless concedes that the women are finally consigned to silence in a male world.[82] Paradoxically, as Philip C. Kolin notes in the Introduction to his annotated bibliography of *Shakespeare and Feminist Criticism*, many studies of women's distinctive language in the plays have in fact focused on their silence.[83]

Sometimes, however, Shakespeare's women speak when male critics and directors would prefer them to be silent, and this is especially evident when they talk about sexuality. George Bernard Shaw revealed himself to be a true Victorian when he remarked of Beatrice that 'In her character of professed wit she has only one subject, and that is the subject which a really witty woman never jests about, because it is too serious a matter to a woman to be made light of without indelicacy.'[84] In *Wooing, Wedding and Power* Irene Dash points out that the part of the sexually outspoken Princess in *Love's Labour's Lost* has often been severely abbreviated, both on stage and in expurgated editions, in a series of attempts to save her from 'vulgarity' and to make her speech more 'ladylike' by post-Renaissance standards.[85] In his paper in this volume William C. Carroll discusses the issue of female sexuality and linguistic obscenity – an area which still poses problems for editors[86] – while Mary Bly examines the 'bawdy puns' of *Romeo and Juliet* and their transformation in the subsequent dramatic tradition from lyric to burlesque.[87] There has been a renewal of interest in the glossing and annotating of sexual language: Eric Partridge's 1947 classic *Shakespeare's Bawdy* was followed by Frankie Rubinstein's *A Dictionary of Shakespeare's Sexual Puns and Their Significance*.[88]

Both are largely superseded by Gordon Williams's three-volume *Dictionary of Sexual Language in Shakespearean and Stuart Literature* and his *Glossary of Shakespeare's Sexual Language.*[89] It begins to seem that 'indelicacy' was a deliberate and indeed formative element in Shakespeare's drama.

We are not always entirely easy talking about sexuality even today, and we don't always know if we are getting the tone right, but at any event, as I hope I have shown, the topic 'Shakespeare and Sexuality' has generated a great deal of language, both spoken and written, witty and serious, and this volume is unlikely to be the last word on it.

A version of this essay was first published in *Shakespeare Survey 46* (1994)

NOTES

1 (Cambridge, Mass., 1990), p. 149.
2 (New York and London, 1991). Dusinberre's book was reissued by Macmillan in 1996 with a substantial new Preface entitled 'Beyond the Battle?'
3 (Baltimore, 1980).
4 (Berkeley, 1981).
5 (London, 1981).
6 (New Brunswick, N.J., 1983).
7 (Toronto, 1987).
8 (London, 1992).
9 (London, 1992).
10 In *Political Shakespeare* edited by Jonathan Dollimore and Alan Sinfield (Manchester, 1985), pp. 88–108.
11 (Oxford, 1988).
12 (Chicago, 1980).
13 *Renaissance Quarterly*, 40 (1987), 707–42.
14 *English Literary Renaissance*, 18 (1988), 5–10.
15 In *The Matter of Difference* edited by Valerie Wayne (Hemel Hempstead, 1991), pp. 117–28.
16 Translated by Alan Sheridan (New York, 1979).
17 'Images of Women in Shakespeare's Plays', *Southern Humanities Review*, 11 (1977), 145–57.
18 (New York, 1981).
19 'The Character of Hamlet's Mother', *Shakespeare Quarterly*, 8 (1957), 201–6. When Heilbrun reprinted this as the first essay in her collection *Hamlet's Mother and Other Women* (New York, 1990), pp. 9–17, she commented in the Introduction that as a critic of Shakespeare in 1957 'I was a feminist waiting for a cause to join' (p. 2).

20 *Shakespeare Quarterly*, 28 (1977), 296–316.
21 In *Alternative Shakespeares* edited by John Drakakis (London, 1985), pp. 95–118.
22 See below, p. 198.
23 (London, 1995).
24 (London, 2001).
25 (London, 1999).
26 (London, 1997).
27 (London, 1997).
28 (London, 1999).
29 (London, 1987).
30 (London, 1991).
31 (Berkeley, 1985).
32 (Berkeley, 1991), p. 169.
33 See below, pp. 92–115.
34 In *Hidden From History: Reclaiming the Gay and Lesbian Past* edited by Martin Duberman, Martha Vicinus and George Chauncey Jr (New York, 1989), pp. 90–105.
35 (London, 1982). See also Bruce R. Smith's *Homosexual Desire in Shakespeare's England* (Chicago, 1992).
36 (New York, 1985).
37 See below, pp. 146–67.
38 (Chicago, 1985).
39 In *Human Sexuality in the Middle Ages and Renaissance* edited by Douglas Radcliff-Umstead (Pittsburgh: University of Pittsburgh Publications on Middle Ages and Renaissance, 1978), pp. 135–52.
40 *South Atlantic Quarterly*, 88 (1989), 127–47.
41 *Journal of Homosexuality*, 8 (1983), 113–26.
42 *Shakespeare Survey 37* (1984), 55–68.
43 *Shakespeare Quarterly*, 38 (1987), 19–33.
44 See below, pp. 72–91.
45 As cited in n. 9 above.
46 In *Erotic Politics: The Dynamics of Desire in the Renaissance Theatre*, edited by Susan Zimmerman (New York and London, 1992), pp. 150–69.
47 (Manchester, 1995).
48 (Cambridge, 1997).
49 (Durham, North Carolina, 1994).
50 (London, 1992).
51 (Oxford, 1991).
52 (London, 1975).
53 (Brighton, 1983).
54 *English Literary Renaissance*, 14 (1984), 367–91.
55 *Criticism*, 28 (1986), 121–43.
56 *Renaissance Drama*, 17 (1986), 53–81.
57 *South Atlantic Quarterly*, 88 (1989), 7–29.

58 *Shakespeare Quarterly*, 39 (1988), 418–40.
59 In *The Woman's Part: Feminist Criticism of Shakespeare* edited by Carolyn Ruth Swift Lenz, Gayle Greene and Carol Thomas Neely (Urbana, 1980), pp. 17–34.
60 *New Theatre Quarterly*, 3 (1987), 120–30.
61 *Shakespeare Bulletin*, 4 (1986), 23–5.
62 *Comparative Drama*, 20 (1986), 349–62.
63 *PMLA*, 102 (1987), 29–41.
64 In *Performing Feminisms* edited by Sue-Ellen Case (Baltimore, 1990), pp. 196–206.
65 In *Alternative Shakespeares* edited by John Drakakis (London, 1985), pp. 166–90.
66 *Shakespeare Survey* 32 (1979), 63–72.
67 As cited in n. 9 above, pp. 122–44.
68 As cited in n. 25 above, pp. 24–5, 34.
69 (Ann Arbor, 1994).
70 (Cambridge, 1994).
71 (Cambridge, 1996).
72 See below, pp. 183–200 and 168–82.
73 (London, 1996).
74 (London, 1997).
75 (London, 1998).
76 (London, 1994).
77 (London, 1987).
78 *Renaissance Drama*, 18 (1987), 43–65.
79 In *Shakespeare and the Question of Theory*, edited by Patricia Parker and Geoffrey Hartman (London, 1985), pp. 95–115.
80 *PMLA*, 101 (1986), 186–202.
81 *Selected Papers from the West Virginia Shakespeare and Renaissance Association*, 11 (1986), 50–61.
82 *Renaissance Papers* 1986 (1987), 43–51.
83 As cited in n. 2 above, p. 42.
84 In *Shaw on Shakespeare*, edited by Edwin Wilson (Harmondsworth, 1969), p. 156.
85 As cited in n. 18 above, pp. 14–20.
86 See below, pp. 14–34.
87 See below, pp. 52–71.
88 (London, 1984, second edition 1989).
89 (London 1994 and London 1997).

Language and sexuality in Shakespeare

William C. Carroll

'New plays and maidenheads', according to the Prologue of *The Two Noble Kinsmen*,

> are near akin:
> Much followed both, for both much money giv'n
> If they stand sound and well. And a good play,
> Whose modest scenes blush on his marriage day
> And shake to lose his honour, is like her
> That after holy tie and first night's stir
> Yet still is modesty, and still retains
> More of the maid to sight than husband's pains.
>
> (Prol. 1–8)

The endless renewal of the spoken word, the play whose every performance is almost but not quite the originary 'first night's stir', is comparable here to the virgin whose maidenhead is taken yet 'still is modesty', still *seems* 'more of the maid' than not. I want to take up here some of the ways in which plays and maidenheads are related, how Shakespeare's dramatic language represents sexuality. It will be necessary to narrow the focus considerably, of course – in terms of language and sexuality in Shakespeare, here, if anywhere, is God's plenty. My argument will therefore only concern female sexuality as a production of male discourse, and I mean to use the term 'sexuality' rather than 'gender' because I will examine the biological semantics at work in the plays. Some feminist theorists have argued that female sexuality is, in patriarchal discourse, unrepresentable – conceptually available only as lack, invisibility, or negation.[1] I will pursue that position through the different, sometimes contradictory ways in which the language of several early modern writers, particularly Shakespeare, represented female sexuality and biology. Ultimately, I will examine some of the mystifications of the Tudor–Stuart discourse of virginity, the

14

ne plus ultra, so to speak, of female sexuality – looking particularly at how certain modes of discourse registered the presence or absence of virginity.

To begin with, female sexuality in Shakespeare's plays is invariably articulated as linguistic transgression – that is, a verbal replication of female obliquity. Often, the ordinary relation between signifier and signified has slipped, been dislocated or even reversed, the linguistic equivalent of the world turned upside down.[2] The chief rhetorical figure here is the pun. It's not surprising that Dr Johnson termed the pun Shakespeare's 'fatal Cleopatra', employing the supreme Shakespearian example of female sexuality to indicate how Shakespeare's masculine persuasive force, to borrow Donne's term, was weakened and deflected by the 'irresistible' fascinations of the feminized quibble. For the heroic, manly playwright, 'a quibble is the golden apple for which he will always turn aside from his career, or stoop from his elevation'.[3] In employing this terminology of swerve, fall, and decline, Johnson touches on something important about the sexualized energy of the pun, as a linguistic field of subversion and transgression.[4] Yet Johnson has also suggestively reversed the actual analogy by transforming the beautiful Atalanta, who abandoned her race with Hippomenes to pick up the golden apples, into the male playwright distracted by effeminizing verbal structures. This gender reversal is necessary for Johnson's understanding of unstable language as feminine and therefore seductive. Johnson thus suggests part of my argument here: that patriarchal discourse equates destabilizing verbal forms and female sexuality.

The pun and its inversion, the malapropism, permit the introduction into utterance of female sexuality without ever seeming to name or recognize it. The references may be comic – as in the Latin lesson in *The Merry Wives of Windsor*, and the English lesson in *Henry V*, with its mispronunciations of 'foot' and 'count' – or they may be sinister – as in the references to 'country matters' and 'country forms' in *Hamlet* and *Othello* – but such linguistic forms continually enact some type of subversion of the master discourse. When Bottom assures his fellows that they will meet in the woods, 'and there we may rehearse most obscenely' (*Dream* 1.2.100–1), we have little reason to doubt him.[5]

This kind of wordplay permits the eruption of female sexuality into ordinary utterance. In *Love's Labour's Lost*, for example, Costard has been put in Armado's custody as punishment for his transgression with Jaquenetta:

ARMADO   Sirrah Costard, I will enfranchise thee.
COSTARD   O, marry me to one Frances! I smell some *l'envoi*, some goose, in
    this.
ARMADO   By my sweet soul, I mean setting thee at liberty, enfreedoming thy
    person. Thou wert immured, restrained, captivated, bound.

(3.1.117–22)

In a complicated series of misunderstandings, Costard has come to
equate *'l'envoi'* with 'goose', a common slang term for a prostitute. So
his fear is that he will be forced to marry a prostitute named Frances.
Her name, in turn, has come from the mishearing of 'enfranchise' as
'one Frances' – the word for liberation turns into its opposite, signifying
a forced marriage. Costard's linguistic incapacities have created a phan-
tom virago, a loose woman with designs on him. A similar betrayal of
subconscious threats occurs in *The Merry Wives of Windsor*, when Quickly
mishears the answer 'pulcher' as 'polecats' during the Latin lesson. The
lesson continues:

EVANS   What is your genitive case plural, William?
WILLIAM   Genitive case?
EVANS   Ay.
WILLIAM   *Genitivo*: '*horum, harum, horum*'.
QUICKLY   Vengeance of Jenny's case! Fie on her! Never name her, child, if
    she be a whore.   (4.1.52–7)

Thus 'pulcher' becomes a slang word for 'whore', virtually the opposite
of the original word. And in one of Quickly's most remarkable transformations, 'genitive case' becomes 'Jenny's case' – the prostitute by name
and, considering her profession, her most valuable possessive as well;
here a grammatical term itself generates the sexual chimera. '*Horum*',
of course, predictably mutates into a verb. Through a kind of acoustical
genius, Costard and Quickly achieve a creation *ex nihilo*, the fabrication
of comically and sexually aggressive females – two ladies of the night,
Frances and Jenny – from the swerves and frictions of language.

  If puns and malapropisms offer the sexual low road, the eruption of
the carnivalesque sexual into high discourse, then their linguistic opposite
is represented by a far more stylized form of verbal dislocation, the
riddle. However riddles are categorized, one common structural feature
is that 'the referent of the description' is withheld, to be guessed at by
an audience – all signifiers and no signified, in short.[6] This 'temporary
threat of discontinuity' Roger Abrahams aptly terms 'epistemological
foreplay', leading to the riddler's clarifying and satisfying solution to the
problem – providing the absent signified.[7] Shakespeare's plays encode

female sexuality in riddles so as to mystify it in terms of obliqueness or absence. We may think immediately of such examples as the casket riddles in *The Merchant of Venice*, which double the mystification, with one riddle on the outside of each box and another on the inside, leading to another kind of inside/outside riddle, as the treasure chest that contains the woman leads to the woman that contains, and is, the sexual treasure. Bertram's riddle in *All's Well That Ends Well* also relies on synecdoches and verbal dislocations to encode Helen's aggressive (in his view) sexuality: 'When thou canst get the ring upon my finger, which never shall come off, and show me a child begotten of thy body that I am father to, then call me husband; but in such a "then" I write a "never"' (3.2.57–60). Bertram has sworn, in the phrase which suggests my paper's title, 'to make the "not" eternal' (3.2.22), to leave the riddle forever unresolved, epistemological foreplay with no climax.

In Shakespeare's first romance, however, the 'not' does and must remain eternal for Pericles. The riddle he reads encodes incest, the missing signified the daughter of Antiochus:

> I am no viper, yet I feed
> On mother's flesh which did me breed.
> I sought a husband, in which labour
> I found that kindness in a father.
> He's father, son, and husband mild;
> I mother, wife, and yet his child.
> How they may be and yet in two,
> As you will live resolve it you.
> (*Pericles* Sc.1.107–14)

It is worth recalling here that Shakespeare, as Goolden has noted, has altered his sources by making the missing signified of the 'I' in this riddle be, not the father, but the daughter.[8] This change not only 'sharpens the focus on the princess', as Gorfain notes,[9] but defines female sexuality as absence – and, if the riddle is answered, as transgression. In a final example, when Mariana appears before the Duke at the end of *Measure for Measure*, her riddling responses to his questions lead him to conclude, 'Why, you are nothing then; neither maid, widow, nor wife!" (5.1.176–7). But the Duke's 'nothing' is then re-presented in Mariana's riddling self-proclamation:

> My lord, I do confess I ne'er was married,
> And I confess besides, I am no maid.
> I have known my husband, yet my husband
> Knows not that ever he knew me.
> (5.1.183–6)

Once again, the power of negation, of the 'not', becomes the defining category of a woman's sexuality. Mariana's riddle that 'my husband / Knows not that ever he knew me' anticipates the paradox of the former virgin who 'still retains / More of the maid to sight', but also begins to lead us toward darker and more tragic moments in the plays, particularly to Othello, who kills the wife he knew not he knew.

If puns and riddles occlude female sexuality by displacing it from the plays' high discourse, we might expect a less oblique representational strategy in the names given to female sexuality, and to the female genitalia specifically, but the realm of the referential, as we will see, is no less one of mystification. Usually, the name given to the female sex organs in Shakespeare's plays is a variant of the patriarchal metaphors of absence or containment: the O, the pit, ring, case, box, casket, the subtle hole, her C's, U's, and T's, the lake, pond, swallowing tomb, the placket, chimney, the fault,[10] and so on. Here are the images, now familiar from psychoanalytic and philological scholarship, of absence, emptiness, darkness, fall, invisible depth. From the 'unhallowed and bloodstained hole' (2.3.210) and 'detested, dark, blood-drinking pit' (2.3.224) of *Titus Andronicus*, to the 'sulphurous pit' (*Lear* F 4.5.125) of *Lear*, Shakespeare produces one misogynistic representation after another; virtually all of them suggest that the female genitalia, in one way or another, locate 'hell . . . darkness . . . burning, scalding, stench, consumption' (*Lear* F 4.5.124–5).[11]

The most contested and paradoxical category of semantic description, however, is the category of the virgin, who is metonymically defined by the names given to her hymen. The religious and psychological value of virginity was of course under interrogation in early modern England. On the one hand, the cult of the Virgin Mary taught, as Marina Warner has noted, 'that the virginal life reduced the special penalties of the Fall in women and was therefore holy. Second, the image of the virgin body was the supreme image of wholeness, and wholeness was equated with holiness'. The virgin body was believed to be perfectly sealed up, 'seamless, unbroken'. This belief was based in part on inaccurate medical knowledge – 'the hymen was thought to seal off the womb completely . . . caulking the body like tar on a ship's timbers', as Warner notes, though Renaissance anatomists, as we will see, were not as certain as this formulation.[12] The virgin's body, to employ a vocabulary derived from Bakhtin, is 'classical', with its key orifice closed, rather than 'grotesque'. The hymen thus became the most important fetishized commodity possessed by a woman, a barrier both physical and spiritual, a sign from God marking the Second Eve. As Mary Douglas has shown, the 'body's boundaries can represent any boundaries which are threatened or precarious';[13] the hymen is an ultimate threshold, a barrier to men, marking the fall into sexuality, the transition from maiden to woman, the making of the virgin not. The hymen's liminal status gives it an enormous symbolic importance as a construct of patriarchal discourse.[14]

The cult of the Virgin, however, was under attack in Reformation England, and even Queen Elizabeth's appropriations of Catholic iconology as the Virgin Queen did not overcome the sceptics and iconoclasts.[15] Elizabeth's own dalliances were public gossip, even her monthly gynaecological status, and Ben Jonson could speculate to Drummond of Hawthornden that Elizabeth 'had a Membrana on her which made her uncapable of men, though for her delight she tryed many, at the comming over of Monsieur, ther was a French Chirurgion who took in hand to cut it, yett fear stayed her & his death'.[16] There was also a strong libertine tradition which demystified and subverted the value of virginity. Catullus, for one, furnished the Renaissance its standard comparison between the natural world and sexuality, pre-eminently through the unplucked flower that loses its bloom (LXII. 39–47). He also commodifies virginity, suggesting that the maidenhead can be precisely divided to reflect the economic stakes of those who have invested in it:

> Your maidenhead [*virginitas*] is not all yours but
>   in part your parents';
> Your father has a third, your mother is given a
>   third,
> Only a third is yours.   (LXII.62–4)[17]

This passage stands behind Chapman's continuation of 'Hero and Leander',[18] among other texts, and leads to paradoxical arguments that virginity is not a something, an intact hymen, but a nothing. Marlowe's witty argument, in 'Hero and Leander' Sestiad I, is typical. Virginity and marriage, the narrator argues, are completely different:

> This idol which you term virginity
> Is neither essence subject to the eye,
> No, nor to any one exterior sense,
> Nor hath it any place of residence,
> Nor is't of earth or mould celestial,
> Or capable of any form at all.
> Of that which hath no being, do not boast;
> Things that are not at all, are never lost.
>   (1.269–76)

The libertine argument may be aimed at seduction, but it also turns on a definition of absence and negation that can lead in more disturbing directions. Iago taps into the vision of the 'not', the no-thing, when he tells Othello: 'Her honour is an essence that's not seen. / They have it very oft that have it not' (*Othello* 4.1.16–17). The handkerchief may be offered as a substitute membrane which can be seen, handled, and passed back and forth, but virginity itself is one of those 'things that are not at all', 'they have it very oft that have it not'. The thing itself can be known only through signs, thereby permitting a semiotic slippage which can be manipulated by an Iago for his own ends.

Paroles' dialogue on virginity with Helen in *All's Well That Ends Well* follows the same line of sophistic logic. His argument proceeds from the libertine assumption: 'It is not politic in the commonwealth of nature to preserve virginity', because 'loss of virginity is rational increase' (1.1.124–6).[19] Virginity is a paradoxically self-annihilating commodity: 'by being once lost [it] may be ten times found; by being ever kept it is ever lost... 'Tis a commodity will lose the gloss with lying: the longer kept, the less worth' (129–30, 150–1). Time forbids the quotation of this entire dialogue, but it ends with an elaborate personification which inverts the gender and age of the virgin:

Virginity like an old courtier wears her cap out of fashion, richly suited but unsuitable, just like the brooch and the toothpick, which wear not now. Your date is better in your pie and your porridge than in your cheek, and your virginity, your old virginity, is like one of our French withered pears: it looks ill, it eats drily, marry, 'tis a withered pear – it was formerly better, marry, yet 'tis a withered pear.   (1.1.152–60)

Turning the young maiden into the old courtier, this passage moves toward an equation between the hymen and male impotence; for every intact virgin, it seems, another male has failed. Helen's response to Paroles – 'Not my virginity, yet...' (line 161)[20] – provides the first instance of the rhetoric of negation which resurfaces later in the play in the central riddle, already quoted, in which Bertram says 'I have wedded her, not bedded her, and sworn to make the "not" eternal' (3.2.21–2), and in Diana's challenge to the King in the final scene, 'Good my lord, / Ask him [Bertram] upon his oath if he does think / He had not my virginity' (5.3.186–8).

The language which Shakespeare employs to signify virginity thus generally trades on various forms of paradoxical negation, but the names given to the hymen itself suggest both positive and negative categories. The name 'hymen', to begin with, signifies both the god of marriage, and marriage generally, as well as the physical membrane; the same word thus figures the object which defines the virgin, and the ritual which demands the loss of that object.[21] The state of virginity thus exists only as a condition of potential loss. The god of marriage makes two formal appearances in Shakespeare: first, at the end of *As You Like It*, to 'join in Hymen's bands' (5.4.127) the four couples, and again in the opening scene of *The Two Noble Kinsmen*, accompanied by a traditionally dressed virgin, 'encompassed in her tresses, bearing a wheaten garland' (1.1.1s.d.). Neither play includes a description of the god himself.[22]

More metaphorically, the hymen is a 'maidenhead', a usage which the *OED* dates from the mid-thirteenth century. Shakespeare uses the term frequently, often in the sense of a commodity, a thing to be acquired or taken, or a trophy of male conquest and possession. Thus Jack Cade asserts in *The First Part of the Contention* (*2 Henry VI*): 'There shall not a maid be married but she shall pay to me her maidenhead, ere they have it' (4.7.118–20). But Shakespeare also understands the symbolic inversion at work in this name, by which the head of a maiden becomes a maidenhead, resulting at times in fantasies of punishment and dismemberment.[23] In *Romeo and Juliet*, Samson promises to be civil with the maids:

> I will cut off their heads.
> GREGORY   The heads of the maids?
> SAMSON   Ay, the heads of the maids, or their
>   maidenheads, take it in what sense thou wilt.   (1.1.22–5)

This displacement figures in several of the plays, but particularly in *Measure for Measure*, where the plot lines converge in the figure of the executioner, Abhorson, and his new assistant, the bawd Pompey. As Ragozine's head is substituted for Claudio's head, so is Mariana's maidenhead substituted for Isabella's.[24]

The hymen is further objectified as a *valuable* object; thus Laertes warns Ophelia not to open 'your chaste treasure. . . / To [Hamlet's] unmastered importunity' (*Hamlet* 1.3.31–2). Virginity is a rare jewel but, as Marlowe puts it in 'Hero and Leander', 'Jewels being lost are found again, this never; / 'Tis lost but once, and once lost, lost for ever' (11.85–6). In *Pericles*, Boult threatens 'To take from you [Marina] the jewel you hold so dear' (*Pericles* Sc.19.180), following the Pander's (or Bawd's) command to him, 'Crack the ice of her virginity, and make the rest malleable'

(Sc.19.167–8). Thus virginity is valuable, rigid, reflective, and fragile – an irresistible challenge to possess, not a spiritual state but merely a physical condition.

In perhaps the most common metaphoric name, virginity is an unplucked flower, usually a rose; to penetrate the hymen is to deflower. The metaphoric origins of this ancient comparison are easy enough to imagine, and the usage in Shakespeare, and certainly in all of Renaissance literature, is pervasive; I will mention here only the 'little western flower' struck by the 'bolt of Cupid', in *A Midsummer Night's Dream*, 'Before, milk-white; now, purple with love's wound' (2.1.165–7). Some contemporary scientific treatises, however, literalized the flower metaphor in their anatomical descriptions. In *The Anatomie of the Bodie of Man* (1548), for example, Thomas Vicary uses the metaphor of 'deflouring' but reserves the term 'flowres' as a specific name for the menses, a term which had become common usage among Renaissance anatomists, midwives, and physicians.[25] In his *Microcosmographia* (1615), however, Helkiah Crooke brings biology and metaphor more closely together. 'The Caruncles [small pieces of flesh and membrane] are foure', Crooke says in his description of the hymen, 'and are like the berries of the Mirtle, in every corner of the bosome one'. All these parts and others, taken 'together make the forme of the cup of a little rose halfe blowne when the bearded leaves are taken away. Or this production', he goes on, 'with the lappe or privity may be likened to the great Clove Gilly-flower when it is moderately blowne' (223 [sic: actually 235]). No wonder Perdita, just five years earlier, did not want 'streaked gillyvors, / Which some call nature's bastards' (*The Winter's Tale* 4.4.82–3) in her garden. Crooke's attempt to bring the semantic domains of metaphor and biology together was echoed in other anatomies, including the anonymous *Aristotle's Master Piece*, where the hymen

is like the bud of a rose half blown, and this is broken in the first act of copulation with man: and hence comes the word *Deflora* to deflower; whence the taking of virginity, is called deflowering a virgin: for when the rose bud is expanded, virginity is lost.[26]

The flower is thus both a metaphor and, through acts of transference and supposed observation, allegedly also a close description of the thing itself.

Crooke goes on to further definitions of the hymen: 'It is called *Hymen quasi Limen*, as it were the entrance, the piller, or locke, or flower of virginity' (223 [sic: 235]), and later, 'they call it *Claustrum virginitatis, the lock of virginity*: for which their opinion they bring testimonies out of the holy scriptures' (255) – namely, the custom of displaying the virginal blood on the wedding sheets. Some anatomies also offer as a name the term '*Cento*', which translates as 'patchwork'. Thus the liminal threshold must be locked and contained, yet the membrane itself is almost indescribably fragile, mere threads.[27]

Shakespeare employs one name which puns on all the dislocations and mystifications that we have already examined – that is, the virgin knot (thus my title again). What was a virgin knot? It is equated with but apparently distinct from the so-called marriage knot and the true-lover's knot. The true-lover's knot is the iconographic image of the elaborately encoiled and overlapping thread, with no beginning or end, which unites true lovers via a 'knot formed of two loops intertwined' (*OED*) – a kind of early Möbius strip, used as an *impresa* or perhaps worn on the sleeve; the *OED* offers examples from the fourteenth century. Examples may be seen as well in portraits of the time – such as that of Sir Henry Lee (1568) in the National Portrait Gallery – in emblem books, and, in *The Two Gentlemen of Verona*, in Julia's proposal to 'knit' up her hair 'in silken strings / With twenty odd-conceited true-love knots' (2.7.45–6). The 'true-love' was also a kind of flower which was said to resemble the true-lover's knot – which leads us back to the flower of the hymen itself.[28]

The marriage knot, on the other hand, was the mystic union of two lovers through marriage, what Milton termed 'the inward knot of marriage, which is peace & love' and 'the holy knott of marriage'.[29] The marriage knot could not be dissolved by man, as Spenser noted: 'His owne two hands the holy knots did knit, / That none but death for ever can divide' (*Faerie Queene* 1.12.37.1–2); marriage is 'the knot, that ever shall remaine' (*Amoretti* 6.14).[30] Shakespeare's usage is straightforward: Warwick in *The True Tragedy of Richard Duke of York (3 Henry VI)* refers to the 'nuptial knot' (3.3.55), Capulet plans to 'have this knot knit up tomorrow morning' between Juliet and Paris (*Romeo* 4.2.24), and in *Cymbeline* those who marry are said 'to knit their souls . . . in self-figured knot' (2.3.114–16). The knot of love may also indissolubly link friends or family: Gloucester in *1 Henry VI* refers to the 'knot of amity' to be gained through the alliance with France (5.1.16), Malcolm describes 'those strong knots of love' which are Macduff's family (*Macbeth* 4.3.28), and Agrippa claims the marriage between Antony and Octavia will make Antony and Octavius 'brothers, and . . . knit your hearts / With an unslipping knot' (*Antony* 2.2.132–3). Hippolyta in *The Two Noble Kinsmen* elaborates the metaphor in this description of the friendship of Pirithous and Theseus:

> Their knot of love,
> Tied, weaved, entangled with so true, so long,
> And with a finger of so deep a cunning,
> May be outworn, never undone.
>
> (1.3.41–4)

The marriage knot or true-lover's knot cannot be 'undone', 'untied', or 'dissolv'd', then. It is for ever.[31]

But the virgin knot is something else. In *Pericles*, Marina is determined to preserve her honour:

> If fires be hot, knives sharp, or waters deep,
> United I still my virgin knot will keep.
> Diana aid my purpose.
>
> (Sc.16.142–4)

And Prospero warns Ferdinand not to be another Caliban with Miranda:

> If thou dost break her virgin-knot before
> All sanctimonious ceremonies may
> With full and holy rite be ministered . . .
>
> (*Tempest* 4.1.15–17)

And so Bertram's riddle in *All's Well* turns on this pun – 'I have wedded her, not bedded her, and sworn to make the "not" eternal' (3.2.21–2) – on both the marriage knot and the virgin knot; he resists the eternal knot by refusing to untie the physical knot. Clearly, the virgin knot – an external figure for the hymen within – is meant to be 'untied' or broken in marriage. But what kind of a knot is it? a square knot? a double half-hitch? surely not a sailor's knot? For Othello, the word conveys everything ugly about what he thought had been his virgin wife: turning the fountain of his life into 'a cistern for foul toads / To knot and gender in' (*Othello* 4.2.63–4).

There were at least two contending mythological accounts of the virgin knot. In 'Hero and Leander' Sestiad v, Chapman refers to the general union of lovers in his long narrative of Hymen's own wedding. The god of marriage himself was eternally bound, when Juno's priest took

> the disparent silks, and tied
> The lovers by the waists, and side to side,
> In token that thereafter they must bind
> In one self sacred knot each other's mind.
>
> (v.355–8)

But if the 'sacred knot' will never be dissolved, another ritual is also invoked:

> The custom was that every maid did wear,
> During her maidenhead, a silken sphere
> About her waist, above her inmost weed,
> Knit with Minerva's knot, and that was freed
> By the fair bridegroom on the marriage night,
> With many ceremonies of delight.
>
> (v.389–94)

Minerva – said to be a perpetual virgin in some Renaissance accounts – seems a plausible choice here, yet Chapman's identification of the knot with Minerva is probably a mistake, as D. J. Gordon has suggested.[32]

A second mythological account – certainly the traditional one – is given by Ben Jonson in his masque *Hymenai*, where the eternal knot and the knot to be dissolved seem to blend together. 'Reason' describes the dress of the bride, including

> The zone of wool about her waist,
> Which, in contrary circles cast,
> Doth meet in one strong knot that binds,
> Tells you, so should all married minds.
>
> (lines 173–6)[33]

The description of the 'personated bride' in the stage directions offers a bit more information: 'her zone, or girdle about her waist, of white wool, fastened with the Herculean knot' (lines 51–2). Jonson's own footnote offers this explanation: 'That was *nodus Herculeanus* [Hercules' knot], which the husband at night untied in sign of good fortune, that he might be happy in propagation of issue, as Hercules was, who left seventy children' (p. 517). Jonson cites as his authority Sextus Pompeius Festus, who indeed specifies the number seventy, though the great majority of authorities suggested a more modest number: Rabelais, for instance, describes Hercules as one of the 'certain fabulous fornicators . . . who made women of fifty virgins in a single night'. Even Christian critics of pagan eroticism, such as Clement of Alexandria, held the line at fifty, as Jonson himself did in *The Alchemist* (2.2.39).[34] The knot of Hercules, in turn, may be associated with the Amazonian belt, the 'golden belt of Thermodon', as Golding translated it (*Metamorphoses* IX.233). In one of his twelve labours, Hercules defeated the Amazon Hippolyta and seized the belt or girdle she wore, freeing the way, in effect, for Theseus' capture of Hippolyta. The figure of the Amazon, as several scholars have shown, represents an effeminizing, demonized female power, suppressed and contained within patriarchal discourse.[35] Queen Elizabeth, herself frequently compared both to Minerva and to an Amazon, is pictured in two of the Armada portraits with an elaborate knot on her dress precisely in front of her genitals; her virginity is thus signified as intact, just as the maidenhead of England is now safe from the Spanish attack.[36]

But whether the virgin knot derives from Hercules, from Minerva, or from biological semantics, it also remains a 'not', a negation. If it is understood as the '*Hymen quasi Limen*', it is a liminal no-thing, perhaps a knot or puzzle to be undone, a zero, a 'nothing'.[37] Some contemporaries speculated that there was no such thing as the hymen as a matter of biological fact. In his long section on the female reproductive system in *De usu partium*, the premier reference work in the period, Galen never mentions the hymen, and indeed, there seemed to early modern writers no defined *use* for the hymen – except to mark by its absence the loss of virginity. Adherents of the so-called one-sex model of the human body, moreover, either do not mention the hymen or cannot relate it to anything equivalent in the male system.[38] In *Microcosmographia*, Crooke is consistently definitive in his comments, but turns exceedingly tentative in his description of the hymen, referring to what 'many will have to bee a slender membrane ... This they say is broken in the devirgination'. For the 'true History of the Hymen', though, Crooke refers to other texts rather than to any actual observation (233 [sic: 235]). In the 'Questions' at the end of this chapter, moreover, Crooke's answers raise more questions: 'Almost all Physitians thinke that there is a certain membrane ... which they call Hymen. This membrane they say is perforated in the middest' (255). In examining the claim that a virgin will bleed when the hymen is first deflowered – the sole function of the hymen from a male point of view – Crooke invokes textual precedent, but it is not clear: '*Falopius* yeeldeth to this opinion, *Columbus* writeth that he hath seene it, [but] *Laurentius* sayeth' that after many dissections of young maidens 'hee could never finde it though he searched curiously for it with a Probe; which (sayth he) might have beene felt to resist the Probe if there had beene any such thing, and therfore he thinketh that it is but a meere fable. Yet notwithstanding thus far he giveth credite to *Columbus* and *Falopius*, that hee thinketh there is sometimes such a membrane found', but it may be only an 'Organicall disease' or malformation. The letting of blood by the virgin, then, may not always occur, and is no sure sign of virginity. 'Wee must therefore', Crooke concludes, in a passage which must have unsettled many a man at the time, 'finde out some other locke of Virginitie' (256). Similarly, in *The Anatomy of Melancholy* (1621), Robert Burton takes up the argument about whether the sign of virginity is the hymeneal blood, quoting authorities from the Bible, the Greeks, the Egyptians, the Carthaginians, and so forth; revealing the instability of this sign of virginity, Burton concludes that as a test for virginity, hymeneal blood is 'no sufficient trial', according to some authorities, 'And yet others again defend it.'[39] A similar doubt is registered in *Aristotle's Master Piece*, where the anonymous author describes various ways in which the requisite signs of the hymen's presence may fail to appear. The conclusion registers a zone of uncertainty and potential anxiety:

> when a man is married and finds the tokens of his wife's virginity, upon the first act of copulation, he has all the reason in the world to believe her such, but if he finds them not, he has not reason to think her devirginated, if he finds her otherwise sober and modest: Seeing the Hymen may be broken so many other ways, and yet the woman both chaste, and virtuous. Only let me caution virgins to take all imaginable care to keep their virgin zone entire, that so when they marry, they may be such as the great Caesar wished his wife to be, not only without fault but without suspicion also.[40]

But no wife can be without a 'fault', in all the senses of that term; the 'tokens' of virginity are unstable, and if the husband 'finds them not, he has not reason to think' his wife is not a virgin. Ambrose Parey, on the other hand, is not tentative or qualifying at all:

> it is worth observation, that in all this passage there is no such membrane found, as that they called *Hymen*, which they feigned to be broken at the first coition. Yet notwithstanding *Columbus, Fallopius, Wierus,* and many other learned men of our time think otherwise, and say, that in Virgins a litle above the passage of the urine, may be found and seene such a nervous membrane, placed overtwhart [sic] as it were in the middle way of this necke, and perforated for the passage of the courses [i.e. menses]. But you may finde this false by experience.
>
> (Book 3, p. 130)

Parey notes the contradictions among different authorities, including midwives, as to the supposed location of the membrane. Those who rely on the appearance of hymeneal blood as the sign of virginity are making a mistake, he argues, giving as one incredible example a story of prostitutes who have learned to *counterfeit* virginity, by putting into their vaginas 'the bladders of fishes, or galles of beasts filled full of blood, and so deceive the ignorant and young lecher, by the fraud and deceit of their evill arts, and in the time of copulation they mix sighes with groanes, and womanlike cryings, and the crocodiles teares, that they may seeme to be virgins, and never to have dealt with man before' (Book 24, p. 938). Virginity is here reduced to one of the performing 'arts', constituted by nothing more than a set of manipulable signs; but as we have seen, even the existence of virginity's physical manifestation, the hymen, was always constituted by secondary and tertiary signs and emblems. That these could be manipulated, or could not be relied upon to convey any truth about women, is the surprising discovery of much contemporary medical discourse, which questions the very existence of the hymen. If the virgin might actually be a harlot, then the 'lock' of virginity is no sure thing. Maybe, maybe not. The evidence of the hymen's presence depends on the status of the sign, which can only (perhaps) point to its absence. As Parey mused on the contradictions of the hymen, 'But truly of a thing so rare, and which is contrary to nature, there cannot be any thing spoken for certainty' (Book 24, p. 938).

Thus the mystery of virginity that attracts, confuses, and bedevils many of the male characters in Shakespeare's plays, the fetishized commodity that is and is not. The plays circle round this mystification through an oblique language of indirection and negation. The not/knot pun slides further and further from its signified, unable to name it but unable to escape it. Flute tells us, 'A paramour is, God bless us, a thing of naught' (*Dream* 4.2.14), allowing sexual transgression and emptiness to mate in a pun. Ophelia takes up Hamlet's suggestive pun in similar language:

HAMLET   Be not you ashamed to show, he'll not shame to tell you what it
    means.
OPHELIA   You are naught, you are naught.   (3.2.137–40)

And Richard III confounds Clarence's guard,

> Naught to do with Mrs Shore? I tell thee, fellow:
> He that doth naught with her – excepting one –
> Were best to do it secretly alone.
>   (*Richard III* 1.1.99–101)

We may even begin to hear more complex resonances in Viola's para-doxical self-declarations: 'I am not that I play' (*Twelfth Night* 1.5.177) and 'I am not what I am' (3.1.139).

In the Shakespearian language of sexuality, then, a woman is not a virgin whose knot is nought because she has been naught. Virginity is continually invoked, described, celebrated, occluded, denied, and de-nounced, and language can only obliquely represent it. It remains a kind of negation *ex creatio*. 'What I am and what I would', Viola tells the audience, 'are as secret as maidenhead' (*Twelfth Night* 1.5.206–7).

First published in *Shakespeare Survey 46* (1994)

NOTES

1 One of the best discussions of sexuality in the early modern period is Mary Beth Rose, *The Expense of Spirit: Love and Sexuality in English Renaissance Drama* (Ithaca, 1988).

2 For a recent analysis of the crisis of the sign in this period generally, see Barry Taylor, *Vagrant Writing: Social and Semiotic Disorders in the English Renaissance* (Toronto, 1991). The 'world turned upside down' trope, in relation to women, is analysed in Natalie Zemon Davis's classic essay, 'Women on Top', in *Society and Culture in Early Modern France* (Stanford, 1975).

3 *Samuel Johnson: Rasselas, Poems, and Selected Prose*, ed. Bertrand H. Bronson (New York, 1958), p. 252.

4 There is a substantial body of critical commentary on the Renaissance use of the pun; see in particular the luminous work of M. M. Mahood, *Shakespeare's Wordplay* (London, 1957), and Sigurd Burckhardt, *Shakespearean Meanings* (Princeton, 1968). See also William C. Carroll, *The Great Feast of Language in 'Love's Labour's Lost'* (Princeton, 1976).

5 Freud remarks that the malaprop 'does not possess [any inner] inhibition as yet, so that he can produce nonsense and smut directly and without compromise' (Sigmund Freud, *Jokes and Their Relation to the Unconscious*, ed. James Strachey (New York, 1960), p. 185).

6 Roger D. Abrahams, 'The Literary Study of the Riddle', *Texas Studies in Language and Literature*, 14 (1972), p. 187. On the distinction between 'oppositional' and 'non-oppositional' riddles, see Alan Dundes, 'Toward a Structural Definition of the Riddle', in *Analytic Essays in Folklore* (The Hague, 1975).

7 Abrahams, 'The Literary Study of the Riddle', p. 182.

8 P. Goolden, 'Antiochus's Riddle in Gower and Shakespeare', *Review of English Studies*, n.s. 6 (1955), 245–51.

9 Phyllis Gorfain, 'Puzzle and Artifice: The Riddle as Metapoetry in "Pericles" ', *Shakespeare Survey 29* (1976), p. 14. Ruth Nevo describes this riddle as 'dream work methodized', in *Shakespeare's Other Language* (London, 1987), pp. 39–41.

10 See John H. Astington, ' "Fault" in Shakespeare', *Shakespeare Quarterly*, 36 (1985), 330–4. See also Janet Adelman's suggestive comments on this pun in *Hamlet*, in *Suffocating Mothers* (London, 1992), pp. 23–4, 252–3.

11 Shakespeare uses a few terms that appear in contemporary anatomies and midwifery books – the mother, the lap – but they are exceptions to the general pattern. The 'mother' was the uterus (cf. Lear's 'O, how this mother swells up toward my heart', *Lear* F 2.2.231). The 'Lap or Privities' was 'that part into which the necke of the wombe determineth, and is seated

outwardly at the forepart of the share bone, and is as it were a skinny ad-
dition of the necke, as *Galen* speaketh ... aunswering to the prepuce or
foreskin of a man' (Helkiah Crooke, *Microcosmographia: A Description of the
Body of Man* (London, 1615), p. 237; subsequent textual references are to
this edition). Hamlet's request of Ophelia – 'Lady, shall I lie in your lap?'
(*Hamlet* 3.2.107) – is thus quite explicit, as the ensuing dialogue indicates.
The best overview of English Renaissance gynaecological knowledge is
Audrey Eccles, *Obstetrics and Gynaecology in Tudor and Stuart England* (Kent,
Ohio, 1982).

12 Marina Warner, *Alone of All Her Sex: The Myth and the Cult of the Virgin Mary*
(New York, 1976), pp. 72–4.

13 Mary Douglas, *Purity and Danger: An Analysis of the Concepts of Pollution and
Taboo* (London, 1984), p. 115. For a discussion of the ways in which 'sexual
states and functions are used as markers of social identity', using modern
ethnographic evidence, see Kirsten Hastrup, 'The Semantics of Biology:
Virginity', in *Defining Females*, ed. Shirley Ardener (New York, 1978).

14 Cf. the answer in *The Problemes of Aristotle, with other Philosophers and Phisitions*
(London, 1597) to the Question, 'Why doth a woman love that man exceed-
ing well, who had hir maidenhead?': 'Is it bicause that as the matter doth
covet a forme of perfection, so doth a woman the male? or is it by reason of
shamefastnes? for as that divine *Plato* saith, shamefastnes doth follow love.
It is reason that the love and esteeme of him who loosed the bonds of hir
credite and shame. Or is it bicause the beginning of great pleasure, doth
bring a great alteration in the whole, bicause the powers of the minde are
greatly delighted, and sticke and rest immoveably in the same? And therefore *Hesiodus* giveth counsell to marry a maide' (14^v). In his essay on 'The
Taboo of Virginity', Freud offers a more sophisticated but equally gender-
biased explanation of the same alleged phenomenon: 'The maiden whose
desire for love has for so long and with such difficulty been held in check,
in whom the influences of environment and education have formed resistances, will take the man who gratifies her longing, and thereby overcomes
her resistances, into a close and lasting relationship which will never again
be available to any other man. This experience brings about a state of "thral-
dom" in the woman that assures the man lasting and undisturbed possession
of her and makes her able to withstand new impressions and temptations
from without' (Sigmund Freud, *Sexuality and the Psychology of Love*, ed. Philip
Rieff (New York, 1963), p. 70).

15 On the Elizabethan appropriation of the cult of the Virgin, see Frances A.
Yates, *Astraea: The Imperial Theme in the Sixteenth Century* (London, 1975), pp.
29–120; Roy Strong, *The Cult of Elizabeth* (Berkeley, 1977); Louis Adrian
Montrose, '"Shaping Fantasies": Figurations of Gender and Power in
Elizabethan Culture', *Representations*, 2 (1983), 61–94; and C. L. Barber
and Richard P. Wheeler, *The Whole Journey: Shakespeare's Power of Development*
(Berkeley, 1986), pp. 23–38.

16 Carole Levin, 'Power, Politics, and Sexuality: Images of Elizabeth I', in *The*

Politics of Gender in Early Modern Europe, eds. Jean R. Brink, *et al., Sixteenth Century Essays and Studies*, 12 (1989), 95–110; *Ben Jonson*, ed. C. H. Herford and Percy and Evelyn Simpson (Oxford, 1925–52), 1.142.

17 Guy Lee, ed., *The Poems of Catullus* (Oxford, 1990), p. 75.

18 Stephen Orgel, ed., *Christopher Marlowe: The Complete Poems and Translations* (Harmondsworth, 1971), 'Hero and Leander', Sestiad v.473–8. Textual quotations from Marlowe and Chapman are from this edition.

19 Erasmus makes this argument in *Proci et puellae* (1523); see *The Colloquies of Erasmus*, trans. Craig R. Thompson (Chicago, 1965, pp. 86–98). For a concise discussion of the Renaissance doctrine of Increase, with special attention to Shakespeare's sonnets, see J. W. Lever, *The Elizabethan Love Sonnet* (London, 1956), pp. 189–201. Donne (the attribution is in doubt) argues in Paradox XII, 'That Virginity is a Vertue', that 'surely nothing is more unprofitable in the Commonwealth of *Nature*, then they that dy old maids, because they refuse to be used to that end for which they were only made ... *Virginity* ever kept is ever lost' (John Donne, *Paradoxes and Problems*, ed. Helen Peters (Oxford, 1980), pp. 56–7). Cf. Comus' argument in Milton's 'Comus': 'List Lady, be not coy, and be not cozen'd / With that same vaunted name Virginity; / Beauty is nature's coin, must not be hoarded, / But must be current, and the good thereof / Consists in mutual and partak'n bliss, / Unsavory in th'enjoyment of itself. / If you let slip time, like a neglected rose / It withers on the stalk with languish'd head' (*John Milton: Complete Poems and Major Prose*, ed. Merritt Y. Hughes (New York, 1957), lines 737–44, p. 107). Even the anti-libertine argument employed the same rhetoric, as may be seen in the thirteenth-century homily, *Hali Meidenhad*: 'Maidenhood is a treasure that, if it be once lost, will never again be found. Maidenhood is the bloom that, if it be once foully plucked, never again sprouteth up' (*Hali Meidenhad*, ed. Oswald Cockayne (London, 1866), p. 10).

20 Helen's line strikes me as not necessarily a textual crux, as some editors have thought – thus Bevington's *The Complete Works of Shakespeare*, 1.1.165n, as well as the Riverside edition – but as her serious musing on Paroles' comic paradoxes: '*Not* my virginity'.

21 So in Catullus' famous wedding song, the god is summoned by the singing of virgins: ' "o Hymenaee Hymen, / o Hymen Hymenaee", / ut lubentius, audiens / se citarier ad suum / munus, huc aditum ferat / dux bonae Veneris, boni / coniugator amoris' (LXI. 39–45). [' "O Hymeneal Hymen, / O Hymen Hymeneal", / So that the more gladly, hearing / Himself summoned to his proper / Duty, he may make approach here / As the bringer of good Venus / And good love's uniter': Lee, *Poems of Catullus*, pp. 58–9.]

22 Cartari, in *Le imagini de i'dei* (Lyons, 1581), offers an illustration of Hymen with the following commentary: 'Hymen was shown by the ancients in the form of a handsome young man crowned with a diversity of flowers, in his right hand a lighted torch and in his left hand a red veil (or it could be saffron) with which new brides covered their head to face the first time they went to their husbands. And the reason for this ... is that the wives of priests among

the ancient Romans almost always wore a similar veil. Because they were not allowed to divorce, as others were, the covering of the bride with the veil came to mean the desire for the marriage never to be dissolved. This does not preclude also the symbolic meaning of the chaste modesty of the bride, which is the same as Pudor, respected by the ancients so much that it was worshipped like a god' (quoted in John Doebler, *Shakespeare's Speaking Pictures* (Albuquerque, 1974), p. 37).

23 Cf. Lear's vision of the simpering dame, 'Whose face between her forks presages snow' (*Lear* F 4.5.117).

24 In *Pericles*, Boult tells Marina, 'I must have your maidenhead taken off, or the common executioner shall do it' (Sc.19.153–4).

25 Thomas Vicary, *The Anatomie of the Bodie of Man* (1548), eds. F. J. and Percy Furnivall (London, 1888), pp. 77–8. According to Ambrose Parey, the term 'flowers' is used 'because that as in plants the flower buddeth out before the fruits, so in women kinde this flux goeth before the issue, or the conception thereof' (*The Workes of that famous Chirurgion, Ambrose Parey*, trans. Thomas Johnson (London, 1634), Book 24, p. 945). Textual references are to this edition; I will refer to Parey by his Englished name rather than Pare. James Rueff, in *The Expert Midwife* (London, 1637), employs the same terminology of deflowering (also describing former virgins as 'robbed of their best Iewll' (Book 2, p. 59).

26 *The Works of Aristotle, The Famous Philosopher* (New York, 1974), p. 18. This description is quoted again in *Aristotle's Experienced Midwife* (in *The Works*, pp. 80–1), and in *Aristotle's Last Legacy* (in *The Works*, p. 233). The textual history of these spurious works is obscure; Eccles locates copies of the *Master Piece* from 1694, the *Last Legacy* from 1690, and the *Midwife* from 1700, but all are 'certainly derived from much older works' (Eccles, p. 12). In the case of the *Problems of Aristotle* – usually included with the other three works – printed copies exist from 1595. In Hoby's translation of Castiglione's *Courtier* (1561), however, Lord Gasper reports 'a great Philosopher in certaine Problemes of his, saith' that a woman always loves the man who 'hath been the first to receive of her amorous pleasures' (Baldassare Castiglione, *The Book of the Courtier*, trans. Sir Thomas Hoby (London, 1928), p. 199) – i.e. the passage from *The Problemes of Aristotle* quoted in note 14, above. The modern editor cites Aristotle's *Physics* as a source, but Thomas Laqueur (*Making Sex: Body and Gender from the Greeks to Freud* (Cambridge, Mass., 1990), p. 277, n. 23) reports that this idea cannot be found there. The reason is that it comes from the spurious *Problemes*, apparently from an edition much earlier than the earliest known version listed in the STC. By 1615, the idea has become completely conventional: 'Whence is the Proverb (as it hath been said) *Maydens love them that have their maydenhead*' (Richard Brathwaite, *A Strappado for the Divell* (London, 1615), M3^r).

27 '*Claustrum*' was also used in *Aristotle's Master Piece*, pp. 10, 18. For '*Cento*', see Rueff, *The Expert Midwife*, Book 2, p. 52.

28 For Sir Henry Lee's portrait, see Roy Strong, *Gloriana: The Portraits of Queen*

Elizabeth I (New York, 1987), p. 141, plate 149. Cf. the title of Richard Brathwaite's excruciatingly long re-telling of the Pyramus and Thisby story: *Loves Labyrinth: Or the True-Lovers Knot* (London, 1615). The *OED* gives *Hamlet* 4.5.39 as a reference to the true-love flower, where Ophelia sings of 'sweet flowers. / Which bewept to the grave did – not – go / With true-love showers'. Cf. also Vaughan's remarkable poem, 'The Knot', where the heavenly Virgin is addressed: 'Thou art the true Loves-knot; by thee / God is made our Allie, / And mans inferior Essence he / With his did dignifie. / For Coalescent by that Band / We are his body grown, / Nourished with favors from his hand / Whom for our head we own. / And such a Knot, what arm dares loose, / What life, what death can sever? / Which us in him, and him in us / United keeps for ever'. (*The Complete Poetry of Henry Vaughan*, ed. French Fogle (New York, 1964), lines 5–16, p. 302). Phillip Stubbes complains of the fashion in 1583, noting the 'sleeves . . . tyed with true-looves knottes (for so they call them)' (Phillip Stubbes, *Anatomy of the Abuses in England*, ed. F. J. Furnivall (London, 1877–9), 1.74).

29 *The Complete Prose Works of John Milton*, ed. Ernest Sirluck (New Haven, 1959), *D.D.* 2.269.31, *M.B.* 2.467.30. The author of *Hali Meidenhad* notes: 'Look around, seely maiden, if the knot of wedlock be once knotted, let the man be a dump or a cripple, be he whatever he may be, thou must keep to him' (p. 32).

30 J. C. Smith, ed., *Spenser's Faerie Queene* (Oxford, 1909), 1.12.37.1–2; Ernest de Selincourt, ed., *Spenser's Minor Poems* (Oxford, 1910).

31 Milton allows that 'the knot of marriage may in no case be dissolv'd but for adultery' (*Complete Prose Works*, *D.D.* 2.240.29), while Donne prays in erotic language for a separation from the knot in 'Holy Sonnet XIV': 'Yet dearly I love you, and would be loved fain, / But am betrothed unto your enemy, / Divorce me, untie, or break that knot again, / Take me to you, imprison me, for I / Except you enthral me, never shall be free, / Nor ever chaste, except you ravish me' (*John Donne: The Complete English Poems*, ed. A. J. Smith (London, 1976), p. 314). Cf. Leantio's dying words for Bianca in Thomas Middleton's *Women Beware Women*, ed. J. R. Mulryne (London, 1975): 'My heart-string and the marriage-knot that tied thee / Breaks both together' (4.2.44–5).

32 In 'Chapman's Use of Cartari in the Fifth Sestiad of "Hero and Leander"', *Modern Language Review*, 39 (1944), 280–5, D. J. Gordon suggests that Chapman inferred an allusion to Minerva in Cartari's phrase, 'In quo Deam Virginensem vir invocabat'; yet in other passages of Cartari which Chapman has obviously read, the identification with Hercules is quite clear: 'Cingulum id Herculano nodo vinctum'. Cartari, in turn, is simply paraphrasing (as he acknowledges) Sextus Pompeius Festus: 'Hunc Herculaneo nodo vinctum' (*Sexti Pompei Festi: De Verborum Significatu Quae Supersunt Cum Pauli Epitome*, ed. Wallace M. Lindsay (London, 1913), p. 55). Chapman may have made an association with Minerva's shield, with which the maiden warrior-goddess defended her virtue. On the iconography of Minerva's shield, see James Nohrnberg, *The Analogy of the Faerie Queene*

(Princeton, 1976), pp. 456–7. For a broader study, see Rudolf Wittkower, 'Transformations of Minerva in Renaissance Imagery', *Journal of the Warburg Institute*, 2 (1938–9), 194–205.

33 Ben Jonson, *The Complete Masques*, ed. Stephen Orgel (New Haven, 1969). Textual references are to this edition. In *Aristotle's Master Piece*, 'the Zone, or girdle of chastity', is defined as the hole in the middle of the hymen, through which the menses flow (p. 18). The terminology of the 'Zone' may derive from Catullus' famous phrase, 'zonam soluere virgineam', 'to undo a virgin's girdle' (Lee, *Poems of Catullus*, LXVII.28, p. 112).

34 *The Five Books of Gargantua and Pantagruel*, trans. Jacques Le Clercq (New York, 1936), p. 390; *Clement of Alexandria*, trans. G. W. Butterworth (London, 1919), p. 69. Sextus Pompeius Festus seems to have been the first to escalate the number ('septuaginta'), which was also copied by Cartari. Natalis Comes (Chapter 7 of the *Mythologiae*) gives the number as fifty. At some point, moreover, a further escalation in Hercules' sexual power took place, as he is said not just to impregnate fifty (or seventy) virgins, but to do it in a single night (so Jonson at *Alchemist* 2.2.39).

35 See Celeste Turner Wright, 'The Amazons in Elizabethan Literature', *Studies in Philology*, 37 (1940), 433–56; Winfried Schleiner, '*Divina virago*: Queen Elizabeth as an Amazon', *Studies in Philology*, 75 (1978), 163–80; Gabriele Bernhard Jackson, 'Topical Ideology: Witches, Amazons, and Shakespeare's Joan of Arc', *English Literary Renaissance*, 18 (1988), 40–65; and Simon Shepherd, *Amazons and Warrior Women: Varieties of Feminism in Seventeenth-Century Drama* (New York, 1981).

36 See Strong, *Gloriana*, pp. 130 (pl. 138) and 132 (pl. 139). In other portraits, a pearl or other jewel holds the same symbolic place on her dress – pp. 127 (pl. 136), 129 (pl. 137), and 151 (pl. 168).

37 In a very suggestive essay, David Willbern traces 'Shakespeare's Nothing', in *Representing Shakespeare*, eds. Murray M. Schwartz and Coppélia Kahn (Baltimore, 1980). See also the brilliant commentary on the sexual economy of the 'O' in James L. Calderwood, *A Midsummer Night's Dream* (London, 1993).

38 Thomas Laqueur's definitive study, *Making Sex: Body and Gender from the Greeks to Freud*, has no entry in its Index under 'hymen'; the subject is significantly absent throughout. Neither of the two most popular midwifery books available in England in this period – Eucharius Roesslin, *The byrth of mankynde* (London, 1540; 13 editions), and James Guillemeau, *Child-Birth or, The Happy Deliverie of Women* (London, 1612; 2 editions) – ever mentions the hymen, even in their descriptions of the female reproductive system. In *The Sicke Womans Private Looking-Glasse* (London, 1636), John Sadler makes a single, one-line reference to the hymen (Chapter 1, p. 5).

39 Robert Burton, *The Anatomy of Melancholy*, ed. Holbrook Jackson (London, 1932), 3.3.2 (p. 284).

40 *Aristotle's Master Piece*, in *The Works of Aristotle, The Famous Philosopher*, p. 20.

Death and desire in Romeo and Juliet

Lloyd Davis

I

The action of *Romeo and Juliet* occurs between two speeches proclaiming the lovers' deaths – the prologue's forecast of events and the prince's closing summary. The vicissitudes of desire take place in this unusual period, after life yet before death. It is a kind of liminal phase in which social and personal pressures build to intense pitch before they are settled. Such liminal tension, as Victor Turner suggests, is the very stuff of which social dramas are made.[1] It figures a mounting crisis that envelops those observing and taking part in the unfolding action. At the same time, this temporal setting has a range of interpretative implications.

With the lovers' deaths announced from the start, audience attention is directed to the events' fateful course. The question is less what happens than how it happens. By framing the action in this way, the prologue triggers various generic and narrative effects. First, it establishes the play as 'a tragedy of fate' similar to Kyd's *The Spanish Tragedy*, which gives 'the audience a superior knowledge of the story from the outset, reducing the hero's role to bring into prominence the complex patterns of action'.[2] In turn, this generic marker initiates a compelling narrative, poised between prolepsis and analepsis, as opening portents of death are played off against background details and further intimations in the following scenes.[3] The tension between these hints and flashbacks fills the narrative with foreboding. The breakneck speed of events (in contrast to the extended time frame of Arthur Brooke's version, a few days as opposed to nine months)[4] sees the ordained end bear relentlessly on the lovers. They are caught between a determining past and future.

The narrative has a further generic analogue. Gayle Whittier suggests that the play develops through a contrast between sonnet lyricism and tragedy that is finally reconciled in death: 'the "spoken lines" of the

35

Prologue predestine the plot of the play to be tragic from without, even as the spirit of Petrarchan poetry spoken by Romeo to Juliet finally necessitates their tragic deaths from within'.[5] What first appears as thematic conflict between two of the period's key literary modes makes way for a troubling similarity. The spirit of Petrarchism is revealed as tragically fatal and idealized romance collapses.

In this view, *Romeo and Juliet* stages the outcome of unfulfillable desire. Although it appears to reverse the erotic story told in the Sonnets, the dramatic narrative ends up paralleling the failing course of identity and desire which can be traced through those poems. There the poet reluctantly finds his desire shifting from the self-gratifying potential figured by the youth to the disarming dark lady, who offers instead 'a desire that her very presence at the same time will frustrate'.[6] This pattern initially seems to be inverted in the play – Romeo willingly renounces self-centred longing for Rosaline, Juliet tests and proves her self-reliance, both find true love in each other. However, their love ends in reciprocal death, with the Petrarchan images fatally embodied and materialized. The links between love and death unveil a dark scepticism about desire, despite bursts of romantic idealism. They convey a sense of futility and ironic fate which Romeo momentarily feels but is able to forget for a time, 'my mind misgives / Some consequence yet hanging in the stars / Shall bitterly begin his fearful date / With this night's revels' (1.4.106–9).

Such scepticism appears in many subsequent literary and psychoanalytic conceptions, where possibilities of romantic union are queried.[7] These questions carry implications about selfhood and desire and about ways of representing them. In theories and stories of divorce or isolation, selfhood is not effaced but conceived as incomplete; as Barbara Freedman puts it, 'The denial of self-presence doesn't negate presence but redefines it as a distancing or spacing we always seek but fail to close'.[8] Characters cannot attain their goals, and the inability to claim satisfaction affects desire as much as selfhood. Proceeding from an uncertain source, desire remains 'predicated on lack, and even its apparent fulfilment is also a moment of loss'.[9] In this view, desire and presence are forever intertwined: 'Differantiated [*sic*] presence, which is always and inevitably differed and deferred, and which in consequence exceeds the alternatives of presence and absence, is the condition of desire'.[10] They forestall each other's wholeness yet continue to provide the self with images of consummation, contentment and victory – the curtsies, kisses, suits, livings and battles which Mercutio's dreamers envisage but cannot clasp, 'Begot of nothing but vain fantasy, / Which is as thin of substance as the air, / And more inconstant than the wind' (1.4.98–100).

The recurrence of this viewpoint in fiction and theory suggests that *Romeo and Juliet* stages a paradigmatic conflict between ways of representing and interpreting desire. The play affects these possibilities by placing idealized and tragic conceptions of desire and selfhood in intense dialogue with each other. This dialogue continues to be played out in literary and theoretical texts since, as Alan Sinfield notes, notions of sexuality and gender are 'major sites of ideological production upon which meanings of very diverse kinds are established and contested'.[11] *Romeo and Juliet* informs and illustrates a cultural history of desire in which images of romantic fulfilment or failure carry great importance.

As well as being part of this history, Shakespeare's play has two other distinctive temporal features. First, as noted above, it unfolds over a charged time span. Time allows desire to be acted out but also threatens its fulfilment, by either running out or not stopping. This equivocal link affects desire's tragic course in *Romeo and Juliet*, 'as the time and place / Doth make against' the characters (5.3.223–4).

Secondly, its depiction of desire reverberates with erotic tropes from earlier traditions – Platonic, Ovidian, Petrarchan, as well as popular sayings. These tropes are used by the characters to talk and think about relationships, but they are also challenged for not allowing the gap between self and other to be bridged. They are unfulfilling since it feels as if they belong to someone else; as Astrophil puts it, 'others' feet still seemed but strangers in my way'.[12] The lovers are often dissatisfied with or unsure about the words of others. Their discontent grows from early dismissals such as Romeo's 'Yet tell me not, for I have heard it all' (1.1.171) and 'Thou talk'st of nothing' (1.4.96), or Juliet's 'And stint thou, too, I pray thee, Nurse' (1.3.60), to deeper disquiet over the inability of this language to match their experience: 'Thou canst not speak of that thou dost not feel' (3.3.64); 'Some say the lark makes sweet division; / This doth not so, for she divideth us' (3.5.29–30). The corollary of their frustration with the language of others and of the past is the value they put on their own: 'She speaks. / O, speak again, bright angel' (2.1.67–8); 'every tongue that speaks / But Romeo's name speaks heavenly eloquence' (3.2.32–3).

Like the lovers, the play also seeks to revise existing rhetorical conventions. It reworks these tropes into personal, tragic terms which underlie later literary and psychological conceptions. Hence, in addition to exemplifying Stephen Greenblatt's point that 'psychoanalysis is the historical outcome of certain characteristic Renaissance strategies',[13] *Romeo and Juliet* shows that these strategies develop in response to earlier discourses. The play's pivotal role in later depictions of desire stems from the way it juxtaposes historical and emergent conceptions.

These complex temporal and rhetorical effects are hinted at in the Prologue, which repeatedly sets past, present and future against each other. 'Our scene' is initially laid in a kind of continuous present, yet one that remains hanging between 'ancient grudge' and 'new mutiny'. Likewise, the 'star-crossed lovers take their life' in a present whose intimations of living and loving are circumscribed by 'the fatal loins' of 'their parents' strife'. As the birth-suicide pun on 'take their life' hints, sexuality is already marked by violence and death, its future determined by the past's impact on the present. The Prologue ends by anchoring the staging of 'death-marked love' in the here and now of the audience, who attend 'the two-hours' traffic of our stage'. It anticipates a successful theatrical conclusion, with the play's performance 'striv[ing] to mend' what the lovers 'shall miss' – a kind of closure that their desire cannot realize. In contrast to the simple linear Chorus to Act 2, which culminates in the lovers' union, the rebounding moments of the Prologue displace consummation with death.[14]

A complicity between sex and death is well known in Renaissance texts. Its function in *Romeo and Juliet* is, however, distinguished by temporal shifts which define the characters' relations. While the lovers in a poem such as Donne's 'The Canonization' exceed worldly time and place, and their post-coital condition is eternally celebrated, in Shakespeare's play the links between past and present, social and personal, cannot be transcended. The intense oneness felt by the lovers appears to signify mutual presence, but such intersubjective moments are overlaid with social and historical pressures. The drama alternates between instants of passion, when time seems to stand still, and inevitable returns to the ongoing rush of events. This contrast is manifested not only in the characterization and plot but in the interplay of underlying traditions, sources and tropes. The play reiterates and revises these conventions, confirming a conception of desire that speeds not to its goal but its end. In this conception personal presence can exist only as a transient, illusory sign of desire.

II

One of the main influences *Romeo and Juliet* has had on later depictions of love lies in its celebration of personal desire. The force of this celebration comes partly from its dramatic mode, staging the lovers' experiences for a 'live' audience. In the decades after the play was first performed, poetry (till then, the key romantic discourse) was changing from oral to written modes. Until the rise of the novel, drama remained the pre-eminent form for presenting love stories, and stage performance could give these tales the confessional tones which earlier forms of poetic recitation doubtless achieved. The Prologue enacts this shift by relocating the love sonnet in the drama, a move again underlined by the verse which the lovers will soon share in Act 1, scene 5.

On stage, the impact of the 'personal' can come across in different ways – through physical, verbal, even interpersonal performance. In *Romeo and Juliet* these forms of presence concentrate in the protagonists' unshakeable love. It seems to assume an essential quality which captures the 'diachronic unity of the subject'.[15] This unity underwrites numerous adaptations of and responses to the play, from elaborate stage productions, operas and ballets, to more popular versions such as the American musical *West-Side Story* or the Australian narrative verse of C. J. Dennis's *A Sentimental Bloke*, whose colloquial tones add to the impression of true romance. For many audience groups, each of these transformations once again discovers the play's 'spirit', which surpasses local differences to reveal truths about desire and 'ourselves'.

The director's programme notes to a recently well-received production in Australia illustrate this kind of response. The mixed tones of confession and authority sway the audience to accept his views:

My fascination with this play continues. Considerable research over the years has taken me twice to Verona and Mantua, but the conflict in Bosnia has brought the work urgently closer. I first considered a Muslim-Christian setting several months before the tragedy of Bosko and Admira ... A study of the text supplies no religious, class, nor race barriers between the 'two households' and this makes Shakespeare's vision all the more powerful. When differences are minimal, ancient grudges seem the more difficult to understand. Yet they remain with us today, passed on by our parents. It seems the one thing we teach the next generation is how to maintain rage and other forms of prejudices. Thus this work is as much about young people in the Brisbane Mall today as it is about the hot days in medieval Verona ... The human spirit, as portrayed by the 31 year old playwright, is a thing of wonder to be nurtured and treasured.[16]

The paradoxical effects of citing 'real' personal and political situations are first to detach the drama from its own historical concerns and then to efface the ideological grounds of the current crisis. The revelation of 'human spirit' triumphs over any tragic significance. Indeed, the play's freedom from material contexts testifies to its, its author's, and our affirming 'vision'. This viewpoint recalls Coleridge's claim that Shakespeare is 'out of time', his characters 'at once true to nature, and fragments of the divine mind that drew them'.[17]

Because it hides sexual, class and ethnic factors behind archetypal human experience, this sort of perception of Shakespeare's work becomes a target of materialist criticism:

> Idealised and romanticised out of all dialectical relationship with society, it [Shakespeare's work] takes on the seductive glamour of aestheticism, the sinister and self-destructive beauty of decadent romance . . . this 'Shakespeare myth' functions in contemporary culture as an ideological framework for containing consensus and for sustaining myths of unity, integration and harmony in the cultural superstructures of a divided and fractured society.[18]

In relation to sexual issues, universal images of the personal in *Romeo and Juliet* can be seen as helping to naturalize notions of desire which reinforce an 'ideology of romantic love' in terms of 'heterosexualizing idealization' and the 'canonization of heterosexuality'.[19] Personal romance and desire are revealed as authoritative codes which conceal and impose official sexuality.

The kinds of ideological impacts that the 'personal' registers may be intensified *or* interrogated by the generic effects of 'Excellent conceited Tragedie', as the Quarto titles announce. The combination of personal experience and tragic consequence can turn *Romeo and Juliet* into an account of contradictory notions of desire and identity, in line with Jonathan Dollimore's recognition that, notwithstanding traditions of celebration 'in terms of man's defeated potential', tragedy questions ideological norms.[20] The genre's ambiguous drift to 'radical' or cathartic ends sees the play assume a kind of meta-textual disinterestedness, distanced from final interpretations as it seems to reflect on how desire may be conceived and staged. This distance can be observed in the play's citing and reworking of tropes and conventions from existing discourses of love and romance. The intertextual traces reveal continuities and changes in the depiction of desire, keyed to social and historical notions of the personal and interpersonal.

Platonism is traditionally seen as offering a set of tropes that affirm selfhood and desire as forms of true being despite possibilities of loss.[21] In the *Symposium*, for instance, Socrates defines love as desire for what one lacks, either a specific quality or a lost or missing element of the self. Aristophanes goes so far as to image love as a 'longing for and following after [a] primeval wholeness . . . the healing of our dissevered nature'. The *Symposium* deals with this incipiently tragic situation by redirecting desire to the heavens; in a comedic resolution, love's lack is fulfilled by catching sight of 'the very soul of beauty . . . beauty's very self'.[22] Such vision provides the model for Renaissance Petrarchism.

This model is famously reproduced in Pietro Bembo's Neoplatonic paean to divine love at the close of Castiglione's *The Courtier*. He recounts 'a most happie end for our desires', as the courtier forsakes sensual desire for a wiser love that guides the soul: 'through the particular beautie of one bodie hee guideth her to the universall beautie of all bodies . . . Thus the soule kindled in the most holy fire of true heavenly love, fleeth to couple her self with the nature of Angels'. This 'most holy love' is 'derived of the unitie of the heavenly beautie, goodnesse and wisedom', and in narrating its course Bembo himself undergoes an ecstatic loss of identity. He speaks as if 'ravished and beside himselfe', and emphasizes that 'I have spoken what the holy furie of love hath (unsought for) indited to me'.[23] Speaking and experiencing true desire are related forms of self-transcendence, and Bembo can rejoice in the loss of selfhood.

Similar experience underpins the double structure of Edmund Spenser's *Fowre Hymnes*, first published in 1596, around the time *Romeo and Juliet* was written. The hymn in honour of earthly love characterizes the lover as Tantalus, feeding 'his hungrie fantasy, / Still full, yet neuer satisfyde . . . For nought may quench his infinite desyre'. This figure is recast in the corresponding hymn of heavenly love, where the poet renounces his earlier poems – 'lewd layes' which showed love as a 'mad fit' – for a lover linked to 'high eternall powre'.[24] In these instances, the lack or absence which motivates love is conceived positively, part of a spiritual response which lifts the lover beyond temporal identity. Through its philosophic or poetic utterance, the self is not destroyed but surpassed.

However, the link between lack and love can also affect selfhood less positively, even fatally. Classical texts again offer tropes and characters to Renaissance authors. Ovid depicts less drastic versions of desire and self-loss in the changes that Jove makes to pursue various nymphs. These can be read in varying ways – on the one hand, a carnivalesque switching of sexual roles for the sake of pleasure; on the other, a sequence of illusory identities that offers no final fulfilment. Though Jove's transformations bring different degrees of satisfaction, none is tragically oriented (at least for himself). In contrast, the tale of Narcissus sets desire and self-hood in irresolvable conflict. In Arthur Golding's 1567 translation of the *Metamorphoses*, Narcissus gazes into the pond to find that 'He knowes not what it was he sawe. And yet the foolishe elfe / Doth burn in ardent love thereof. The verie selfe same thing / That doeth bewitch and blinde his eyes, encreaseth all his sting'.[25] His desire cannot be satisfied, and the attempt to do so pains and then destroys selfhood.

Opposing notions of genre, time and character underlie these figures of ecstasy and loss. Platonic and Neoplatonic transcendence is marked by timelessness and selflessness. It brings narration and character to an end, as the self enjoys eternal fusion with the other. In comparison, Ovidian images of disguised or deluded self-loss entail conflict within or between characters. These interactions rely on distinct, often opposed, figures who respond to each other through time. Their fates frequently impose eternities of lonely, unfulfilled selfhood.

Platonic images of true desire and identity are invoked in Shakespeare's comedies during the 1590s; but even there, as characters move to romantic union, they are usually questioned. The disguises, confusions and mistakes through which love's destiny is reached may suggest random or enforced effects that unsettle 'nature's bias'. In a less equivocal way, Shakespeare's use of Ovidian images of desire and selfhood tends to limit or foreclose positive readings, especially where narcissistic traces are discerned. This tendency takes place in both comic and tragic genres: 'Like Ovid's tales, Shakespeare's comedies never lose sight of the painfulness and the potential for the grotesque or for disaster wrought by love's changes . . . If part of the Ovidianism of the comedies is their potential for violence and tragedy, it would seem logical to expect that Ovidianism to be developed in the tragedies'.[26] In *Venus and Adonis*, for example, the humour of the goddess's overweening desire and her beloved's petulance changes to grim consequence. 'The field's chief flower' (line 8) is mournfully plucked, recalling Narcissus's end, 'A purple flower sprung up, chequered with white, / Resembling well his pale cheeks, and the blood / Which in round drops upon their whiteness stood' (lines 1168–70). The characters have shared an ironic desire whose deathly goal was unwittingly imaged by Venus, 'Narcissus so himself himself forsook, / And died to kiss his shadow in the brook' (lines 161–2). As noted earlier, comparable effects occur throughout *Romeo and Juliet*, where moments of romantic union are disrupted by ongoing events that undercut their idealism. The mixed genres in these tales represent desire as a hybrid of the comic, tragic and ironic.[27]

Related images of threatening or incomplete desire and self-transformation are repeated through many sixteenth- and seventeenth-century texts, from the angst of sonneteers to Montaigne's musings in the *Apologie of Raymond Sebond* on 'The lustfull longing which allures us to the acquaintance of women, [and] seekes but to expell that paine, which an earnest and burning desire doth possesse-us-with, and desireth but to allay it thereby to come to rest, and be exempted from this fever'.[28] As most of these references suggest, this notion of erotic jeopardy is almost always tied to masculine conceptions of desire and selfhood. The pains of desire are indulged if not celebrated, and they may convert to misogyny, as in Hamlet's tirade against Ophelia or Romeo's charge that Juliet's beauty 'hath made me effeminate' (3.1.114).

This attitude echoes through Romeo's early laments about Rosaline. As Coleridge noted, he is 'introduced already love-bewildered':[29] 'I have lost myself. I am not here. / This is not Romeo; he's some other where' (1.1.194–5). Amid these tones of despair a self-satisfied note can be heard. The early Romeo is a 'virtual stereotype of the romantic lover',[30] whose role-playing brings a kind of egotistic reassurance. The lament for self-loss becomes proof of self-presence, a 'boastful positiveness',[31] with Romeo still to know the unsettling force of desire.

From this point, the play proceeds by exploring the limits of the Platonic, Ovidian and Petrarchan tropes. The seriousness of narcissistic absorption is questioned (underlined by Mercutio's quips at romantic indulgence);[32] yet the full consequence of desire is not realized in Platonic union but deferred to its aftermath. None of the conventional models can quite convey what is at stake in the lovers' story, and the discourse of desire must be revised.

III

Clearly, then, *Romeo and Juliet* invents neither tragic nor personal notions of desire. Both are strongly at work in Shakespeare's direct source, Brooke's *The Tragicall Historye of Romeus and Juliet* (1562): the threats to selfhood caused by love; the workings of 'False Fortune' and 'wavering Fortunes whele'; an intense desire that can be quenched 'onely [by] death and both theyr bloods'; time as tragic and ironic, first intimated in woe at Juliet's 'untimely death' and then gaining full significance as Romeus's man tells him 'too soone' of her end.[33]

While it reiterates these ideas, Shakespeare's play also develops and sharpens the connections among desire, the personal and the tragic. The lovers create new images of individuality and of togetherness in order to leave their worldly selves behind. Yet their efforts remain circumscribed by social forces. The ironic result is that the ideal identities the lovers fashion in order to realize their desire become the key to its tragic loss. Self-transcendence can be experienced but not as a kind of timeless ecstasy; instead it becomes entwined with unfulfilled desire.

The play personalizes desire in ways which constantly alternate between idealism and failure. As Kay Stockholder notes, threats to desire are 'externalized' and the lovers consciously create 'a radiant world apart by attributing all inimical forces to surrounding circumstance'.[34] In this reordering of reality, desire becomes part or even constitutive of private, individual identity. Romeo and Juliet's love is secret from others and transgresses the roles imposed by their families. In *The Petite Pallace of Pettie his Pleasure* (1576), George Pettie considered this opposition the key to the story: 'such presiness of parents brought Pyramus and Thisbe to a woful end, Romeo and Julietta to untimely death'.[35] In *A Midsummer Night's Dream* and *Romeo and Juliet*, resisting or contesting patriarchal authority allows a temporary move towards selfhood.

Through this contest, love appears to be one's own, yet both plays show the impossibility of holding onto it. The personal is as elusive as it is idealized, destined to slip back into constraining and distorting social forms. In retrospect, we may see this elusiveness pre-figured in the lovers' first meeting, an intense bonding that occurs amid an elaborate ritual of masks and misrecognition. The symbolic means through which love must be expressed will prevent its consummation.[36] For the moment, however, love beholds a single object of desire, whose truth authenticates the lover and recreates both their identities: 'Deny thy father and refuse thy name, / Or if thou wilt not, be but sworn my love, / And I'll no longer be a Capulet . . . Call me but love and I'll be new baptized. / Henceforth I never will be Romeo' (2.1.76–93).

The nexus between identity and desire is strengthened by the need for secrecy. Hidden and equivocated as the lovers move between private and public realms, secret desire endows selfhood with interiority and intention. It grants a depth of character, and even if its longings are not fulfilled inner experience is confirmed. Juliet's cryptic replies to her mother's attack on Romeo reveal private pleasure couched in pain: 'O, how my heart abhors / To hear him named and cannot come to him / To wreak the love I bore my cousin / Upon his body that hath slaughtered him!' (3.5.99–102). Like secret desire, the obstacles to fulfilment sharpen internal experience and give it a kind of sensuous reality: 'runaways' eyes may wink, and Romeo / Leap to these arms untalked of and unseen. / Lovers can see to do their amorous rites / By their own beauties' (3.2.6–9).

This deep desire and selfhood develop in terms of intentionality – desire *for* someone, effected through imagination, speech and action.

Desire marks the self as agent, and tragic desire portrays the onus of agency. It is felt sharply by Juliet before she takes the friar's potion, 'My dismal scene I needs must act alone' (4.3.19), and by Romeo as he enters the Capulet tomb 'armed against myself' (5.3.65). In this sense, the play's depiction of desire is linked to representations of subjectivity that emerge during the sixteenth century. It reflects the important role that tropes such as the secret, with its social and personal disguises, have in discourses which are starting to inscribe both an inner self and the individual as agent.

Even as it invests in such notions of selfhood, at its most intense desire in *Romeo and Juliet* surpasses individual experience and realizes an intersubjective union. The lovers re-characterize each other as much as themselves: 'Romeo, doff thy name, / And for thy name – which is no part of thee – / Take all myself' (2.1.89–91). Again this effect has generic analogues, as we see the lovers' discourse moving beyond single-voiced Petrarchism. They share exchanges which reveal 'not only the other's confirming response, but also how we find ourselves in that response'.[37] Unlike contemporary sonnet sequences, which portray the poet by stifling the woman's voice (just as Romeo invokes and silences Rosaline), the play is marked by the lovers' dialogues. This reciprocity is epitomized by the sonnet they co-construct and seal with a kiss at their first meeting (1.5.92–105).[38] It is a highly suggestive moment, capturing the separateness of the lovers' world and speech from others, and also rewriting the dominant 1590s genre for representing desire. The sonnet is re-envoiced as dialogue, its meanings embodied in the climactic kiss. At the same time, the heightened artifice of the scene intimates its transience. The lovers start another sonnet but are interrupted by Juliet's garrulous nurse, who foreshadows the dire interventions of others. A further irony is also implied – as noted earlier, their union will be ended by events that literalize poetic tropes of love and death: Romeo really does die 'with a kiss' (5.3.120), and Juliet falls in eternal sexual embrace, 'O happy dagger, / This is thy sheath! There rust, and let me die' (5.3.168–9).[39]

The deaths verify the Prologue's vision of inescapable ties between sex and violence. Not only can the lovers not escape the eternal feud that frames them, they even play parts in it, responding impulsively, at the threshold of nature and nurture, to news of Mercutio's and Tybalt's deaths. For a moment their union bows under its violent heritage as each impugns the other: 'O sweet Juliet, / Thy beauty hath made me effeminate, / And in my temper softened valour's steel' (3.1.113–15);

'did Romeo's hand shed Tybalt's blood? · · · O serpent heart, hid with a flow'ring face!' (3.2.71–3)

Other characters also link sex and violence, suggesting that the connection has become naturalized and accepted. The Capulet servants joke aggressively about raping and killing the Montague women (1.1.22–4). The friar parallels birth and death, 'The earth, that's nature's mother, is her tomb. / What is her burying grave, that is her womb' (2.3.9–10), and is later echoed by Romeo, who calls the Capulet crypt a 'womb of death' (5.3.45). The friar also connects 'violent delights' to 'violent ends' (2.5.9), and the lovers' suicides suggest a final fusing of love and death. Yet as different interpretations maintain, this fusion's meaning may be tragic, romantic, or both. The lovers are 'consumed and destroyed by the feud' and seem to rise above it, 'united in death'.[40]

The final scene thus accentuates the connections among selfhood, death and desire. It caps off the discourse of tragic desire announced by the Prologue – a tradition of failed love known through numerous European novellas, the second volume of *The Palace of Pleasure* (1567), and two editions of Brooke's *Tragicall Historye* (1562, 1587). The action has thus had a doubly repetitive stamp, not only replaying this oft-told tale but restaging what the Prologue has stated. Foreknowledge of the outcome plays off against moments of romantic and tragic intensity, and triggers a kind of anxious curiosity that waits to see the details of the deaths – the near misses of delayed messages, misread signs, plans gone awry.

Through this repetitive structure, the play affirms precedents and conditions for its own reproduction as if anticipating future responses. Before ending, it even shows these possibilities being realized. The grieving fathers decide to build statues of the lovers, and the prince's final lines look forward to 'more talk of these sad things', in an effort to establish once and for all what desire's tragic end might mean (5.3.306). As Dympna Callaghan observes, the play not only 'perpetuates an already well-known tale', but its closure is predicated on 'the possibility of endless retellings of the story – displacing the lovers' desire onto a perpetual narrative of love'.[41]

Patterns of repetition weave through the play as well as framing it. Characters constantly restate what has previously been staged – in the first scene Benvolio explains how the opening brawl started, and later he recounts details of Mercutio's and Tybalt's deaths and Romeo's involvement; the Chorus to the second act reiterates the lovers' meeting; the Nurse tells Juliet of Tybalt's death; the Capulets and Paris echo each other's lamentations over Juliet's apparent death;[42] and lastly the Friar recaps the whole plot to the other characters after the bodies are found. These instances are part of the effort to explain the violent meaning of events, but as the prince's closing words suggest, something extra needs to be told, 'never was a story of more woe / Than this of Juliet and her Romeo' (5.3.308–9). There is a sense that 'this' version of the story exceeds earlier ones. For all its repetition of tropes and narratives, in closing the play recognizes and stresses a difference from precursors.

Other repetitive designs through the play are used to underline the tension between desire and death. Four meetings and kisses shared by Romeo and Juliet structure the romance plot. They are in counterpoint to four violent or potentially violent eruptions that occur between the male characters, especially involving Tybalt. A muted fifth interruption is provided by the presence of Tybalt's corpse in the Capulet crypt where Juliet and Romeo finally meet and miss each other. These turbulent scenes frame the romantic ones, unsettling the lyric and erotic essence which they seem to capture.

The repetitions and retellings connect with the representation of time in the play, imposing a destructive pressure between the weight of social and family history and personal longings. Social and personal time are opposed, and desire is caught between these conflicting time frames. Social time is frequently indexed through the play, in general terms such as the 'ancient grudge' and through the scheduling of specific events such as Capulet's banquet and Juliet's wedding to Paris. Against this scheme, the lovers' meetings seem to dissolve time, making it speed up or, more powerfully, stop and stand still, as the present is transformed into 'the time of love'.[43] The lovers seek to disregard time and death in their union, 'Then love-devouring death do what he dare – It is enough I may but call her mine' (2.5.7–8). Yet this passionate energy also drives the drama to its finale, and Romeo's words link their union and separation with death. The time of love confronts the passing of its own presence.

In various ways, then, *Romeo and Juliet* renovates tragic desire for the Elizabethans and for subsequent periods. In early scenes it evokes a narcissistic poetics of desire as self-loss and death but moves beyond that to stage a dialogic reciprocal presence. The reappearance of death then inscribes ineluctable external influences – the determinations of time and history which frame desire – and the impossible idealization of self and other which passion seeks but fails to find. In this sense, Shakespeare's play marks a complex intersection between historical and emergent discourses of desire. First, in a period when modern institutions of family, marriage and romance are starting to appear, it translates Platonic, Ovidian and Petrarchan tropes of ecstasy and love into personal notions of desire. Next, it conceives desire as the interplay between passion, selfhood and death. And thirdly, its equivocal staging of love's death anticipates the tension between romantic and sceptical visions of desire that runs through many later literary and theoretical works.

It could be said that the play's symbolic bequest to these works is a notion of desire as lost presence. Though love continues to be celebrated as present or absent or present-in-absence in many texts (in different ways, Herbert's poetry and Brontë's *Wuthering Heights* come to mind), a significant line of literary works explores the interplay among desire, death and selfhood. Like *Romeo and Juliet*, these texts place desire in conflict with time, recounting moments of ideal presence whose future reveals they could never have been. This revision of desire begins with Shakespeare's later tragedies – *Hamlet, Othello, Macbeth* and *Antony and Cleopatra* – where one lover survives, though briefly, to feel the other's loss. It runs from the fallen lovers of *Paradise Lost* ('we are one, / One flesh; to lose thee were to lose myself' [9.958–9]), to the equivocal pairings at the end of Dickens's great novels or the images of foreclosed desire in Henry James's major phase. Its most poignant statement comes at the close of Scott Fitzgerald's *The Great Gatsby*:

the green light, the orgiastic future that year by year recedes before us. It eluded us then, but that's no matter – to-morrow we will run faster, stretch out our arms farther . . . And one fine morning –
So we beat on, boats against the current, borne back ceaselessly into the past.

If *Romeo and Juliet* helps to initiate this tradition, it does so as the last tragedy of desire. For in these later texts the note is of melancholic rather than tragic loss: what hurts is not that desire ends in death but that it ends before death. The present then becomes a time for recounting lost desire, and the self's task is to try to hold the story together. 'The subject's centre of gravity is this present synthesis of the past which we call history', writes Lacan.[44] Like Romeo's last letter, this history reveals the 'course of love' (5.3.286) to those who remain.

First published in *Shakespeare Survey 49* (1996)

NOTES

1 *Drama, Fields, and Metaphors: Symbolic Action in Human Society* (Ithaca, 1974), pp. 40–1 and *passim*.

2 Brian Gibbons, Introduction, in *Romeo and Juliet* (London, 1980), p. 37.

3 On analepsis and prolepsis, see Shlomith Rimmon-Kenan, *Narrative Fiction: Contemporary Poetics* (London, 1983), pp. 46ff.

4 Gibbons, Introduction, p. 54.

5 Gayle Whittier, 'The Sonnet's Body and the Body Sonnetized in *Romeo and Juliet*', *Shakespeare Quarterly*, 40 (1989), 27–41; p. 40.

6 Joel Fineman, *Shakespeare's Perjured Eye: The Invention of Poetic Subjectivity in the Sonnets* (Berkeley, 1986), p. 24.

7 Two of the primary psychoanalytic texts are *Civilization and Its Discontents*, and *Beyond the Pleasure Principle*. A clear reading of this direction in Freud is offered by Jean Laplanche, *Life and Death in Psychoanalysis*, trans. Jeffrey Mehlman (Baltimore, 1976): 'the death drive is the very soul, the constitutive principle of libidinal circulation' (p. 124). Related scepticism underlies Lacan's view of the link between desire and demand. Desire is dependent on demand, but demand, 'by being articulated in signifiers, leaves a metonymic remainder that runs under it . . . an element that is called desire': desire leads only to desire. See *The Four Fundamental Concepts of Psycho-Analysis*, trans. Alan Sheridan (New York, 1981), p. 154; compare Catherine Belsey's gloss of Lacan's view – 'desire subsists in what eludes both vision and representation, in what exceeds demand, including the demand for love' – in *Desire: Love Stories in Western Culture* (Oxford, 1994), p. 139.

8 *Staging the Gaze: Postmodernism, Psychoanalysis, and Shakespearean Comedy* (Ithaca, 1991), p. 110.

9 Belsey, *Desire*, pp. 38–9.

10 Ibid., p. 70.

11 *Faultlines: Cultural Materialism and the Politics of Dissident Reading* (Oxford, 1992), p. 128.

12 *Sir Philip Sidney: Selected Poems*, ed. Katherine Duncan-Jones (Oxford, 1973), p. 117. As discussed below, this first sonnet's turn to a seemingly authentic self is also made in *Romeo and Juliet*.

13 Stephen Greenblatt, 'Psychoanalysis and Renaissance Culture', in *Literary Theory / Renaissance Texts*, ed. Patricia Parker and David Quint (Baltimore, 1986), 210–24; p. 224.

14 'But passion lends them power, time means, to meet, / Tempering extremities with extreme sweet' (2 Chor. 13–14). The Chorus, not included in first Quarto, is reprinted in the Arden edition (see n. 2).

15 Catherine Belsey, *The Subject of Tragedy: Identity and Difference in Renaissance Drama* (London, 1985), p. 34.

16 Aubrey Mellor, 'From the Artistic Director', in Queensland Theatre Company Program for *Romeo and Juliet* (Brisbane, 1993), p. 3.

17 Samuel Taylor Coleridge, *Lectures on Shakespeare and Other Poets and Dramatists*, Everyman's Library (London: Dent, 1914), p. 410.

18 Graham Holderness, Preface: 'All this', in *The Shakespeare Myth*, ed. Graham Holderness (Manchester, 1988), pp. xii–xiii.

19 See Dympna Callaghan, 'The Ideology of Romantic Love: The Case of

Romeo and Juliet, in Dympna Callaghan, Lorraine Helms and Jyotsna Singh, *The Weyward Sisters: Shakespeare and Feminist Politics* (Oxford, 1994), pp. 59–101; Jonathan Goldberg, '*Romeo and Juliet*'s Open Rs', in *Queering the Renaissance*, ed. Jonathan Goldberg (Durham, 1994), 218–35; p. 227; and Joseph A. Porter, 'Marlowe, Shakespeare, and the Canonization of Heterosexuality', *South Atlantic Quarterly*, 88 (1989), 127–47.

20 *Radical Tragedy: Religion, Ideology and Power in the Age of Shakespeare and His Contemporaries* (Chicago, 1984), p. 49.

21 Cf. Michel Foucault, *The Use of Pleasure*, vol. 2 of *The History of Sexuality*, trans. Robert Hurley (New York, 1990), p. 5 and *passim*.

22 *Symposium*, in *The Collected Dialogues of Plato*, ed. Edith Hamilton and Huntington Cairns (Princeton, 1985), 193a–c, 211d–e.

23 Baldassare Castiglione, *The Book of the Courtier*, trans. Sir Thomas Hoby (London, 1948), pp. 319–22.

24 *Fowre Hymnes*, 'A Hymne in Honovr of Love' (lines 197–203) and 'A Hymne in Honovr of Heavenly Love' (lines 8–28), in *Spenser: Poetical Works*, ed. J. C. Smith and E. de Selincourt (Oxford, 1979).

25 *Shakespeare's Ovid: Being Arthur Golding's Translation of the 'Metamorphoses'*, ed. W. H. D. Rouse (Carbondale, 1961), book 3: lines 540–2.

26 Jonathan Bate, *Shakespeare and Ovid* (Oxford, 1993), p. 173. Bate emphasizes Actaeon as another figure of self-consuming desire (p. 19 and *passim*).

27 Cf. George Bataille's conceptions of eros as 'laughable', tragic and 'arousing irony', and of 'The complicity of the tragic – which is the basis of death – with sexual pleasure and laughter': *The Tears of Eros*, trans. Peter Connor (San Francisco, 1990), pp. 53 and 66.

28 Michel de Montaigne, *Essays*, trans. John Florio (London, 1980), vol. 2, pp. 192–3.

29 Coleridge, *Lectures*, p. 103.

30 Harry Levin, 'Form and Formality in *Romeo and Juliet*', in *Twentieth-Century Interpretations of 'Romeo and Juliet': A collection of Critical Essays*, ed. Douglas Cole (Englewood Cliffs, N.J., 1970), 85–95; p. 86.

31 Coleridge, *Lectures*, p. 103.

32 Joseph A. Porter emphasizes that Mercutio's opposition is to romantic love not to sex: *Shakespeare's Mercutio: His History and Drama* (Chapel Hill, 1988), p. 103.

33 Geoffrey Bullough, *Narrative and Dramatic Sources of Shakespeare*, vol. 1 (London, 1966), lines 114, 210, 935, 2420 and 2532.

34 Kay Stockholder, *Dream Works: Lovers and Families in Shakespeare's Plays* (Toronto, 1987), p. 30. In *Love's Argument: Gender Relations in Shakespeare* (Chapel Hill, 1984), Marianne Novy sees that the lovers' private world crystallizes in the aubade of Act 2, Scene 1 (p. 108).

35 Bullough, *Sources*, vol. 1, p. 374.

36 On the interplay among misrecognition, desire and the symbolic, see Catherine Belsey, 'The Name of the Rose in *Romeo and Juliet*', *Yearbook of English Studies*, 23 (1993), 126–42; on the significance of the lovers being masked from each

other, see Barbara L. Parker, *A Precious Seeing: Love and Reason in Shakespeare's Plays* (New York, 1987), p. 142.

37 Jessica Benjamin, *The Bonds of Love: Psychoanalysis, Feminism, and the Problem of Domination* (New York, 1988), p. 21.

38 Edward Snow suggests that the sonnet registers 'an intersubjective privacy' that subdues 'sexual difference and social opposition': 'Language and Sexual Difference in *Romeo and Juliet*', in *Shakespeare's 'Rough magic': Renaissance Essays in Honor of C. L. Barber*, ed. Peter Erickson and Coppélia Kahn (Newark, 1985), pp. 168–92; p. 168; Novy contrasts this scene with the stichomythic exchange between Juliet and Paris at 4.1.18–38 (*Love's Argument*, p. 108).

39 On the love-death oxymoron, cf. Whittier, 'Sonnet's Body', p. 32.

40 Coppélia Kahn, 'Coming of Age in Verona', in *The Woman's Part: Feminist Criticism of Shakespeare*, ed. Carolyn Ruth Swift Lenz, Gayle Greene and Carol Thomas Neely (Urbana, 1980), pp. 171–93; p. 186. Marilyn Williamson regards the deaths as alienating rather than uniting, 'Romeo's suicide fulfills a pattern to which Juliet is both necessary and accidental': 'Romeo and Death', *Shakespeare Studies*, 14 (1981), 129–37; p. 132.

41 Callaghan, 'Ideology', p. 61.

42 See Thomas Moisan, 'Rhetoric and the Rehearsal of Death: the "Lamentations" Scene in *Romeo and Juliet*', *Shakespeare Quarterly*, 34 (1983), 389–404.

43 Julia Kristeva, *Tales of Love*, trans. Leon S. Roudiez (New York, 1987), p. 213.

44 *The Seminar of Jacques Lacan*, Book 1, *Freud's Papers on Technique 1953–1954*, trans. John Forrester (New York, 1991), p. 36. On literature and psychoanalysis as twin discourses of mourning and melancholia, see Julia Reinhard Lupton and Kenneth Reinhard, *After Oedipus: Shakespeare in Psychoanalysis* (Ithaca, 1993), esp. pp. 32–3.

The legacy of Juliet's desire in comedies of the early 1600s

Mary Bly

Romeo and Juliet is a play crowded with lewd puns. Mercutio, Benvolio and Romeo toy with bawdy innuendoes; Gregory, Peter and Sampson delight in the proximity of maidenheads and their own naked weapons; the Nurse both puns and is punned about. The play's lyricism contends with language intoxicated by carnality. Even Juliet, the romantic centre of the play, quibbles with erotic meaning, most notably in her epithalamium of 3.2. Juliet is chaste and desirous, a unique combination in plays of the early 1590s. This essay argues that Juliet's erotic fluency had a marked influence on the shaping of comic heroines in the four to five years after the play's first performances. I look first at Juliet's language, and then at two parodic versions of Shakespeare's heroine, written between 1598 and 1607. *Romeo and Juliet* was often imitated; what interests me are those balcony scenes in which pseudo-Juliets express erotic desire in clever puns. These imitative plays are among the very few extant Renaissance comedies portraying virginal heroines who make self-referential bawdy jokes. It seems that the act of parodying the enormously popular Shakespeare play created an odd sub-genre, that of romantic comedies whose heroines display a ribald humour.[1]

Balcony scenes litter Renaissance plays; the popularity of *Romeo and Juliet* has caused most amorous balcony exchanges to be labelled imitative. I limit my discussion to Henry Porter's *The Two Angry Women of Abington* (1598) and Thomas Dekker's *Blurt, Master Constable* (1607) because these two playwrights explicitly borrow language as well as plot devices from Shakespeare's play.[2] I also look more briefly at the balcony scene in an anonymous play, *The Puritan* (1607). *Romeo and Juliet* was an enduring favourite with Elizabethan audiences; its language apparently filtered into normal conversation. Several works written after 1600 mock those who borrow its verse. For example, Gullio, the foolish courtier of *1*

Return from Parnassus (1606), imitates Mercutio: 'the moone in comparison of thy bright hue a meere slutt, Anthonies Cleopatra a blacke browde milkmaide, Hellen a cowdie.' But Ingenioso (an impoverished scholar) leaps on the theft: 'Marke Romeo and Iuliet: o monstrous theft.'[3] *Romeo and Juliet's* popularity suggests that the dual presence of a balcony scene and 'monstrous theft' would make the connection immediately apparent to a contemporary audience.

Porter and Dekker make two fundamental revisions of *Romeo and Juliet*: their plays end with marriage rather than death, and their heroines display skill at erotic innuendo in conversation, rather than in soliloquy. Punning duels are, of course, found in other Shakespeare plays. Benedick's and Beatrice's witty exchanges are sexually charged, if not explicitly sexually allusive. Yet virginal heroines rarely make bawdy jokes. In the context of romance, heroines tend to stay within conventional lyric guidelines.[4] In *Much Ado About Nothing* (1598), for example, Hero's maid Margaret tries to cheer up the heavy-hearted bride by joking that she will 'be heavier soon by the weight of a man'; Hero scolds her for immodesty: 'Fie upon thee, art not ashamed?' (3.4.25–6). For the most part, erotic innuendo in drama remains the province of marginal characters. Old women, clowns, malcontents and male sidekicks, Parolles, Pandarus, Iago, lewdly mock and are mocked, but it is hard to find a young heroine referring even indirectly to copulation.

Why, then, should these two plays be among the very few whose heroines are ribald jokers? Significantly, the plays are not simple burlesques; they are romantic comedies in their own right, and their connection to *Romeo and Juliet* has so far been considered merely a matter for footnotes. If a blunt expression of lust is an inappropriate statement for a virginal heroine, what is the position of a witty expression of desire? The nature of the expression is clearly important. Porter's and Dekker's heroines are not straightforwardly lustful; they speak in puns. If desire is revealed in clever puns, does that wit protect the heroine from a charge of immodesty? Certainly, the very elaboration of rhetoric involved in puns removes them from clear revelation. Puns impose an order on speech: face-value relinquishes its place to paradox, plain definition to the imagination. For example, Porter's Mall's 'quarterly I must receive my rent' plays on secondary meanings: 'rent' does not, in itself, carry an erotic meaning, although the sexual reference is easily surmised from her definition of 'income' as 'kisses and embraces every day'.[5] Puns, Walter Redfern writes, 'are a means of circumventing taboos, as are euphemisms, which play a similar hide-and-seek game with the listener/reader'.[6] The audience's attention may be redirected from the titillating *double entendre* to admiration of rhetorical cleverness. This argument assumes that erotic puns act as a masking device for desire, that Porter and Dekker are able to circumvent cultural restrictions on female speech by clever phrasing. However, I would argue that bawdy puns do not mask desire but flaunt it.

A bawdy pun is a word placed in such a context that it points to a secondary, sexual, reference, as in Juliet's 'Give me my Romeo, and when I shall die . . .' (3.1.21). Juliet's 'death' is both ceasing to be and erotic ecstasy. The sexual innuendo Juliet uses was a common one in Renaissance literature.[7] It is important to recognize that in the case of a pun as ordinary as this, a Renaissance audience would definitely grasp its double meaning. As James Brown says of puns, 'When we know enough . . . failure to perceive a pun is impossible; we cannot wilfully suspend our ability to see puns.'[8] Obviously, seemingly non-sexual speech often carries an inference of carnal desire, as when Miranda calls Ferdinand a 'thing divine' (1.2.422). But if Miranda had been conscious enough of that carnality to construct a witty play with words, had she offered a bawdy pun, the effect of her statement would have been radically different and quite surprising. Miranda's innocence is stressed throughout *The Tempest*, and her explicit lack of knowledge is echoed in her speech. As an audience grasps the *double entendre* behind Juliet's 'die', they grasp her sexual knowledge and her consciousness of carnal desire at the same time. That sexual knowledge was a dubious virtue in light of Elizabethan conceptions of a chaste young woman's education; it may explain why witty heroines in Renaissance plays rarely offer immodest puns.

It is common for female characters' rhetoric to produce an inadvertent sexual reference, as in Juliet's Nurse's protest: 'thou must stand by, too, and suffer every knave to use me at his pleasure'. Peter replies: 'I saw no man use you at his pleasure. If I had, my weapon should quickly have been out' (2.3.145–8). Eyre's wife Margery in Dekker's *The Shoemaker's Holiday* (1599) provides a similar example. Her robust tone leads to puns – when her husband swears to 'firke' her if she doesn't stop quarrelling, she responds: 'Yea, yea man, you may vse me as you please.'[9] The prolonged scenes between Margery, Firke, and Hodge, in which the servants slyly mock her wrinkles, aged body and social ambition, are typical. These two female characters, the Nurse and Margery, are laughable precisely due to their age, sexual unattractiveness and inadvertent sexual references. It is their choice of words – 'use' interpreted as 'copulate with' – that creates a bawdy innuendo. The sexual pun arises from the word's two interpretations, not from the women's deliberate command of those two meanings.

On the other hand, Juliet's invitation to Romeo in 3.2 – to 'Hood my unmanned blood' – offers an elaborately rhetorical, self-consciously erotic image. Juliet's long soliloquy strings together six separate invocations, each specifically alluding to the physical pleasure she expects that night. The epithalamium's metaphorical flourishes allow her desire to be latent and yet obvious; they are particularly surprising in view of the dense Petrarchan rhetoric of the play.[10] Romeo first loves Rosaline who, in a fine Petrarchan tradition, 'hath forsworn to love' (1.1.220). She is invulnerable to Cupid's arrow, 'in strong proof of chastity well armed' (1.1.207). To Romeo, both Juliet and the absent Rosaline are archetypal Petrarchan mistresses: chaste, undesirous and beautiful. Certainly Romeo believes Juliet and Rosaline to be untouched by desire:

> She will not stay the siege of loving terms,
> Nor bide th'encounter of assailing eyes,
> Nor ope her lap to saint-seducing gold.
> O she is rich in beauty . . .
> (1.1.209–12)

Romeo's construction of Rosaline's beauty ties it directly to her chastity. He also sees Juliet's beauty as ensuring her chastity: 'Beauty too rich for use, for earth too dear' (1.5.46). The energy of Romeo's Petrarchan rhetoric is bound up in fruitless pursuit, rather than in an anticipation of lovers' meeting.

It is Mercutio who envisions union: 'O Romeo, that she were, O that she were / An open-arse, and thou a popp'rin' pear' (2.1.37–8). Mercutio speaks of sex only in puns. Erotic humour predominates. Love, for him, is a chase towards copulation: 'this drivelling love is like a great natural that runs lolling up and down to hide his bauble in a hole' (2.3.84–5). Romeo's solemn poetry sits uneasily in a play where it is ridiculed by Mercutio's banter ('Laura to his lady was a kitchen wench . . . Dido a dowdy, Cleopatra a gypsy, Helen and Hero hildings and harlots' (2.3.37, 39–40)) and mocked by Friar Laurence: 'Thy love did read by rote, that could not spell' (2.2.88). Even Juliet offers a mild rebuke: 'You kiss by th'book' (1.5.109).

Juliet is unsuited to the role of Romeo's Petrarchan mistress. She is desirous, and moreover, she is long-winded in anticipation: 'O, I have bought the mansion of a love / But not possessed it, and though I am sold, / Not yet enjoyed' (3.2.26–8). Juliet is not precisely bawdy – but neither is she modest.[11] Remarkably, Shakespeare gives her the epithalamium

traditionally spoken by a bridegroom. Act 3 scene 2 opens with her invocation to the night: 'Gallop apace, you fiery-footed steeds', an inversion
of Ovid's 'lente currite, noctis equi'.[12] Juliet's soliloquy is a mixture of
plainly expressed invitations and artfully phrased metaphors. Her initial call to Romeo, 'Leap to these arms untalked of and unseen' (3.2.7),
echoes one of the most beautiful passages in Marlowe's *Tragedy of Dido*
(1587):

> If thou wilt stay
> Leap in mine arms; mine arms are open wide;
> If not, turn from me, and I'll turn from thee . . .[13]

The passage comes from Dido's final plea to Aeneas to remain in
Carthage; it is spoken by a sexually knowing woman, intoxicated with
love.

Juliet turns from Marlovian invitation to a lengthy series of sexual
metaphors: 'Come, civil night . . . And learn me how to lose a winning
match / Played for a pair of stainless maidenhoods' (3.2.10, 12–13).
This is a good example of the complexity of Juliet's speech.[14] 'Winning'
is turned to a pun meaning both victorious and appealing. Moreover,
the 'match' Juliet hopes to lose and win is, at once, a wedding and an
erotic game. At the pun's heart, obviously, is the fate of her virginity: it is
a match in which she will lose a 'stainless' maidenhead, while she gains
a 'match' or marriage with Romeo.[15]

The rest of her speech is similarly full of *doubles entendres*:

> Hood my unmanned blood, bating in my cheeks,
> With thy black mantle, till strange love grow bold,
> Think true love acted simple modesty.
>   (3.2.14–16)

Talking to her Nurse, Juliet's linguistic stress turns from sex itself ('true
love acted') to Romeo's beauty. Romeo has a 'flow'ring face'; he is a
'gorgeous palace', a 'mortal paradise of such sweet flesh' (3.2.73, 85,
82). But the epithalamium itself stands as a lyric anticipation of erotic
pleasure:

> Come night, come Romeo; come, thou day in night,
> For thou wilt lie upon the wings of night
> Whiter than new snow on a raven's back.
>   (3.2.17–19)

I would suggest that Juliet's cleverly phrased desire for consummation
acts as a bridge between desirous, tragic heroines and comic plots.

Shakespeare bestowed sexual metaphors on a young heroine; Porter and Dekker follow his example, moving into comedy. They use *Romeo and Juliet* as a distant subtext, fashioning heroines who are virginal and wittily desirous. Like Juliet, these heroines are intensely interested in the fate of their maidenheads, and their wit similarly reveals a specific understanding of sexual congress.

Henry Porter's *The Two Angry Women of Abington* turns *Romeo and Juliet* into a subtext for a comedy. Porter appropriates Juliet's wit; at the same time he manipulates famous bits of the play (such as the balcony scene) to jest at Romeo's lyric dedication. Juliet's nimble metaphors are turned wholly to sexual puns. Porter shapes his heroine, Mall, around the epithalamic Juliet. Mall speaks only in erotic quibbles and sexual metaphors.

The Two Angry Women is constructed around a breach between two neighbouring families, which the fathers hope to patch by marrying their son and daughter. The young couple, Frank and Mall, are introduced, woo and agree to marry in a bare three minutes. Although the plot summary seems in line with conventional romantic comedies, Mall's character is radically opposed to Petrarchan idealization. She is, her brother says, 'a wicked wench to make a jest' (8.25). She is not merely witty, like Rosaline or Beatrice, but lusty, and her jokes are overtly sexual. For example, Mall opens the ninth scene by musing on conies – rabbits but also slang for women:

> Good Lord, what pretty things these conies are;
> How finely they do feed till they be fat!
> And then what a sweet meat a coney is,
> And what smooth skins they have, both black and gray.
> They say they run more in the night than day . . .
> But when that Francis comes, what will he say?
> 'Look, boy, there lies a coney in my way.'
> (9.7–11, 24–5)[16]

Mall's sexual bravado extends past sly puns. When her father asks Mall if she has a mind to marry, she points out that since she is a maid, she ought to 'blush, look pale and wan, / And then look pale again' (3.1 24–5). However, she decides to 'speak truth and shame the devil' (3.1 33). In fact, she has lately 'let restrained fancy loose, / And bade it gaze for pleasure' (3.1 58–9). Mall urges her father to a quick match: 'If I shall have a husband, get him quickly / For maids that wears cork shoes may step awry' (3.163–4). The scene ends with her blunt summary of the evils of letting maids lie alone:

> Lying alone they muse but in their beds
> How they might lose their long-kept maidenheads.
> This is the cause there is so many scapes...
> Therefore, come husband, maidenhead adieu!
> (3.205–7, 10)

Her mother bitterly labels her 'lusty guts'; certainly Mall's forthright acknowledgement of her own physical desire is extraordinary. I would argue that Porter is deliberately abrogating romantic ideals – perhaps most clearly in his veiled mockery of *Romeo and Juliet*.

At various points in *The Two Angry Women of Abington*, *Romeo and Juliet* is invoked as a romantic model, and then burlesqued by Porter's rewriting.[17] We can see an echo of Juliet above, in Mall's response to her father's query: 'hast thou a mind to marry?' (3.120). Lady Capulet asks Juliet a similar question: 'How stands your dispositions to be married?' and Juliet responds 'It is an honour that I dream not of' (1.3.67–8). Mall lampoons Juliet's answer on two levels: she announces that she does dream of marriage, and she rejects a modest answer as dishonest. The textual crux behind the Shakespearian line (Q2 reads 'It is a houre that I dream not of') creates an even sharper counterpart, since Mall specifically alludes to maidens dreaming of that hour:[18]

> How many maids this night lies in their beds
> And dream that they have lost their maidenheads.
> Such dreams, such slumbers I had, too, enjoyed...
> (12.13–15)

Considering that the balcony scene (in which Juliet initiates the idea of marriage) supposedly occurs only a few hours after the scene between Juliet and her mother, Juliet's demure answer does appear conventional rather than truthful. In the balcony scene Juliet actually emphasizes the cultural restrictions on her speech: 'For that which thou hast heard me speak tonight. / Fain would I dwell on form, fain, fain deny / What I have spoke; but farewell, compliment' (2.1.129–31). Mall's refusal to respond with 'close-clipped civility' may also point to Juliet:

> With true-faced passion
> Of modest maidenhead I could adorn me,
> And to your question make a sober cursey,
> And with close-clipped civility be silent;
> Or else say 'No, forsooth,' or 'Aye, forsooth.'
> If I said 'No, forsooth,' I lied, forsooth.
> (3.126–31)

Mall's emphasis on maidenheads is characteristic of Porter's humour: marriage is seen as consummation, not ceremony. Mall and the other characters often conflate the two.

Mall and Frank meet and woo in a balcony scene which apes the parallel scene in *Romeo and Juliet*. Both balcony scenes involve rapid wooing between near strangers. Juliet takes no joy in a contract 'too rash, too unadvised, too sudden' (2.1.160); Frank's reaction is more confident: 'Now in good faith, Phillip, this makes me smile, / That I have wooed and won in so small while' (8.135–6). The scenes are remarkably similar in concept and choreography, but quite different in language, a difference which I would suggest grows from the dominant topic of conversation in each scene. Romeo and Juliet, famously, talk of love; Mall and Frank, of sex.

Mall's brother Phillip brings Frank to her bedroom window. Phillip calls up: ''Tis I.' Mall's response is raucously far from Juliet's dignified 'What man art thou that, thus bescreened in night, / So stumblest on my counsel?' (2.1.94–5). Mall shouts back: ''Tis I? Who I? "I, quoth the dog", or what?' (8.45). Romeo and Juliet speak in verse strewn with loving metaphors: 'thou art / As glorious to this night, being o'er my head, / As is a wingèd messenger of heaven' (2.1.68–70). Their conversation moves adroitly between lyrical metaphors and conventional phrases. Romeo, in particular, strikes extravagant chords in his praise: Juliet is a sun; her eyes are stars; her cheeks are brighter than starlight.

Mall's and Frank's dialogue is diametrically opposed to Romeo and Juliet's balcony scene, in that they fall into metaphors of sexual innuendo, not those of romantic love. They begin by talking of Venus's chariot, punning on the similarity of couch and coach, a joke which also alludes to the 'carting' of prostitutes:

MALL　　I pray, sir, tell me, do you cart the Queen of Love?
FRANK　　Not cart her, but couch her in your eye, And a fit place for gentle love
　　　　to lie.
MALL　　Aye, but methinks you speak without the book.　　　　　　　　(8.61–4)

Mall's 'methinks you speak without the book' is a mocking rewriting of Juliet's 'You kiss by th'book' (1.5.109). Whereas Juliet chides Romeo for his ready command of conventional sonnet conceits, Mall's retort to Frank's play on 'couch' is a direct recognition of the unconventional manner of their conversation. To woo 'by th' book' is to gild one's language with sonnet rhymes and conceits: Romeo and

Frank are quite opposite in this respect. Frank does speak 'without' the book. Mall's brother Phillip had earlier advised Frank to woo her by setting 'such painted beauty on thy tongue / As it shall ravish every maiden sense', a neat summary of sonneteers' ornate love language (8.10–11). Phillip himself speaks in Romeo-esque metaphors. He opens scene 10, one of the nocturnal scenes, with a soliloquy on the night:

> The sky that was so fair three hours ago
> Is in three hours become an Ethiope,
> And, being angry at her beauteous change,
> She will not have one of these pearlèd stars
> To blab her sable metamorphesy.
>
> (10.3–7)

Phillip is faintly echoing Romeo's praise of Juliet:

> O, she doth teach the torches to burn bright!
> It seems she hangs upon the cheek of night
> As a rich jewel in an Ethiope's ear –
> Beauty too rich for use, for earth too dear.
>
> (1.5.43–6).[19]

Porter's use of Romeo's famous speech (also adapted by Dekker in *Blurt, Master Constable*) plays to the audience's theatrical knowledge: much of the humour in this play depends on acquaintance with the language of *Romeo and Juliet*. Phillip's echoing of Romeo refers not only to the play, but to the convoluted phrasing of stately love language in general. However, Frank discards Phillip's advice to use 'painted beauty' in wooing.

Mall's retort to Frank's superficially gallant wish to 'couch' Venus in her eye leads to an even more explicit dialogue:

MALL Where will you have room to have the coachman sit?
FRANK Nay, that were but small manners and not fit.
  His duty is before you bare to stand,
  Having a lusty whipstock in his hand.
MALL The place is void. Will you provide me one?
FRANK And if you please, I will supply the room.
MALL But are you cunning in the carman's lash?   (8.66–72)

The kind of metaphor by which Mall and Frank build a conversation is very different from the parallel set of metaphors which Romeo and Juliet build between them (their play on 'tassel-gentle', for example). Romeo's and Juliet's conceits are elaborately matched: she wears a 'mask of night', he has 'night's cloak'.[20] Mall and Frank build a series of metaphors which point not to conventional conceits but to sexual metaphors. Romantic love, and the metaphors of romantic love, are here replaced by puns of sexual wit. Porter's lovers manipulate a rhyming exchange to create not a sonnet, but an extended set of bawdy riddles about Mall's virginity:

MALL   Nun, votary, stale maidenhead, seventeen-and-upward?
   Here be names! What, nothing else?
FRANK   Yes, or a fair built steeple without bells.
MALL   Steeple, good people? Nay, another cast.
FRANK   Aye, or a well-made ship without a mast.
MALL   Fie, not so big, sir, by one part of four!
FRANK   Why, then ye are a boat without an oar.
MALL   O, well rowed, wit!   (8.102–9)

The relentless puns on male sex organs – or the lack thereof – are helped by the fact that the dialogue falls into couplets. If puns rely on displacement of face-value meanings, rhyming puns allow an even greater disjuncture from apparent sense, and rhyming puns characterize the entire balcony scene. 'I had both wit to grant when he did woo me' Mall says, 'And strength to bear what ere he can do to me' (8.209–10). Frank later echoes her: 'Well, I must bear with her – she'll bear with me' (9.65). I would argue that Mall and Frank are able to dance further into obscenity because their puns tumble onto each other, delighting the ear before comprehension strikes. Gillian Beer writes that the second rhyme word moves in on the first and tricks it into rhyme, 'sound dominates sense'.[21] In one sense a pun is itself a compressed rhyme; fixing one or the other possible definition as correct is less important than grasping the contexts linked together in one syntactic unit.

This joining of contexts makes puns vulnerable to the passing of time. If Mercutio's quibbles with 'prick' are still understood, it is only because of the durability of that particular reference. Mall's joke about the danger of wearing cork heels is a case in point. Many such puns are understandable only with a dictionary in hand. The problematics of phallic references in the language of female characters and, therefore, of boy actors point to another context which may be missed by a modern reader. Porter's *The Two Angry Women of Abington* was written for Henslowe's (adult) company at the Rose; the Admiral's Men is not a company generally discussed as employing *doubles entendres* which reference the boy behind the female

role.[22] But Mall's and Frank's exchange, quoted above, certainly raises
the possibility:

FRANK   Aye, or a well-made ship without a mast.
MALL   Fie, not so big, sir, by one part of four!
FRANK   Why, then ye are a boat without an oar.

On one hand, Frank's jokes refer to Mall as a virgin in need of an oar. At
the same time, the dialogue could be construed as a pointed reference
to the boy actor's smaller sex organ: 'not so big, sir, by one part of four!'
Thus Porter's puns link three contexts: literal meaning, erotic innuendo,
and extra-textual, actorial reference.

When Mall descends from the bedroom she defines the contract between them in rhyming puns:

MALL   Francis, my love's lease I do let to thee,
   Date of my life and thine. What sayest thou to me?
   The entering fine or income thou must pay
   Are kisses and embraces every day,
   And quarterly I must receive my rent.
   You know my mind.
FRANK   I guess at thy intent.
   Thou shalt not miss a minute of thy time.   (8.148–54)

The difference between the two romances is encapsulated in Juliet's wish
for marriage ('thou wilt perform the rite, / And all my fortunes at thy foot
I'll lay, / And follow thee, my lord, throughout the world' (2.1.188–90))
and Mall's demand of 'rent'. In the majority of Renaissance comedies,
well-born heroines speak in Petrarchan measures; low-born females
speak a kind of rolling dialect, marked by indecorous jokes and coinages.
It is a source of extra dramatic interest if a low-born woman is able
to use Petrarchan metaphors. The protagonist of Thomas Heywood's
I The Fair Maid of the West (1610), for example, is a barmaid and later
a tavern owner who loves chastely and expresses herself in Petrarchan
hyperboles. The entire play revolves around this social anomaly. It is
similarly remarkable when well-born heroines play with erotic puns.[23]
By Elizabethan standards, Mall's punning banter with Frank sails
dangerously close to shameful. I would suggest that the popularity of
The Two Angry Women of Abington came at least partially from its heroine's
defiance of the conventions prescribing a well-born maiden's concerns
and behaviour.[24] Wit here is not merely verbal dexterity but the daring
involved in staging a virgin's expression of sexual desire.

In this regard, the discrepancies between the bad quarto (Q1) of *Romeo and Juliet* [1597] and the 'newly corrected, augmented, and amended' Q2, published in 1599, are interesting. Q1 retains only the first four lines of the epithalamium. The Arden editor, Brian Gibbons, suggests the lines may have been cut in anticipation of a provincial audience, and there is some evidence that travelling versions of plays were deliberately shortened in such a way as to tone down sexual content.[25] I would suggest that the excised epithalamium points to the fact that Juliet's expression of erotic desire represented a breach of cultural expectation. Mall's transgressive speech is acknowledged in the play itself: her suitor says her wit is 'held a wonder,' and her brother acknowledges that she can 'make blush / The boldest face of man that ere man saw' (8.127, 5.10–11). The heroine of the anonymous play *The Puritan* has similarly impressed her suitor: 'th'art a mad wench *Moll'*.[26]

If *Romeo and Juliet* influenced Porter's creation of a bawdy heroine, Porter's play, in turn, seems to have garnered an imitator. *The Puritan* was printed in 1607 as having been acted by the Children of Paul's. The play involves foolery plotted by a witty scholar and his nefarious compatriots, who pretend to raise both the devil and a man from the dead, in order to wrangle freedom from prison and the hands of a rich widow and her eldest daughter, Franke. The younger daughter, Moll, is in love with Sir John Penny-dub, and is fluently bawdy: 'Ide as soone vow neuer to come in Bed. / Tut? Women must liue by th'quick, and not th'dead' (A4r, lines 6–7).

The heroine is known as Moll, basically the same name as Porter's Mall, and at various points the *Puritan* Moll appears to echo the earlier character. In *The Two Angry Women*, for example, Mall is agonized by the frustration of her wedding plans: 'A starved man with double death doth die / To have the meat might save him in his eye / And may not have it – so am I tormented' (12.17–19). When the *Puritan* Moll's marriage plans are thwarted, she is similarly wrought: 'A double torment . . . a double curse' (D2r, lines 3, 27). The most notable parallel between the plays is found in *The Puritan*'s balcony scene. Sir John appears below: 'Whewh Mistris Mol, Mistris Mol.' Moll appears above, 'lacing of her clothes'. Like the earlier Mall, she calls 'Who's there?' And just as does Phillip in Porter's play, Penny-dub replies, 'Tis I' (H2, lines 26–7). What ensues is a wild series of puns, instigated solely by Moll, *not* by Penny-dub. In *The Two Angry Women of Abington*, Mall generally answers Frank's sallies with a rhyming couplet; but this Moll is bolder than her predecessor: 'O you'r an early cocke ifayth, who would haue thought you to be so

rare a stirrer' (H2r, lines 28–9). Penny-dub offers to climb into Moll's
bed-chamber, but she refuses. 'No by my faith Sir Iohn, Ile keepe you
downe, for you Knights are very dangerous if once you get aboue' (H2r,
lines 31–32). She explains her refusal by a bawdy quibble: 'Sir Iohn you
must note the nature of the Climates your Northen wench in her owne
Countrie may well hold out till shee bee fifteene, but if she touch the
South once, and come vp to *London*, here the Chimes go presently after
twelue' (H2, lines 34–6 – H2r, lines 1–2).

One subject which seems to mark the group of heroines I discuss in
this paper is an anxious regard for their virginity. Porter's Mall is a gentlewoman who three times explains her urgent desire to lose that virginity.
Her own family jokes about her maidenhead: 'by my troth, my sister's
maidenhead / Stands like a game at tennis: if the ball / Hit in the hole
or hazard, fare well all' (3.327–9). Juliet's epithalamium speaks to the
same issue; hearing Romeo is banished she takes to her bed: 'I, a maid,
die maiden-widowèd. / Come, cords; come, Nurse; I'll to my wedding
bed, / And death, not Romeo, take my maidenhead!' (3.2.135–7). Her
maidenhead is a topic of conversation, notably of the Nurse, but also of
her mother. Quibbles about virginity are common throughout Renaissance drama, particularly when spoken boastfully by male characters
(Sampson's vow that he will cut off the heads of Montague's maids is a
good example). But in these plays virginity skips from the provenance of
Sampson and the Nurse, to that of the upper classes: Juliet's despairing
attention to her maidenhead, Mall's dreams of her wedding night.

Thomas Dekker's *Blurt, Master Constable* (1602) is another play which
exploits the ribald potential of a desirous virgin. Like Porter, Dekker borrows both plot and language from *Romeo and Juliet*. The main plot grows
from the love of Violetta and Fontinelle, who meet at a ball. Fontinelle
is a member of the enemy (France) and is later thrown into prison by
Violetta's aristocratic suitor, Camillo. In Act 4, the lovers are secretly
married by a friar. Thus marked parallels exist between the two plays:
a ball-room scene depicting instantaneous love between members of
warring factions, a secret marriage, even borrowed language. Violetta's
admirer, Camillo, adapts Romeo's praise of Juliet:

And of Beautie what tongue would not speake the best, since it is the Jewell
that hangs upon the brow of heaven, the best cullor that can be laide upon the
cheeke of earth?[27]

Fontinelle also adopts Romeo's language. He refuses to dance: 'bid him
whose heart no sorrow feeles / Tickle the rushes with his wanton heeles'

(1.1.181–2), as does Romeo, who lets 'wantons light of heart / Tickle the sense-less rushes with their heels' (1.4.35–6). Romeo characterizes himself as having a 'soul of lead' (1.4.15); Fontinelle declares he has 'too much lead' in his heart (1.1.183). Falling in love at the ball, Fontinelle is as bombastic and Petrarchan as Romeo: 'Oh what a heaven is love! oh what a hell!' (1.1.212).

The last act appears to offer a startling reversal of Shakespeare's play: Fontinelle falls in love with another woman, a prostitute, and Violetta is forced to arrange a bed-trick to consummate her marriage. Yet one of the aspects of Romeo's character that has interested many commentators is the passion of his initial love for Rosaline, instantly displaced by an equal ardour for Juliet. Fontinelle shows that same inconstancy, and makes a similar use of Petrarchan rhetoric to describe both women. In the last act he defends his (supposed) night with the courtesan, Imperia: 'who dyes / For so bright beauty, is a bright Sacrifice', and returns to language nearly identical to that which he applied to Violetta in the first act: 'She is my heaven; she from me, I am in hell' (5.3.77–8, 183).

If Fontinelle is a Romeo pushed to the extremes of Petrarchan shallowness, Violetta is also a parodied version of Juliet. In the ballroom scene of *Blurt, Master Constable*, Fontinelle dances with another woman, while Violetta watches: 'In troth a very pretty French man; the carriage of his bodie likes me well; so does his footing, so does his face, so does his eye above his face, so does himselfe, above all that can bee above himselfe' (1.1.187–90). Violetta repeatedly swears by her maidenhead and answers respectful questions with bawdy puns: 'What breeds that desire?' asks Camillo when she ends their dance. 'Nay I hope it is no breeding matter; tush, tush, by my maiden-head I will not . . .' (1.1.173–5). As a whole, the play is bawdier than *Romeo and Juliet*; jokes to do with maidenheads embellish virtually every scene, and many of these scenes burlesque Shakespeare's play. In 4.1, for example, a would-be lover tries to climb a rope to his mistress's window, borrowing Romeo's phrasing – 'Ile hang a Jewell at thine eare, sweet night' – but he is doused with urine when he pulls the cord (4.1.20).

The balcony scene in *Blurt, Master Constable* takes place in 3.1, between Violetta, her suitor (but not beloved) Camillo, and her brother Hippolito. Camillo, in response to Fontinelle's presumption in loving Violetta, has thrown the Frenchman into prison. Camillo and Hippolito are accompanied by musicians singing in an effort to 'pleade to a stonie heart' (3.1.120). The scene which ensues is marked by Violetta's lusty wit. She baits the anger of Camillo by risqué references to her desire for

Fontinelle: 'Let him pleade your love for you; / I love a life to heare a man speake French / Of his complection' (3.1.164–6). She uses Fontinelle's nationality as a metaphor for consummation: 'I would undergoe / The instruction of that language rather far, / Than be two weekes unmaried (by my life)' (3.1.166–8). Like Mall, she ties a wish for marriage specifically to a desire for sex: 'Because Ile speake true French, Ile be his wife' (3.1.169). Her defiance is underlined by the boldness of her expression: 'the French-man's mine, / And by these hands Ile have him' (3.1.157–8). After Camillo and Hippolito leave, Violetta receives a letter from the imprisoned Fontinelle. Her response evokes Juliet's wish that night come with her 'black mantle': 'Blest night, wrap *Cinthia* in a sable sheete, / That fearefull lovers may securlie meete' (3.1.188–9).

One very important shift has occurred between Shakespeare's play and its parodic siblings. When Mercutio juggles puns, as in his 'Prick love for pricking, and you beat love down' (1.4.28), he does so to display his wit. He relies for humour on the fact that he has wrangled three priapic references into one sentence. But Juliet's erotic puns and metaphors are not directed, for the most part, at a display of her wit. Eroticized humour does steal into the balcony scene. Romeo cries 'O, wilt thou leave me so unsatisfied?' and Juliet responds 'What satisfaction canst thou have tonight?' (2.1.167–8). Satisfaction, in her hands, becomes a demure play on the sating of desire. But in general Juliet's wordplay does not demand laughing applause. Mall's and Violetta's puns, on the other hand, are spoken in joking exchanges, similar to those Shakespeare gives to Romeo and Mercutio. In fact, Mall's quibbles about Venus's coach can be matched to Mercutio's jokes about Queen Mab's chariot. The Queen Mab speech ends in a bawdy pun: 'This is the hag, when maids lie on their backs, / That presses them and learns them first to bear, / Making them women of good carriage' (1.5.93–5). Yet Mall is not simply a female Mercutio. Her puns, like Juliet's, are self-referential. Juliet's epithalamic images of Romeo lying on her, like snow on a raven, like day on night, are personally referent. Mercutio does not address his own desire; Juliet, Mall and Violetta do. Thus while Mercutio jokes about maids being taught 'to bear', Mall makes the same joke about herself, boasting she has 'strength to bear what ere he can do to me' (8.210).

These women offer self-referential sexual puns, not bawdy quibbles which rise solely from the punning potential of the English language. I would argue that Mercutio's delight in ribald double meanings leads to a different kind of banter than that which Mall and Frank engage in. If Mercutio's quibbles are funny, bawdy puns spoken by virgins are both comic and transgressive. The woman's revelation of desire may strengthen the audience's belief in the romantic relationship being staged, but it also violates a fundamental convention regarding the behaviour of a marriageable young female.

Puns desert surface rationality, turning instead to an emphasis on linguistic cleverness. I would argue that it is this emphasis on cleverness which precludes them from the language of virginal heroines in the majority of romantic comedies. Puns challenge a claim to chastity; the speaker is too knowledgeable. To understand the connotation of 'die' is to reveal carnal knowledge. To apply such a pun to one's own desire is even more damning. Thus these puns cannot operate as a mask, using ambiguity of interpretation to allow transgression of cultural expectations regarding virginal female speech. Not only does the commonplace nature of puns such as Mall's on 'oars' and Juliet's on 'die' preclude a censorious audience member from mistaking them, but the particular parallelism involved in a romantic balcony scene also operates to dispel the necessary ambiguity. The puns of parodic Juliets bring together more contexts than surface meaning and erotic implication. The audience sees yet another balcony scene, yet another desirous 'Juliet'.

I would suggest that the sexual jesting of Porter's and Dekker's heroines certainly looks in part to Juliet's remarkable epithalamium. She expresses, if in metaphor, a joyful anticipation of sexual pleasure not found in the language of a virginal heroine preceding her in English drama. Imitation of this aspect of Juliet's character seems to be divided: on the one side, a few Renaissance balcony scenes stage outspoken, lustful pseudo-Juliets, and on the other, there are the punning pseudo-Juliets I have discussed in this essay. The balcony scene in Jonson's *Poetaster* (1601), for example, takes place between Caesar's daughter, Julia, and the newly banished Ovid. Julia's wrath at Ovid's banishment grows from anticipated celibacy: 'Let me vse all my pleasures: vertuous loue / Was neuer scandall to a Goddesse state.'[28] Notably, *Poetaster* is no romance. Parody traditionally attacks the ideals of a famous predecessor: when Julia hysterically invites Ovid to climb up to her room ('enjoy me amply, still' (4.9.691)), Jonson burlesques Juliet's chastity at the same time as he mocks her sexual desire. Both types of balcony scenes involve a brutalizing of the passion that permeates the Shakespeare play, but Porter's and Dekker's emphasis on punning wit creates a very different kind of burlesque.

In the punning balcony scenes, Juliet's deeply felt sexual metaphors are turned to shallow banter, but the emphasis on wordplay as an appropriate vehicle for a female revelation of desire remains. Shakespeare used puns in two ways in *Romeo and Juliet*: as witty conversation (between Mercutio and Romeo, for example) and as a device by which Juliet expresses erotic anticipation. Dekker and Porter conflate the two. Bawdy conversation turns to self-referential sexual wit, an important shift.

When Porter and Dekker move Mercutio's decorative puns to the central female figure of a romance, the playwrights explicitly renounce the lyric concept of wooing. Their lovers speak 'without the book' as Mall observes. Romantic hyperbole is abandoned for a heady acknowledgement of sexual interest. Petrarchan idealization is mocked as representative of blind foolishness, and desire that grows from bodily appreciation is contrasted to insincere similes comparing eyes to suns. That alteration is certainly foreshadowed in Shakespeare's play. It is Juliet – so adroit at wordplay that reveals carnal desire – who tells Romeo that he kisses 'by th' book,' and begs him not to make empty vows. Perhaps the presence of that distant subtext, *Romeo and Juliet*, can explain why Mall and Violetta are practically unique among Renaissance heroines in their use of bawdy puns. If puns themselves cannot operate as an excuse for the expression of female desire, the faint burlesque of Juliet may. In this case, parody offers protection.

First published in *Shakespeare Survey 49* (1996)

NOTES

1 Since I spend most of this paper discussing bawdy puns, I want to address a problem with terminology. The puns I discuss are difficult to label. 'Bawdy' is a word used by Shakespeare, and it carries a definition, according to *Webster*'s, of humorously coarse. On the other hand, it also has connotations of obscenity and Victorianesque naughtiness. Other adjectives tend to be more pejorative (licentious, lewd, indecent, obscene); I use 'ribald' or 'bawdy' because of the implication of humour as well as sexual reference.

2 Another play which exhibits a similar combination of *Romeo and Juliet* tags, desirous virgins, and ribald jokes is Edward Sharpham's *Cupid's Whirligig* (1607). Sharpham borrows Shakespearian metaphors, describing the court, for example, as a place where 'so many earth-treading starres adornes the sky' (see Capulet's description of his dance, 1.2.22–3). Marston's *Jack Drum's Entertainment* (1600) also stages a parodic balcony scene. Marston satirizes cloying love language, but his Katherine offers no sexual puns. Michael Scott, while making a claim for a parody of Shakespeare's balcony scene in *The Insatiate Countess*, argues that *Romeo and Juliet* was at a height of popularity around 1600. See 'Marston's Early Contributions to "The Insatiate

Countess"'", *Notes and Queries*, n.s. 24, 222 (1977), 116–17, and Andrew Gurr, for a discussion of the play's influence on Henslowe's repertory. *Shakespeare Quarterly*, 38 (1987), 189–200.

3 *1 Return from Parnassus*, *The Three Parnassus Plays*, ed. J. B. Leishman (London, 1949), 3.1.988–92. In another example, John Marston's 10th satire mocks the play's followers: '*Luscus*, what's play'd to-day? Faith now I know / I set thy lips abroach, from whence doth flow / Naught but pure Juliet and Romeo.' 'Satire XI', *The Scourge of Villainie*, *Works*, vol. 3, ed. A. H. Bullen (London, 1887), pp. 37–9.

4 See Linda Woodbridge's discussion of dramatic treatments of female desire, *Women and the English Renaissance: Literature and the Nature of Womankind, 1540–1620* (Urbana, 1984), especially pp. 244–63.

5 Henry Porter, *The Two Angry Women of Abington*, ed. Marianne Brish Evett (N.Y., 1980). Modern editors have divided the play into thirteen scenes. 8.150–2.

6 Walter D. Redfern, *Puns* (Oxford, 1984), p. 91.

7 'Die' is frequently used by female characters, as in Marston's and Barksted's *The Insatiate Countess* (1610). Isabella goes to her nuptial bed reluctantly: 'When my loath'd mate / Shall struggle in due pleasure for his right, / I'll think't my love, and die in that delight!' John Marston and others, *The Insatiate Countess*, ed. Giorgio Melchiori (Manchester, 1984), 1.2.259–61. For further examples, see James Henke, *Courtesans and Cuckolds: A Glossary of Renaissance Dramatic Bawdy (Exclusive of Shakespeare)* (N.Y., 1979), p. 67.

8 James Brown, 'Eight Types of Pun', *PMLA*, 71 (1956), 15–16.

9 Thomas Dekker, *The Shoemaker's Holiday*, *The Dramatic Works*, vol. 1, ed. Fredson Bowers (Cambridge, 1953), 2.3.39. Firke and Hodge view the Wife as a natural butt of sexual innuendo. For example, Hodge: 'Maister I hope yowle not suffer my dame to take downe your iourneymen.' Firke: 'If she take me downe, Ile take her vp, yea and take her downe too, a button-hole lower.' 2.3.29–32.

10 See Gayle Whittier's definitive study of Petrarchan conceits in the play, 'The Sonnet's Body and the Body Sonnetized in *Romeo and Juliet*', *Shakespeare Quarterly*, 40 (1989), 27–41. Also M. M. Mahood, *Shakespeare's Wordplay* (London, 1957), p. 61, and Jill Levenson, 'The Definition of Love: Shakespeare's Phrasing in *Romeo and Juliet*', *Shakespeare Studies*, 15 (1982), 21–3.

11 Juliet's erotic epithalamium has distressed many critics, particularly those from the nineteenth century. I quote from the appendix to the Variorum edition: N.J. Halprin argued in 1845 that bridal ceremonies must have been common in the 1590s: 'hence may be inferred her familiarity with thoughts and expressions not likely in any other way to have obtained entrance into the mind of an innocent and unsophisticated girl of fourteen' (374); Massey in 1866 argues for emendation of the speech, or 'the sole incentive of this appeal for night to come was Juliet's eagerness for the perfecting of her marriage. It is not so. That would make of Juliet a forward wanton, and of her speech an invocation most immodest' (392); and A. de Lamartine

rants in 1865: 'the most scandalous obscenity usurps the place of that virgin purity' (440). *A New Variorum Edition of Romeo and Juliet*, vol. 1, ed. Horace Furness (Philadelphia, 1871).

12 Noted by Harry Levin, 'Form and Formality in *Romeo and Juliet*', *Romeo and Juliet: Critical Essays*, ed. John F. Andrews (N.Y., 1993), p. 49. See Gary McCown's thorough study of the genre of epithalamium in terms of Juliet's speech. McCown points out that the bridegroom should speak the epithalamium and the bride, like Junia in Catullus 61, is supposed to be afraid and weep to demonstrate modesty. '"Runnawayes Eyes" and Juliet's Epithalamium', *Shakespeare Quarterly*, 27 (1976), 150–76.

13 Christopher Marlowe, *The Tragedy of Dido Queen of Carthage*, *Works*, vol. 1, ed. C. F. Tucker Brooke (London, 1933), 5.1179–81.

14 I have tried to limit my discussion of sexual puns to those I think audiences would readily grasp. Frankie Rubinstein finds a more obscure series of puns in the following line from Juliet's epithalamium: 'Spread thy close curtain, love-performing night' (3.2.5): 'Juliet's amorous impatience is conveyed in (1) the spreading of the "close" (genitals) curtain; (2) the love-performing … "night", her "knight", as she calls Romeo in the last line of the scene.' *A Dictionary of Shakespeare's Sexual Puns and their Significance* (London, 1984), p. 251.

15 See Brown, 'Eight Types of Pun', pp. 20, 22.

16 In John Day's *Isle of Gulls*, Dametas uses 'coney' with a similar implication: 'I would thou shouldst know, we olde Courtiers can hunt a Cony, and put her to the squeake, & make her cry out like a young married wife of the first night.' *The Isle of Gulls*, ed. Raymond S. Burns (N.Y., 1980), 1.4.16–19. For an extended discussion of the sexual implications of 'coney', see James Henke's glossary, *Courtesans and Cuckolds*.

17 One of the most exact borrowings occurs between Lady Capulet's 'I would the fool were married to her grave' (3.5.140) and Mistress Barnes's 'I'll rather have her married to her grave' (8.175). R. W. Dent lists Porter and Shakespeare as the only users of the phrase until Fletcher's *The Night Walker* in 1611. See *Proverbial Language in English Drama Exclusive of Shakespeare 1495–1616* (Berkeley, 1984). For a list of all verbal parallels between the two plays, see Evett, *The Two Angry Women*, pp. 51–4. An unlikely argument has been made that Porter's play was written earlier than 1597 and that Shakespeare looked to his play, rather than the reverse. See J. M. Nosworthy, 'The Two Angry Families of Verona', *Shakespeare Quarterly*, 3 (1952), 219–26.

18 The generally accepted reading of this line (an 'honour') is taken, in fact, from Q1 (the 'bad' Quarto). The 'newly corrected' Q2, Q3 and Q4 all read 'It is an houre that I dreame not of.'

19 See Shakespeare's sonnet 27: 'Which like a jewel hung in ghastly night / Makes black night beauteous and her old face new' (27:11–12).

20 See Edward Snow for an intricate analysis of the gender differences in Romeo's and Juliet's use of matched metaphors. 'Language and Sexual Difference in *Romeo and Juliet*', *Shakespeare's 'Rough Magic': Essays in Honor*

of C.L. Barber, ed. Peter Erickson and Coppélia Kahn (Newark, 1985), pp. 168–92.

21 Gillian Beer, 'Rhyming as Comedy: Body, Ghost and Banquet', *English Comedy*, eds. Michael Cordner, Peter Holland and John Kerrigan (Cambridge, 1994), p. 181.

22 Boys' companies are generally singled out as prone to boy-actor innuendo, a fact often attributed to a more exaggerated acting style. On the other hand, considerable work has been done on proposed *doubles entendres* in Shakespeare's plays. Many studies of the erotic potential of transvestism have been recently published: see, for example, Susan Zimmerman's claim that Jacobean playwrights deliberately privileged transvestism for purposes of erotic titillation. 'Disruptive Desire: Artifice and Indeterminacy in Jacobean Comedy', *Erotic Politics: Desire on the Renaissance Stage*, ed. S. Zimmerman (N.Y., 1992), p. 39.

23 Puns and malapropisms, writes William C. Carroll, 'offer the sexual low road, the eruption of the carnivalesque sexual into high discourse . . . ' 'The Virgin Not: Language and Sexuality in Shakespeare', *Shakespeare Survey 46* (1994), p. 109.

24 *The Two Angry Women of Abington* is surmised to have been popular, considering Henslowe paid the sum of £7 (as against a standard £6) for its sequel. The sequel went into production in February 1598, and Porter was paid the final £2 on 12 February. There was apparently a third sequel planned (*The Two Merry Women of Abington*); on 28 February Henslowe records the following payment: 'Lent unto harey porter at the Requeste of the company in earnest of his boocke called ij mery women of abenton the some of forty shellings & for the Resayte of that money he gave me his faythfulle promysse that I shold have alle the boockes wch he writte . . . ' Qtd. Evett, *The Two Angry Women*, p. 5. The only comparable arrangement was made with Chettle. While the entry indicates Porter's desperate financial straits, it also points to the popularity of his first two plays.

25 See *Romeo and Juliet*, ed. Brian Gibbons (London, 1980), p. 8. The British Library owns a copy of the first quarto of Edward Sharpham's *The Fleire*, bowdlerized some time in the seventeenth century with cuts congruent with a provincial performance of the play. Apparently many bawdy jokes, in particular, were cut. See Clifford Leech, 'The Plays of Edward Sharpham: Alterations Accomplished and Projected', *Review of English Studies*, 11 (1935), 70–4.

26 W. S., *The Puritan, or the Widow of Watling Street*, ed. John S. Farmer (London, 1911), p. H2r, line 3.

27 *A Critical Old-Spelling Edition of Thomas Dekker's Blurt, Master Constable*, ed. Thomas Leland Berger (Salzburg, Austria, 1979), 1.1.90–3. See *Romeo* 1.5.44–6.

28 *Poetaster*, Ben Jonson, vol. 4, ed. C. H. Herford and Percy Simpson (Oxford, 1952), 4.9.63–4.

Love in Venice

Catherine Belsey

Love in Venice generally has a poor record. For Othello and Desdemona, as three centuries later for Merton Densher and Kate Croy, things work out badly. Love in Venice withholds happiness from Henri and Villanelle, the protagonists of Jeanette Winterson's novel, *The Passion*. It is fatal, of course, to Thomas Mann's Gustav Aschenbach. And Jessica, the twentieth-century heroine of Erica Jong's *Serenissima*, goes to Venice to play her namesake, and has the misfortune to fall in love with Shakespeare.[1] Though the nature of their tragedies changes with cultural history, Venice is generally no place for lovers.

In the circumstances, this essay, which is about *The Merchant of Venice*, should perhaps have been called 'Love in Belmont'. Belmont, after all, is so evidently the location in the play of happy love. Belmont is a fairytale castle, where three suitors come for the hand of the princess, and undergo a test arranged by her father in order to distinguish between true love on the one hand and self-love and greed on the other. It is a refuge for eloping lovers, who flee the precarious world of capital and interest and trade, to find a haven of hospitality, music, poetry, old love stories retold in the night – and the infinite wealth (without origins) which makes all this possible. Belmont is the conventional critical *other* of Venice, its defining romantic opposite. Belmont, it is widely agreed, is feminine, lyrical, aristocratic – and vanishing – while Venice represents the new world of men, market forces and racial tensions.

And yet it is the relationship between Venice and Belmont which generates the romantic plot of the play. Portia's princely suitors are in the event an irrelevance: true love turns out to rely on credit. And when Portia takes an active hand in the affairs of capital, true love undergoes, I want to argue, a radical transformation which has continuing repercussions for us now.

It is surely perverse in a volume on Politics and Shakespeare to talk about *The Merchant of Venice* without discussing Shylock, who has quite properly come for twentieth-century criticism, particularly since the Second World War, to represent the crucial issue of this puzzling and in many ways disturbing play. The history of anti-semitism in our own epoch demands that this question be accorded full attention. If I say nothing about it, that is not because I regard it as less than central, but only because I have nothing of value to add to the existing debate.[2] And meanwhile, the play also presents a sexual politics which is beginning to be the focus of feminist criticism and the cultural history of gender.[3] This essay is offered as a contribution to that discussion.

A reading of the sexual politics of the play might begin where interest in Shylock ends, in Act 5. The action of the play seems to have been completed already: the conflict, for better or worse, is over. Act 5 constitutes a coda to the main plot, a festival, set in Belmont, of love and concord and sexuality, combining elements of poetry and comedy, just as weddings do. Although it has no part in the main events of the play, Act 5 is conventionally held to complete its 'harmonies', to dissipate tension and reconcile differences.[4] The classic analysis is surely C.L. Barber's:

> No other comedy, until the late romances, ends with so full an expression of harmony as that which we get in the opening of the final scene of *The Merchant of Venice*. And no other final scene is so completely without irony about the joys it celebrates.[5]

It is true that Act 5 *alludes to* harmony in Lorenzo's account of the music of the spheres. But it also reminds us that we cannot hear the celestial concord 'whilst this muddy vesture of decay/Doth grossly close it in' (5.1.64–5), and this way of talking about the body might seem, if not ironic, at least incongruous in an unqualified celebration of the joy of love. So too, perhaps, is the choice of love stories the newly married Lorenzo and Jessica invoke so lyrically: Troilus and Cressida, Pyramus and Thisbe, Dido, Medea (5.1.1–14). Nor does the text select from their tragic narratives moments of reciprocal happiness. On the contrary, Troilus is represented on the walls of Troy, sighing his soul towards the Greek camp and the absent Cressida. Thisbe is fearful and dismayed, Dido already deserted. Medea, gathering enchanted herbs, has not yet murdered her children in revenge for Jason's infidelity, but the text hints at her demonic powers and begins her characterization as a witch.[6]

The stories of Troilus and Cressida, Dido and Aeneas, and Pyramus and Thisbe are also represented on the walls of the temple of Venus in

Chaucer's *Parliament of Fowls* (lines 289–91).[7] The temple, with its near-naked goddess lying on a bed of gold in the scented half-light, is surely a perfect allegory of desire. But desire is predicated on deprivation: love's acolytes in the temple include pale-faced Patience and bitter Jealousy; two young people kneel to the goddess crying for help; the altar-candles flicker, fanned by lovers' sighs. The stories painted on the walls tell more of sorrow than of joy. Happy love, as Denis de Rougemont repeatedly reminds us, so that the phrase becomes a kind of refrain running through *Love in the Western World*, happy love has no history.[8] In Chaucer's poem the parliament of the birds, to which the account of the temple of Venus is no more than a prelude, would have no story at all if Nature simply prevailed, and the fowls unproblematically chose their mates and flew away. But the narrative is sustained by the courtly eagles, all three in love with the same mistress, so that two at least are doomed to despair, and all three compelled to wait in hope and fear and longing.

'The moon shines bright. In such a night as this . . .' The rhythms and the internal rhymes, in conjunction with the climatic conditions, 'When the sweet wind did gently kiss the trees' (*The Merchant of Venice* 5.1.1–2), all serve to contain and dissipate what is most distressing in Shakespeare's classical and Italian narratives transmuted into medieval romance. The effect is thrilling to the degree that pleasure is infused with danger. It is also profoundly nostalgic in that it looks back to a world, fast disappearing in the late sixteenth century, where love was seen as anarchic, destructive, and dangerous. In the play this world is no longer dominant. Love in *The Merchant of Venice* means marriage, concord, consent, and partnership. It means mutual compatibility and sympathy and support. But the older understanding of love leaves traces in the text, with the effect that desire is only imperfectly domesticated, and in consequence the extent to which Venice is superimposed on Belmont becomes visible to the audience.

II

Desire, as characterized in Western culture, is dangerous. It depends on lack: you desire what you don't have; desire fulfilled is desire suspended. Psychoanalytically, desire can be satisfied only at the level of the imaginary, in that it insists upon absolute recognition from the other.[9] Lacan distinguishes desire from demand, the appeal for love which can be formulated – and met. Desire is the residue of demand, the unutterable within or beyond it. Lacan calls it the 'want-to-be' ('manque-à-être') that demand 'hollows within itself'. Because love cannot be fully present in the signifier, desire is brought to light precisely by the signifying chain itself, the otherness of language, in which it can never be met, since language too lacks being.[10]

Western literature presents desire as immoderate, disproportionate, unstable, thrilling precisely because it is hazardous. Villanelle, Jeanette Winterson's web-footed, cross-dressed Venetian croupier heroine, consistently associates desire with gambling, gambling with passion. Both are compulsive and urgent; both risk the possibility of loss. 'Somewhere between fear and sex passion is.'[11] Gustav Aschenbach is paradoxically elated by the discovery of disease in Venice because he senses a correspondence between the concealed, physical threat to the population and the dangerous secret of his own emotional condition.

Desire is perilous because it annihilates the speaking, knowing, mastering subject, the choosing, commanding self so precious to the Free West. Lovers are conventionally speechless (what can they say that would do justice to desire?). They are uncertain, irrational, out of control; transformed, transported, other than they are. Gustav Aschenbach, the rational, disciplined writer, knows that he ought to warn the Polish family about the pestilence and then leave Venice, but he also knows that passion will prevent him from doing either. 'It would restore him, would give him back himself once more; but he who is beside himself revolts at the idea of self-possession.'[12] For these reasons, desire also undermines the *idea* of the self, calling in question the dualism on which it is founded, deconstructing the opposition between mind and body, as each manifests itself in the province of the other.

We know from endless accounts of burning, freezing Petrarchan lovers, still pursuing, still disdained, wrecked and racked by love neglected, that the Renaissance took full account of the element of danger in desire.[13] And we know it too from the efforts of Astrophil to resist his own destruction, from the ambivalence of Antony towards his strong Egyptian fetters, and from countless tragedies of love in the period, most particularly, perhaps, the work of Middleton. Passion turns women to whores; it renders men effeminate, incapable of manly pursuits; it threatens identity, arousing fears that subjectivity itself is unstable.[14]

Bassanio is able to solve the riddle of the caskets not only because he sees through outward show, but also because he alone among the suitors recognizes the appropriate emblem of desire: 'thou meagre lead / Which rather threaten'st than dost promise aught, / Thy paleness moves me more than eloquence . . . ' (3.2.104–6).[15] The Prince of Aragon thinks of his own desert, and the silver casket acts as a mirror for his narcissism, revealing the portrait of a blinking idiot (2.9.30–2, 50, 53). Morocco resolves to take his own desert for granted (2.7.31–4) and thinks of Portia's value: 'never so rich a gem / Was set in worse than gold' (2.7.54–5). The golden casket contains death, the destiny of those who serve mammon. Only Bassanio is motivated by desire and knows that lovers give and hazard all they have. His choice vindicates Portia's conviction: 'If you do love me, you will find me out' (3.2.41).

Even in his triumph Bassanio displays all the symptoms of passion: he is bereft of words; only his blood speaks in his veins, reducing subjectivity to sensation. Turmoil within the subject confounds the familiar system of differences: 'Where every something being blent together / Turns to a wild of nothing save of joy / Expressed and not expressed'. And in case it should all be too easy from now on, he willingly accepts the new hazard that Portia has set him: 'when this ring / Parts from this finger, then parts life from hence' (3.2.175–84). Even Portia's picture, which is no more than her 'shadow', is full of metaphorical dangers. Her parted lips are sweet friends *sundered*; her hair is a spider's web, 'A golden mesh t'untrap the hearts of men / Faster than gnats in cobwebs'. And in a strange, baroque conceit, Bassanio argues that the rendering of her eyes should surely have blinded the painter: 'having made one, / Methinks it should have power to steal both his / And leave itself unfurnished' (3.2.118–29).

III

Riddles too are traditionally dangerous because they exploit the duplicity of the signifier, the secret alterity that subsists in meaning. They prevaricate, explicitly deferring and obscuring the truth. Riddles demonstrate that meaning is neither single nor transparent, that words can be used to conceal it. They show that language itself seduces and betrays those who believe themselves to be in command of it, who imagine it to be an instrument for their use, at their disposal. Riddles equivocate: Portia is what many men desire; but so is death. His own portrait is what Aragon deserves precisely because he supposes that he deserves Portia.

'What has one voice, and goes on four legs in the morning, two legs in the afternoon, and three legs in the evening?' The sphinx posed her riddle to the Thebans, and each time they got it wrong, she devoured one of them. In the play suitors who fail to solve the riddle of the caskets undertake never to marry. Penalties of this kind are common. Riddles are posed by the wise to isolate the foolish. Solomon delighted in them. They feature prominently in the book of Proverbs. The riddle for Portia's hand has the sacred character of a trial by ordeal. As Nerissa explains:

Your father was ever virtuous, and holy men at their death have good inspirati-
ons; therefore the lottery that he hath devised in these three chests of gold, silver,
and lead, whereof who chooses his meaning chooses you, will no doubt never
be chosen by any rightly but one who you shall rightly love.   (1.2.27–32)

Traditionally riddles are no joke. It is only the Enlightenment regulation of language, with its insistence on the plain style, affirming the transparency of the signifier, that relegates riddles to the nursery,[16] along with ogres and fairies and all the remaining apparatus of the uncanny.

In folk-tales riddles are a common way of exalting the humble and meek. The youngest of three brothers or the poorest of three candidates has only ingenuity or virtue to draw on. Success depends on quick wits or the help of a grateful friend. One of the commonest situations in folk-tales is a contest for the hand of the princess, and the motif of winning a bride by solving a riddle goes back to the Greek romances, and reappears in the middle ages.[17] Bruno Bettelheim proposes a broadly Freudian interpretation of this recurrent phenomenon:

Solving the riddle posed by a particular woman stands for the riddle of woman
in general, and since marriage usually follows the right solution, it does not seem
farfetched that the riddle to be solved is a sexual one: whoever understands the
secret which the other sex presents has gained his maturity.[18]

In a broadly Lacanian reformulation of this proposition it could be argued that the riddle for the hand of the princess is a riddle about the nature of desire, and that the text of *The Merchant of Venice* comes close to making this explicit. In the presumed source in the *Gesta Romanorum*, where the protagonist, interestingly, is a woman, the inscription on the lead vessel is providential: 'Who so chooseth mee, shall finde that God hath disposed for him'.[19] Shakespeare's change locates the meaning of the lead casket firmly in the realm of the secular and the sexual.

Moreover, riddles could be said to enact at the level of the signifier something of the character of desire. Both entail uncertainty, enigma. Both are dangerous. Riddles tease, torment, elude, challenge, and frustrate. Once the answer is known the riddle ceases to fascinate, just as desire evaporates once the *otherness* of the other is mastered. Both riddles and desire depend on a sense of the unpresentable within the process of representation, though desire imagines a metaphysical presence, a real existence elsewhere, while riddles refer to the unpresented, the meaning which is not there but which can be found, and found nowhere else but there.[20] In this sense the wooing of Portia displays a perfect appropriateness, a ceremonial decorum which endows it with all the traditional impersonality of the Anglican marriage service itself (this man. . .this woman, making a formal undertaking).[21]

IV

The riddle for Portia's hand is posed, appropriately enough, by a dead father, and solved by the romantic hero. Portia, who also has immoderate desires, cannot act on them but waits, a sacrificial virgin, for the happy outcome of the ordeal (3.2.111–14, 57). The news from Venice, however, changes everything. Antonio's predicament also poses a riddle: how can he fulfil his contract without losing his life? This time, Bassanio stands helplessly by while Portia and Nerissa turn to men, and Portia-as-Balthasar finds the equivocation which releases her husband's friend: flesh is not blood. An apparently archetypal and yet vanishing order is radically challenged by cross-dressed women who travel from Belmont to Venice and, uniquely in Shakespearian comedy, intervene not only in the public world of history, but specifically in the supremely masculine and political world of law, with the effect of challenging the economic arrangements of the commercial capital of the world.

And then in the final episode of the play it is the women who produce a series of equivocations which constitute yet another riddle, this time concerning the meaning of gender difference within a new kind of marriage, where a wife is a partner and a companion. The exchanges in Act 5 between Lorenzo and Jessica about old tales of love and death and the unheard music of the spheres are interrupted by the voice of Portia (5.1.110, 113), and her first words to them constitute a riddle to which, of course, the audience knows the answer: 'We have been praying for our husbands' welfare, / Which speed (we hope) the better for our words' (5.1.114–15). The remainder of the play (almost 180 lines of it) consists largely of a series of increasingly bawdy puns and double entendres about rings, and this festival of plurality at the level of the signifier poses a riddle about sexual identity which presumably pleases the audience, but entirely baffles Bassanio.

George Puttenham discusses riddles in his handbook for vernacular writers, *The Arte of English Poesie*, printed in 1589. For Puttenham, with his clear humanist and Renaissance commitments, riddles are already becoming childish, though it is possible to see more in them than children might.

My mother had an old woman in her nurserie, who in the winter nights would put us forth many prety riddles, whereof this is one:

> *I have a thing and rough it is*
> *And in the midst a hole Iwis:*
> *There came a yong man with his ginne,*
> *And he put it a handfull in.*

The good old Gentlewoman would tell us that were children how it was meant by a furd gloove. Some other naughtie body would peradventure have construed it not half so mannerly.[22]

Evidently for Puttenham riddles are engaging, harmless equivocations or ambiguities (unless they're unduly lewd), and the answer can be deduced from the terms of the puzzle itself, though it is not necessarily the first solution a grown-up might think of.[23]

But Puttenham also identifies another category of equivocation, this time profoundly disturbing, to which Steven Mullaney has drawn attention. This is the kind that seduces and betrays Macbeth, because it lies like truth, making it impossible to tell where truth resides. Puttenham calls this figure *amphibology*, and he condemns it roundly as a threat to order. Amphibologies are frequently without evident human or social origin: they emanate from oracles, pagan prophets – or witches, of course. And they particularly constitute the figure of insurrection, misleading the people in times of rebellion,

as that of Iacke Straw, & Iacke Cade in Richard the seconds time, and in our time by a seditious fellow in Norffolke calling himself Captaine Ket and others in other places of the Realme lead altogether by certaine propheticall rymes, which might be constred two or three wayes as well as that one whereunto the rebelles applied it.[24]

Amphibologies depend on an indeterminacy of meaning which only events can resolve. Puttenham has no patience with them because they have unexpected consequences, and because he associates them with challenges to the social order.

It is difficult to identify with any confidence a clear formal distinction between Puttenham's amphibologies and his riddles. Both depend on ambiguity; both prevaricate and equivocate. Both use words to conceal what is meant, paradoxically bringing out into the open the hidden alterity of meaning. The difference seems to lie in the question of mastery. Riddles promise closure: the old woman in the nursery has the answer, and the children can expect to be told if they have guessed correctly. Like Macbeth, however, Captain Ket has to wait until experience reveals the truth. The proof of the pudding is deferred until it is too late to be any use. Amphibologies mislead. Riddles install the knowing subject: amphibologies undermine the subject's power to know and consequently to control events.

The riddles posed by Portia and Nerissa in the rings episode of *The Merchant of Venice* mostly concern the sex of the lawyer. 'In faith, I gave it to the judge's clerk. / Would he were gelt that had it for my part', Graziano stoutly affirms (5.1.143–4). The clerk *is* 'gelt', of course, to the extent that in the Renaissance, as in a different way for Freud, women are incomplete men,[25] and the pleasure for the audience lies in identifying a meaning which is not available to the speaker.

NERISSA   The clerk will ne'er wear hair on's face that had it.
GRAZIANO   He will an if he live to be a man.
NERISSA   Ay, if a woman live to be a man.
GRAZIANO   Now by this hand, I gave it to a youth. . .   (5.1.158–61)

All these utterances are true. By a radical transgression of the differences that hold meaning in place, the youth and the woman are the same person, though Nerissa and the woman she speaks of are not the same. The speed of the exchanges requires some agility on the part of the audience, though not, perhaps, the degree of mobility needed to follow the dizzying series of shifts in the meanings Portia attributes to the 'doctor':

> Since he hath got the jewel that I loved,
> And that which you did swear to keep for me,
> I will become as liberal as you.
> I'll not deny him anything I have,
> No, not my body nor my husband's bed:
> Know him I shall, I am well sure of it.
> Lie not a night from home. Watch me like Argus.
> If you do not, if I be left alone,
> Now by mine honour, which is yet mine own,
> I'll have that doctor for my bedfellow.
>   (5.1.224–33)

Here Bassanio once again confronts three apparently exclusive options. First, the doctor is a woman (but not Portia, whose honour is still her own), and the woman has taken the 'jewel' that Bassanio promised, by marrying her, to keep for Portia herself. Second, the doctor is a man, and Portia is willing to share her bed with him. And finally the doctor is Portia, her bedfellow when she is alone. Each of the options contains part of the answer. No wonder Bassanio is baffled, and Portia has to spell out the truth for him (5.1.269–70).

The full answer to the riddle of the rings is that Portia has more than one identity. There is a sense in which the multiple meanings here recapitulate the action of the play. Portia has always been other than she is. The fairytale princess, a sacrificial virgin, as she characterized herself, was not only 'an unlessoned girl' but also (and in the same speech) 'the lord / Of this fair mansion, master of my servants, / Queen o'er myself' (3.2.159, 167–9). Evidently to be an heiress is already to disrupt the rules of gender. But her marriage in conjunction with her Venetian journey (and the deferred consummation confirms them as inextricable) invests her with a new kind of polysemy. The equivocations and doubles entendres of Act 5 celebrate a sexual indeterminacy, which is not in-difference but multiplicity.

In this sense the episode of the rings surely resembles Puttenham's category of amphibology rather than his concept of the riddle. The answer cannot be deduced from the terms of the puzzle itself. At one level, of course, the solution to the ambiguities and equivocations of the scene is readily available: the doctor and his clerk are also women. That knowledge sustains all the puns and resolves all the contradictions, and thus ensures for the audience the pleasure of mastering a succession of rapidly shifting meanings. This pleasure may help to account for the feeling of harmony which so many critics derive from Act 5. But there is another sense in which the implications of the episode are more elusive. The double act between Portia and Nerissa takes their performance beyond the realm of the individual, endowing it with a representative quality, and the reference back through the text which the episode invites, suggests a more metaphysical question: what, in a world where Belmont encounters the values of Venice, does it mean to be a wife?

Portia claims the ring in return for rescuing Bassanio's friend and thus, indirectly, Bassanio himself. Like Britomart, the lady becomes a warrior, and the equal of her man. 'If you had known,' she says to Bassanio, 'half her worthiness that gave the ring...' (5.1.199–200). The role of desire is fully acknowledged in the casket scene, and the importance of sexual difference is repeatedly affirmed in the bawdy double meanings of Act 5. This is evident in the final pun, delivered, appropriately, by Graziano: 'Well, while I live I'll fear no other thing / So sore, as keeping safe Nerissa's ring' (5.1.306–7), though Stephen Orgel points out that an element of indeterminacy remains even here. Anatomical rings may be

82   CATHERINE BELSEY

masculine as well as feminine, and the preceding lines are: 'But were the day come, I should wish it dark / Till I were couching with the doctor's clerk'. But the other non-sexual, non-differential 'half' of Portia's worthiness as a wife is made apparent in her performance as Bassanio's fellow-warrior, partner and friend. The solution to the riddle of the rings is thus a utopian vision of the new possibilities of marriage. The riddle does not originate with Portia and Nerissa, nor even entirely with their author, for all his familiar human wisdom. On the contrary, it is the effect of a specific cultural moment when the meaning of marriage is unstable, contested, and open to radical reconstruction.[26] The riddle is also deeply socially disruptive in its fundamental challenge to the patriarchal order.

In the episode of the rings happy love acquires a history by superimposing a similitude on the existing difference. The otherness which is the condition of desire is brought into conjunction with a comradeship which assumes a parallel, a likeness of values and dispositions. The gap that lies between these two 'halves' of what constitutes conjugal worth is dramatized both in the disjunction between the two parts of Act 5 and in the multiple identity that is required of Portia.

V

If the term 'wife' absorbs the meaning of 'friend', what place in the signifying chain, what specific difference is left for the meaning of friendship? We can, of course, reduce the metaphysical burden of Antonio's apparently unmotivated melancholy to disappointed homoerotic desire. This is a possible reading and not one that I wish to discredit.[27] Certainly the play constructs a symmetry between Antonio and Portia. It is Antonio who assures Bassanio, 'My purse, my person, my extremest means / Lie all unlocked to your occasions' (1.1.138–9), but it might equally have been Portia who said it (see 3.2.304–5). And certainly in Acts 4 and 5 this symmetry turns into the contest between two kinds of obligation which is evident in the episode of the rings. But my view is that the play here presents to the audience the implications of a contest for meaning, including the meaning of sexuality, which throws into relief something of the distance between the culture of Renaissance England and our own.

In court in Act 4 Bassanio declares:

> Antonio, I am married to a wife
> Which is as dear to me as life itself,

> But life itself, my wife, and all the world
> Are not with me esteemed above thy life.
> I would lose all, ay, sacrifice them all
> Here to this devil, to deliver you.
>
> (4.1.279–84)

Bassanio's priorities are surely shocking to a modern audience. Men are not supposed to prefer their friends to their wives. On the contrary, in our normative society, while adolescent sexuality is allowed to include homosocial or even homoerotic desire, this phase is supposed to be left behind by adults, who 'naturally' privilege heterosexual marriage. (At least one recent reading of *The Merchant of Venice* takes this pattern of 'normal' development for granted.[28])

But Bassanio's position is not without a Renaissance pedigree. In Sir Thomas Elyot's *The Governour* (1531) Titus and Gysippus grow up together and are inseparable until Gysippus falls in love and decides to marry. But when Titus meets his friend's proposed bride, to his own horror, he instantly falls in love with her too. Overcome by the double anguish of desire and disloyalty, Titus takes to his bed. At last Gysippus prises the secret out of him, and once he knows the truth he is easily able to resolve the problem. The friends agree to substitute Titus for Gysippus on the wedding day. Thus friendship is preserved. Gysippus is publicly embarrassed, and has to leave town for a time, but otherwise all is well, and Elyot triumphantly cites the story as an 'example in the affectes of frendshippe'.[29] The values here resemble those of Chaucer's *Knight's Tale*, where love tragically destroys chivalric friendship. The relationship between Palamon and Arcite is heroic; love, on the other hand, is high folly, according to Theseus, and the text does nothing to counteract this view (lines 1798–9). According to Geron's aphoristic assessment of the priorities in Lyly's *Endimion*,

Love is but an eye-worme, which onely tickleth the heade with hopes, and wishes: friendshippe the image of eternitie, in which there is nothing moveable, nothing mischeevous . . . Time draweth wrinckles in a fayre face, but addeth fresh colours to a faste friende, which neither heate, nor cold, nor miserie, nor place, nor destiny, can alter or diminish. (3.4.123–36)[30]

Eumenides accepts this evaluation, chooses friendship, and is rewarded with love too.

When Damon is falsely accused of spying in the play by Richard Edwards, his friend Pithias volunteers to take his place in prison and to be executed if Damon fails to return in time. The hangman finds this remarkable:

> Here is a mad man I tell thee, I have a wyfe
>   whom I love well.
> And if iche would die for her, chould iche
>   weare in Hell:
> Wylt thou doo more for a man, then I woulde
>   for a woman(?)

And Pithias replies firmly, 'Yea, that I wyll' (lines 1076–80).[31] It is not clear how seriously we are invited to take the values of the hangman, but it is evident that Pithias is right about the supreme obligations of friendship in this most pedagogic of plays, written in the 1560s by the Master of the Chapel Royal for the Children to perform. Even as late as *The Two Noble Kinsmen* in 1613 the conflicting claims of marriage and friendship are matter for debate – this time between women. Hippolyta reflects without rancour on the affections of Theseus, divided between herself and his friend Pirithous:

> Their knot of love,
> Tied, weaved, entangled, with so true, so long,
> And with a finger of so deep a cunning,
> May be outworn, never undone. I think
> Theseus cannot be umpire to himself,
> Cleaving his conscience into twain and doing
> Each side like justice, which he loves best.
>   (1.3.41–7)

Hippolyta finally concludes that Theseus prefers her (1.3.95–7), but not before Emilia has put the case for friendship between members of the same sex as the stronger force: 'the true love 'tween maid and maid may be / More than in sex dividual' (1.3.81–2). In the end Hippolyta and Emilia agree to differ.

Both *The Governour* and *Endimion* are cited by Bullough as possible sources of *The Two Gentlemen of Verona*, where Valentine offers his beloved Silvia to his friend Proteus.[32] Bullough finds Valentine's gesture 'Quixotic', as presumably most twentieth-century commentators would.[33] And indeed the play has so enlisted our sympathy for Julia that we cannot want Proteus to accept his friend's generosity. Elsewhere too Shakespeare's texts tend to opt, however uneasily, for the nuclear couple. Othello, who should prefer his wife, tragically listens to his friend. More specifically, in *Much Ado About Nothing*, which is chronologically closer to *The Merchant of Venice*, Beatrice's imperative to Benedick on behalf of her cousin also foregrounds the conflicting obligations of lovers and friends.

The loyalty of Beatrice to Hero is absolute, and at the moment when Benedick declares his love for Beatrice, her immediate concern is Hero's honour. Beatrice's challenge necessarily threatens the loyalty of Benedick to Claudio.

BENEDICK   Come, bid me do anything for thee.
BEATRICE   Kill Claudio.
BENEDICK   Ha! Not for the wide world.   (4.1.289–91)

Whether or not Benedick's moment of recoil is played as comedy, the play goes on in the event to realign him explicitly as Beatrice's 'friend' (4.1.319) and thus as Claudio's enemy. Later the text reverts to this issue when, in the course of a series of teasing exchanges, an instance of the verbal friction characteristic of desire,[34] Beatrice sets up an opposition between Benedick's friendship and his 'heart'. But this time, she opts for friendship with Benedick even at the price of love:

BENEDICK   ... I love thee against my will.
BENEDICK   In spite of your heart, I think. Alas, poor heart. If you spite it for my sake I will spite it for yours, for I will never love that which my friend hates.   (5.2.61–4)[35]

This *is* comedy. The play's treatment of the issue is more complex: Beatrice's challenge to Benedick to fight for her evokes classical myth and medieval romance, rather than the new model of marriage. At the same time, we are invited to understand that Benedick qualifies as a husband to the degree that he is prepared to sacrifice his friend. It is no surprise, therefore, that in *The Merchant of Venice* Bassanio's declaration that his friend comes first does not go unchallenged. At once Balthasar, uniquely in the court scene, draws the attention of the audience to his/her other identity: 'Your wife would give you little thanks for that / If she were by to hear you make the offer' (4.1.285–6). When Bassanio surrenders the ring to Balthasar it is in response to Antonio's persuasion, and the conflict of obligations is made explicit:

> My Lord Bassanio, let him have the ring.
> Let his deservings and my love withal
> Be valued 'gainst your wife's commandëment.
>   (4.1.446–8)

Bassanio subsequently excuses himself to Portia in the vocabulary of chivalry:

> Even he that had held up the very life
> Of my dear friend. What should I say, sweet lady?

I was enforced to send it after him.
I was beset with shame and courtesy.
My honour would not let ingratitude
So much besmear it.

(5.1.214–19)

And here, perhaps, is a pointer to the residual meaning of friendship in
the period. Georges Duby gives a graphic account of the life of chivalry
among the 'youth' of twelfth-century France. These men constituted a
substantial proportion of the audience, and therefore, no doubt, much of
the motive, for the new romantic love stories and troubadour poems of
the period. A version of their image survives in ideal form in the nostalgic
culture of late sixteenth-century England, most obviously in texts like
The Faerie Queene, in response to the Queen's enthusiastic cultivation of
the heroic and courtly ideal.

Duby's 'youths' were fully-grown knights who were not yet fathers.
This stage of life might last, it appears, for upwards of twenty years.
During this period the 'youth', often accompanied by a slightly more
experienced 'youth', or as one of a group of fast friends who loved each
other like brothers, roamed in pursuit of adventure and, more specifically,
in quest of a wife. The eldest son could expect in due course to inherit
his father's property. But in a world where the patrimony was expected
to provide a living for the couple as well as a marriage settlement for the
wife, younger sons had usually little to hope for outside a career in the
church, unless they could locate an heiress, secure her father's approval
and marry her.

Since the life of the 'youth' was violent and dangerous, whole male
lineages were in practice eliminated, and rich women were not as rare
as might be expected, though only a tiny minority of the 'youth' could
hope to secure one. In the mean time, groups of men, officially celibate,
lived and fought together. We may assume that in such circumstances the
virtue of loyalty was paramount: at least in their idealized, literary form,
the knights were conventionally bosom friends and inseparable com-
panions. Once married, and a father, the knight gave priority to his own
establishment, though he might well retain some of his former comrades
in his household, and indeed help them to find suitable brides.[36]

Duby's account gives no indication of a conflict between love and
friendship. In a chivalric culture love endangers friendship when it becomes rivalry, as *The Knight's Tale* shows, but wives do not supplant friends:
their rôle is quite different. The new model of marriage in the sixteenth
century, however, identified wives precisely as friends, and the texts of

the period bring to light some of the uncertainties and anxieties which attend the process of redefinition. Antonio is sad because he is in mourning for friendship. Of course, Portia does it nicely. She gives the ring to Antonio to give back to Bassanio, so that Antonio feels included. But he knows from the beginning of the play that things will never be the same again.

And what about the place of homoerotic desire? Perhaps we shall never know. Eve Kosofsky Sedgwick is surely right to urge that 'the sexual context of that period is too far irrecoverable for us to be able to disentangle boasts, confessions, undertones, overtones, jokes, the unthinkable, the taken-for-granted, the unmentionable-but-often-done-anyway, etc.'[37] It seems unlikely that medieval knights were as chaste as the chivalric code required. On the other hand, while sodomy was consistently identified as an abominable crime, homosexual acts were very rarely prosecuted in England in the middle ages or the Renaissance.[38] In practice the whole issue seems to have generated relatively little anxiety. Stephen Orgel in a brilliant contribution to the cultural history of the sixteenth century argues that homosexual acts were perceived as less dangerous to men than heterosexual love, because it was association with women which was effeminating.[39]

A single example may indicate the difficulty we have in construing the meanings of a vanished culture. In *The Two Noble Kinsmen* the relationship between Palamon and Arcite is treated in remarkable detail. They love each other; they lighten each other's imprisonment. Arcite declares, apparently without embarrassment, that since imprisonment will prevent them from marrying, 'We are one another's wife, ever begetting / New births of love' (2.2.80–1). At the same time, it is clear that their explicit sexual preferences are heterosexual. The whole plot depends on this. And besides, the text makes clear that they admire each other greatly for their former heterosexual conquests (3.3.30–42).

Possibly our difficulty resides in the plurality of the word 'love'? Palamon loves Arcite; Arcite loves Palamon; but both Palamon and Arcite love Emilia. Perhaps it is not only our difficulty: Palamon explicitly distinguishes between love and desire, in order to be sure that his cousin is really his rival. 'You love her then?' 'Who would not?' 'And desire her?' (2.2.159–61). It could be argued, then, that the play sets up its own system of differences: that while love might or might not be sexual, desire is erotic in this text. It could be argued, were it not for Palamon's final words to the dying Arcite, which surely deconstruct any such opposition:

O cousin,
That we should things desire which do cost us
The loss of our desire! That nought could buy
Dear love, but loss of dear love.

(5.1.109–12)

Here heterosexual passion and homosocial friendship are defined in exactly the same terms: both are dear love; both are desire. It remains for the audience to determine whether Palamon's words are best understood as conflating difference (one love, one desire, at the price of its similitude) or as turning to account the difference within the signifier (one love, one desire, at the cost of its distinguishing, differentiating other).

VI

A tentative history of our own cultural moment emerges from all this. Our more carefully regulated meanings impose narrow limits on the range of possibilities available to us. Since Freud we have learned that all intense emotion is 'really' sexual; since the Enlightenment we have known how to classify and evaluate deviance; and since *The Merchant of Venice* we have known that marriage, which includes every imaginable adult relationship, ought to be enough for anyone.

I wonder...

First published in *Shakespeare Survey 44* (1992)

NOTES

1 I owe this reference to Kristina Engler.
2 For an account of the debate (and selective bibliography) see Walter Cohen, *Drama of a Nation: Public Theater in Renaissance England and Spain* (Ithaca, 1985), pp. 196–7. See also Cohen's own analysis, pp. 195–211; Thomas Moisan, ' "Which is the Merchant here? and Which the Jew": Subversion and Recuperation in *The Merchant of Venice*', in *Shakespeare Reproduced: The Text in History and Ideology*, ed. Jean E. Howard and Marion F. O'Connor (New York, 1987), pp. 188–206; Kiernan Ryan, *Shakespeare* (London, 1989, pp. 14–24; and John Drakakis, '*The Merchant of Venice*, or Christian Patriarchy and its Discontents', in *Mortal Shakespeare: Radical Readings*, ed. Manuel Barbeito (Santiago de Compostela, 1989), pp. 69–93.
3 See for example Linda Bamber, *Comic Women, Tragic Men: A Study of Gender and Genre in Shakespeare* (Stanford, 1982), pp. 109–33; Keith Geary, 'The Nature of Portia's Victory: Turning to Men in *The Merchant of Venice*', *Shakespeare Survey 37* (1984), 55–68; Lars Engle, ' "Thrift is Blessing": Exchange and Explanation in *The Merchant of Venice*', *Shakespeare Quarterly*, 37

(1986), 20–37; Karen Newman, 'Portia's Ring: Unruly Women and Structures of Exchange in *The Merchant of Venice*', *Shakespeare Quarterly*, 38 (1987), 19–33; Jean Howard, 'Crossdressing, the Theatre, and Gender Struggle in Early Modern England', *Shakespeare Quarterly*, 39 (1988), 418–40.

4 See for example Lawrence Danson, *The Harmonies of 'The Merchant of Venice'* (New Haven, 1978), pp. 170–95.

5 C. L. Barber, *Shakespeare's Festive Comedy: A Study of Dramatic Form and its Relation to Social Custom* (Princeton, NJ, 1959), p. 187.

6 The specific reference is to Ovid, *Metamorphoses* vii, 162ff. Medea treats Aeson with rejuvenating herbs. When the daughters of Pelias subsequently ask for her help, she deliberately offers them inefficacious herbs and thus causes them to bring about his death. I owe this point to Michael Comber. See also Jonathan Bate, 'Ovid and the Mature Tragedies: Metamorphosis in *Othello* and *King Lear*', *Shakespeare Survey 41* (1989), 133–44, pp. 134–5.

7 Geoffrey Chaucer, *Works*, ed. F. N. Robinson (London, 1957).

8 Denis de Rougemont, *Love in the Western World*, trans. Montgomery Belgion (Princeton, NJ, 1983), p. 15 and *passim*.

9 Jean Laplanche and J.-B. Pontalis, 'Wish (Desire)', *The Language of Psychoanalysis*, trans. Donald Nicholson-Smith (London, 1973), pp. 481–3. Cf. Jacques Lacan, *Écrits: A Selection*, trans. Alan Sheridan (London, 1977), p. 58.

10 Lacan, *Écrits*, pp. 263, 265.

11 Jeanette Winterson, *The Passion* (London, 1988), p. 62. Cf. pp. 55, 66.

12 Thomas Mann, *Death in Venice, Tristan, Tonio Kröger* (London, 1955), p. 74.

13 See Scott Wilson, 'Racked on the Tyrant's Bed: The Politics of Pleasure and Pain and the Elizabethan Sonnet Sequences', *Textual Practice*, 3 (1989), 234–49.

14 Laura Levine, 'Men in Women's Clothing: Antitheatricality and Effeminization from 1579–1642', *Criticism*, 28 (1986), 121–43; Stephen Orgel, 'Nobody's Perfect: Or Why Did the English Stage Take Boys for Women?', *South Atlantic Quarterly*, 88 (1989), pp. 7–29.

15 Freud argues that Bassanio's choice (which is really a choice between three women) betrays an acknowledgement of ineluctable death, masked as the choice of a desirable woman (Sigmund Freud, 'The Theme of the Three Caskets', *Complete Psychological Works*, SE 12, ed. James Strachey (London, 1958), pp. 291–301). Sarah Kofman, developing Freud's argument, sees the episode as a representation of the 'ambivalence' (or duplicity) of love: the wish for love is superimposed on the awareness of death, but the imagery prevents the complete success of the process, so that the audience is satisfied at the level of fantasy but also at the level of the intellect (Sarah Kofman, 'Conversions: *The Merchant of Venice* Under the Sign of Saturn', in *Literary Theory Today*, eds. Peter Collier and Helga Geyer-Ryan (Cambridge, 1990), pp. 142–66).

16 Mark Bryant, *Dictionary of Riddles* (London, 1990), p. 51.

17 Stith Thompson, *The Folktale* (Berkeley, 1977), pp. 153–8.

18 Bruno Bettelheim, *The Uses of Enchantment: The Meaning and Importance of Fairy Tales* (London, 1978), p. 128.
19 John Russell Brown, ed., *The Merchant of Venice* (London, 1959), p. 173.
20 Wyatt exploits the parallel in his riddles of forbidden desire. See for example 'A ladye gave ne a gyfte she had not' ... and 'What wourde is that that chaungeth not?', *The Collected Poems of Sir Thomas Wyatt*, ed. Kenneth Muir and Patricia Thomson (Liverpool, 1969), pp. 238, 36.
21 The view that Bassanio is no more than a fortune-hunter who desires Portia only, or primarily, for her money seems to me anachronistic, probably filtered by Victorian fiction, where love and money are commonly opposed.
22 George Puttenham, *The Arte of English Poesie*, ed. G. D. Willcock and A. Walker (Cambridge, 1936), p. 188.
23 William Dodd identifies a structural analogy between riddle and comedy, which also sets a puzzle and finally solves it, though not in the most obvious way. See *Misura per misura: la transparenza della commedia* (Milano, 1979), pp. 203ff.
24 Puttenham, *Arte*, pp. 260–1. Steven Mullaney, 'Lying Like Truth: Riddle, Representation and Treason in Renaissance England', *ELH*, 47 (1980), 32–47.
25 Stephen Greenblatt, 'Fiction and Friction', *Shakespearean Negotiations: The Circulation of Social Energy in Renaissance England* (Oxford, 1988), pp. 66–93.
26 See Catherine Belsey, 'Disrupting Sexual Difference: Meaning and Gender in the Comedies', in *Alternative Shakespeares*, ed. John Drakakis (London, 1985), pp. 166–90; *The Subject of Tragedy: Identity and Difference in Renaissance Drama* (London, 1985), pp. 129–221. Eighty years later it would be possible for a good woman to propose that it would be 'nobler' to be her husband's friend than his wife (John Dryden, *Troilus and Cressida* 2.1.143–5, *Works*, vol. 13, ed. Maximillian E. Novak (Berkeley, 1984)). I owe this point to M. C. Bradbrook.
27 This has been a recurrent interpretation of the play at least since Tillyard toyed with the idea in 1966. See Danson, *Harmonies*, pp. 34–40.
28 W. Thomas MacCary, *Friends and Lovers: The Phenomenology of Desire in Shakespearean Comedy* (New York, 1985), especially pp. 167–8.
29 Sir Thomas Elyot, *The Governour* (London, 1907), p. 183.
30 John Lyly, *Endimion, The Complete Works*, ed. R. Warwick Bond (Oxford, 1902), 3 vols., vol. 3. Cf. Elyot, *The Governour*, II.xi, and Montaigne, 'Of Friendship', cited in Eugene Waith, ed., *The Two Noble Kinsmen* (Oxford, 1989), p. 50.
31 Richard Edwards, *Damon and Pythias* (Oxford, 1957).
32 Geoffrey Bullough, *Narrative and Dramatic Sources of Shakespeare*, vol. 1 (London, 1957), pp. 203–17.
33 Bullough, *Sources*, vol. 1, p. 203.
34 Greenblatt, 'Fiction and Friction', pp. 88–91.
35 I owe this point to A. D. Nuttall.
36 Georges Duby, 'Youth in Aristocratic Society', *The Chivalrous Society*, trans. Cynthia Postan (London, 1977), pp. 112–22. I owe this connection to Mary

Beth Rose, *The Expense of Spirit: Love and Sexuality in English Renaissance Drama* (Ithaca, 1988), pp. 178–235, though she reads the texts with a rather different emphasis.

37 Eve Kosofsky Sedgwick, *Between Men: English Literature and Male Homosocial Desire* (New York, 1985), p. 35.

38 For a discussion of the available evidence see David F. Greenberg, *The Construction of Homosexuality* (Chicago, 1988).

39 Orgel, 'Nobody's Perfect'.

Male sexuality and misogyny

Michael Hattaway

To begin with, a description of an excellent but disconcertingly polit-ically correct production of *Measure for Measure* by Compass Theatre Company.[1] The group, directed by Neil Sissons, is a small one and, as with Peter Brook's *A Midsummer Night's Dream*, they generated a stunning new reading of the text by doubling members of the cast. Isabella and Mistress Overdone were played by the same actress; Angelo, Claudio, and Barnardine by one actor, and the authority figures of the Duke and Elbow by another. The revelation of the production came with the recog-nitions of the last scene. In that final sequence, the Friar is unmasked as the Duke: in this production, in a resonantly quoted gesture, Angelo was also stripped down – the cast wore modern dress – to the long-johns he had worn as Claudio in prison. At the Duke's question 'Which is that Barnardine?' (5.1.477), the actor simply adopted the half-crazed man-nerisms he had deployed for Barnardine during the short sequence that follows.

David Westbrook had played Angelo as a compulsively smiling, be-spectacled, and totally bald young man whose first act on acquiring power was to tidy the Duke's desk. He looked like the most danger-ous sort of train-spotter who revealed his true day-dreams as he wrestled Isabella to the ground at the end of 2.4. Handy-dandy, which was which? The doubling of the actors led to an equation of the 'naturalness' of Claudio's 'tilth and husbandry' with the depravity of Angelo the 'virgin violator': Claudio was merely Angelo in disguise, and, more horribly, Angelo was Claudio in disguise. The Duke's second question, 'What muffled fellow's that?' (5.1.485) acquired another, generalized, meaning – the production ended with the Duke, a comfortable, cherubic, humorous fellow, chortling to himself centre stage. He too, it turned out, was 'muf-fled': the director had highlighted the moment when he had 'pardoned'

Isabella for refusing to lay down her chastity, and his plan to bring her 'heavenly comforts of despair/When it [was] least expected' (4.3.107–8) was thereby revealed as part of a long-hatched plan to get her into his bed. One might go further: the doubling of Isabella and Mistress Over-done suggested that both, in a patriarchal world, were transgressors. By proposing to Isabella, the Duke was at once exercising his power over a woman who had challenged his authority and seeking to turn into fact the fantasy of taking sexually an unattainable woman. Men without their little brief authority were indeed poor forked creatures: Angelo/Claudio had to be comforted and led off by a horrified Isabella (Helen Franklin) who looked back at the Duke her 'saviour' with an expression that would have been apt if Elbow had propositioned her.

This was undoubtedly brilliant and, equally undoubtedly, a post-feminist production. The insight of the production was of our time, and there is no evidence either in the text or even in my sense of what a per-formance would have meant to contemporaries that would enable me to dismiss it out of hand on critical or 'historical' grounds. Indeed I want to examine and try to explain, if not to condone, some of the appalling attitudes towards women within other plays that productions of this kind may expose. They lay bare a disconcerting degree of misogyny[2] – to such an extent that I am prepared in this context, to speak of 'Shakespeare's works' rather than 'Shakespearian texts'. Shakespeare's plays of love – in tragedy, comedy, and romance – often expose ploys of hatred. The tones of 'happy' romantic comedy are so continually displaced that we might concede that what Lactantius deemed to be the subjects of an-cient comedy, 'the debauching of virgins and the amours of strumpets',[3] apply equally to Shakespeare in the Renaissance. I shall end by draw-ing attention to particular passages where it is obvious that misogyny is problematized.

These days, however, for a man 'reading as a woman' there is much discomfort, not only because one is invited to accept guilt on behalf of one's masculine forebears – and that's dangerous – but equally because, by endorsing the kind of statement the Compass production made, there is a danger of suppressing all that is erotic and enjoyable – in Renais-sance terms, perhaps, what is 'wanton' or 'frolicsome' – and embittering all relationships between the sexes. For Shakespeare's plays explore not only the connections between sex and power but those between sex and pleasure. I do not want to launch here into another reading of Madonna as a cultural icon, but I do want to suggest that the Compass Company's reading suppresses what George Orwell called, in his wonderful essay on the art of Donald McGill (the artist who produced 'vulgar' seaside postcards), the Sancho Panza view of life, one of the 'two principles, noble folly and base wisdom [that] exist side by side in nearly every human being'.[4] There is admittedly little cheerful relishing of sexual vulgarity of this sort in *Measure for Measure*. Lucio is relevant, but Lucio is hard to define. We might take his jibes at Angelo's sexuality as merely sniggering clubroom prattle, and feel that Shakespeare undercuts his role as a positive foil to sexual puritanism by having him abandon Kate Keepdown. Alternatively we may hear in his lines the sardonic tones and the verbal conceits of Pietro Aretino, the scourge of princes.

Concerning the wanton, we might consider the sort of values that are associated with, say, Costard in *Love's Labour's Lost* who seems simply 'happy' to consort with his wench. Again, however, I need to qualify as I am aware that there are dangers of attributing a happy and unconstrained sexuality to what were in those days called the base members of society. Freud may have been as guilty of this idealization when he wrote of the unproblematized sexuality of 'primitive man'[5] as Margaret Mead was when writing of the Samoans. Moreover, it is not just male clowns who celebrate sexual desire: Beatrice and Margaret in *Much Ado* (3.4), Rosaline and Maria in *Love's Labour's Lost* (4.1) speak 'greasily'. In cases like this, are the politically correct simply going to attribute this 'feminine bawdy' to the proclivities of a voyeuristic male author? Rather, to quote Orwell again, sexy talk represents 'a sort of saturnalia, a harmless rebellion against virtue'[6] – for there are dangers under the present cultural regime that a neo-Bowdlerism may become prevalent.[7] Man may be a giddy thing, but male desire will not go away – nor need it be the driving force of a chauvinist or imperialist strategy. It may on occasion even be reciprocated.

Woven into what follows is a general analysis of misogyny in Shakespearian texts. I want, after some preliminary remarks about evidence and some account of contemporary debates, to think about possible psycho-analytical, social, and cultural explanations – perhaps descriptions is a better word – of Renaissance misogyny. I list these by order of convenience: it is impossible for me to prove *either* that the social is base and the others superstructure, *or* that the psychological is prior to either by virtue of being transhistorical. In particular texts we may come across the displacement of class hostilities onto gender but we can set this up as no over-arching explanation. My descriptions tend to the psycho-analytical[8] and ideological; they are less transparent than the terms in which the *querelle des femmes* was conducted in early modern England.

'Jane Anger's' *Protection for Women* (1589), and, a generation or so later, the texts associated with the play *Swetnam the Woman Hater* (1620), for example, are essentially rhetorical exercises.[9] The authors simply trade *idea* for *idea*, reversing the direction of masculine railing by looking out alternative *topoi* and *exempla* from the scriptures and the church fathers to confound Aristotle and expose how, as the mysterious 'Jane Anger' says, men 'confess we are necessary, but . . . would have us likewise evil'.[10] Nor do I want to deal here with the 'humorous' type of the stage misogynist and his formal diatribes.[11]

I want to concentrate on three plays – *Love's Labour's Lost*, *All's Well That Ends Well*, and *The Winter's Tale* – in order to explore some of the particular connections made in the Renaissance between male sexuality and blood. Because blood is a metonym not only for a humour but also for social rank, I shall be invoking what I said about Costard and implying that both Renaissance misogyny and our own 'anti-sexism' may well be products of élite cultures. Both may stem from what Orwell called 'high sentiments'[12] – and high sentiments can be dangerous.

EROS AND METAPHOR

To begin with language. It was well said of D. H. Lawrence that the representation of sex in his novels is a way of 'talking about something else', an area where 'Eros becomes metaphor'.[13] We are now equally aware of a hermeneutic circle, that 'something else' is often a way of talking about sex, and that consequently gender and, possibly, desire itself, at the centre of our experience, is as conditioned by social forms and pressures as any other aspect of life. What we take to be the most intimate, the most authentic, the most unmediated is, because we can position it only within language, as much a social as a private phenomenon. The private is but an internalization of the social or, as Michel Foucault put it, 'there is no experience which is not a way of thinking'.[14] According to a 'hard' reading, sexuality is not just a biological drive but 'a way of fashioning the self "in the experience of the flesh", which itself is "constituted from and around certain forms of behaviour" . . . Like the whole world for Nietzsche, . . . sexuality is "a sort of artwork" '.[15]

Like woman, man is not born but made.[16] *Literary Love*, the title of a notable book by A. J. Smith, deconstructs itself – or turns out to be about far more than it proclaims. Because of this mediation in and by language, the authentic experience is endlessly deferred; desire is bound to be unfulfilled either because it fails to match the imaginary or, having matched it, reveals itself to be thereby inauthentic. (I do not think it is too far-fetched to claim that a consideration of the play of style in *As You Like It* leads to a profound questioning of whether the romantic is in fact authentic. Orlandos may be happier wooing their Ganymedes than wedding their Rosalinds.)

Donne's writings provide a convenient site for the investigation of the relationship between language and desire – if we can distinguish them. One need only invoke, from the second Satire, Coscus, once a poet and now a lawyer, who 'woos in language of the Pleas and Bench'.[17] Although Coscus is a fool, he, like all of us, can woo (and feel?) only in the language of another trade or practice. Eros is unattainable except through metaphor.

Donne's epigram 'On Manliness' gives us another example. The language game upon which it depends reveals that manliness is a construction:

> Thou call'st me effeminate, for I love women's joys;
> I call not thee manly, though thou follow boys.

The grammar of the poem serves to defamiliarize the word 'women's'. It can be a subjective or an objective genitive: the voice of the poem may be confessing that he enjoys what women enjoy or that he enjoys women. Experience in this world can be explained only by metaphor, and 'spiritual' or Platonic love rendered and experienced only by the language of this world. Biological division, sex, gives its name to 'sex' in the sense of desire – an unobvious case of metonymy (or is it synecdoche, the part for the whole?). In what might be the first use of the word 'sex' in its modern sense of carnal desire,[18] Donne seems to claim that desire is always driven by something else:

> This ecstasy doth unperplex,
>   (We said) and tell us what we love,
> We see by this, it was not sex,
>   We see, we saw not what doth move.

What, then, doth move?

BLOOD AND PARADISAL MARRIAGE

To the men of the Renaissance, the answer was simple, 'Blood' or 'Flesh and blood'. This is the reply churlish that the Duchess' Younger Son offers in *The Revenger's Tragedy* when he is asked what moved him to the rape of Antonio's wife.[19] Blood, of course, was one of the humours. To those with bad faith, like this Younger Son, it gave an excuse for transgressive behaviour; for Shakespeare's Angelo it is the centre of a tragic predicament: 'Blood, thou art blood' (2.4.15). It was a sign of a curse, ambiguously signifying lust and murder,[20] as we hear in De Flores' rebuke to Beatrice-Joanna in *The Changeling*: 'A woman dipped in blood, and talk of modesty'.[21] For sage Ben Jonson blood was part of a signifying system. He solved the brain/mind problem by arguing that a description of a physical condition could only be a metaphor for a mental condition.[22]

'Blood' therefore is what Empson called a complex word. Let us consider a moment in *All's Well* when the Countess is bidding farewell to her son:

> Be thou blessed, Bertram, and succeed thy father
> In manners as in shape. Thy blood and virtue
> Contend for empire in thee, and thy goodness
> Share with thy birthright.
>
> (1.1.58–61)

'Blood' and 'virtue': the context suggests that these designate aspects of nature and nurture, inherited and acquired qualities. These words, however, are disconcertingly ambiguous: 'blood' can mean rank ('birthright') as well as 'good breeding',[23] 'virtue', manliness or mettle as well as goodness. This turns out not to be a simple binary opposition, but a quaternary one. When we deconstruct the passage we realize that there is an ideological agenda contained in it: rank gives licence to desire, and goodness depends on sexual valour.[24] The Countess is being proleptic, anticipating both Bertram's rejection of Helen and his (thwarted) attempt on Diana's virginity.

In another key we might notice how what we might have understood, before Foucault, as a biological imperative, desire, is described by the clown of the play, Lavatch, as something experienced by the 'other', in this case the body of the subject:

COUNTESS Tell me thy reason why thou wilt marry.
LAVATCH My poor body, madam, requires it. I am driven on by the flesh, and he must needs go that the devil drives. (1.3.27–30)

The passage economically evokes a fierce Pauline Christianity that has generated, as the clown's plain speaking demonstrates, what Donne calls a 'serpent love',[25] an alienated sexuality. This ascription of desire to the blood and its demonization together constitute one part of what I would term a complex disorientation syndrome.

To analyse it, we might start with the physical. Anatomy was imperfectly understood, or rather what we take to be the empirical, something to be seen, was 'seen as' a version of the ideological. As Thomas Laqueur has claimed in his important analysis of the 'one-sex model' of Renaissance sexuality, most anatomists of the period sought to reveal similarities and not differences between cadavers of what we take to be the 'opposite' sexes, with a view of course to demonstrate that woman was but an imperfect version of the man.[26] It followed that they held both semen and the menses to be versions of blood. In the Hippocratic tradition, 'sperm, a foam much like the froth on the sea, was first refined out of the blood; it passed to the brain; from the brain it made its way back through the spinal marrow, the kidneys, the testicles, and into the penis. Menstrual blood, a phethora or leftover of nutrition is, as it were, a local variant in this generic corporeal economy of fluids and organs.'[27] Accordingly, we read in Thomas Vicary's *The Anatomy of the Body of Man*, 1577: 'And further it is to be noted that this sperm that cometh both of man and woman is made and gathered of the most best and purest drops of blood in all the body; and by the labour and chafing of the testicles or stones, this blood is turned into another kind, and is made sperm. And in man it is hot, white, and thick, wherefore it may not spread nor run abroad of itself, but runneth and taketh temperance of the woman's sperm, which hath contrary qualities, for the woman's sperm is thinner, colder, and feebler'.[28] This reinforces the over-valuation of the masculine and the devaluation of the feminine: we read in a misogynistic text of 1599, 'Woman ... [is] not framed for any respect or use than for a receptacle of some of our excremental humours':[29] woman is 'the pits'.

What we are meeting, in these patriarchal texts (which arguably served as documents of control rather than as descriptions of experience) is a deeply ambivalent attitude towards sexuality, both male and female. On the one hand it is a manifestation of manliness (*virtù*), on the other it is the enemy of goodness (virtue). Moreover because, in the Augustinian tradition, desire, since the fall, has not been voluntary, desire, like drink, makes and mars a man, causes him to lose control.[30] In a figure used in the 1615 translation of Varchi's *The Blazon of Jealousy*, *voluptas* supplants *voluntas*.[31] Or, to put it another way, misogyny may well imply misandry. The rules that were framed to control the behaviour of women served of course to control the behaviour of men. If a man 'fell' for a woman, it was easy to blame the *cause* of that fall, which was, paradoxically, the idealized object of his desire. In some cases this might be projected back onto the subject. So Othello, when he is vaunting of his success in winning Desdemona, sums it up in his half-proud, half-shamefaced line, 'I do confess the vices of my blood' (1.3.123).

We see this fear of women – or is it hatred? – registered in *Love's Labour's Lost*. The men of Navarre are young bloods, men of high degree in the prime of their youth. They proclaim that they are devotees of art (they are seeking fame), and that study, based on reason, is all too vulnerable to 'affections':

> Therefore, brave conquerors – for so you are,
> That war against your own affections
> And the huge army of the world's desires
>   (1.1.8–10)

'Affections' means here both perturbations or diseases (*OED*, affection *sb* 10) and desires.[32] But in order to put down desire the men put down the cause of disease and desire – women. This 'happy' comedy is, we may come to feel, shot through with misogyny:

DUMAINE
>   I would forget her, but a fever she
>   Reigns in my blood and will remembered be.   (4.3.93–4)

In the subplot Armado, he who would combine the male roles of Mars and Mercury, explores the 'bitter-sweet' pun of *amare-amaro*:[33] 'Love is a familiar; love is a devil. There is no evil angel but love' (1.2.163–5).

Biron, who in the first set of wit in the play casts himself as the 'natural' man, unwilling to repress his desires, has a set speech later where his satirical wit serves only to reveal a comic unease that well may rest upon a degree of residual misogyny:

> What? I love, I sue, I seek a wife? –
> A woman, that is like a German clock,
> Still a-repairing, ever out of frame,
> And never going aright, being a watch,
> But being watched that it may still go right ...
>
> And I to sigh for her, to watch for her,
> To pray for her – go to, it is a plague
> That Cupid will impose for my neglect
> Of his almighty dreadful little might.
>   (3.1.184–98)

This is the sort of jocularity we find in misogynist texts like *Les quinze joyes de mariage*, translated anonymously in 1509 as *The fyftene Joyes of maryage* and again in 1603 as *The Batchelar's Banquet*,[34] probably by Robert Tofte who seems to have specialized in this sort of work.[35] If we read the text in this 'hard' manner we may conclude that Biron's great set speech in praise of love later in the play ('Have at you, then, affection's men at arms'[36]) is mere opportunistic rhetoric.

The way in which social form empowers feeling is manifest in Biron's lines

> For every man with his affects is born,
> Not by might mastered, but by special grace.[37]
>
> (1.1.149–50)

This second line needs unpacking. 'Affects' is a pun: it means both 'affections' and 'affectations', has to do with both humours and manners. In this comedy, as it happens, the 'affects' *are*, we might conclude, mastered, not, as is usual in comedy, by will or change but by 'grace'. The Princess and her ladies come upon the scene as, to pick up Biron's phrase, 'special graces'. The phrase has a specific meaning – it derives from Calvin who distinguishes 'special graces' from 'gifts of nature'. 'Special graces', he writes, 'God ... diversely and to a certain measure dealeth among men that are otherwise ungodly'.[38] The ladies are, moreover, related to the classical tradition, to figures of Venus and the three Graces.[39] Artists customarily depicted the Graces with two figures facing and one with her back to the viewer[40] – which may explain the joke where all turn their backs on the masquers (5.2.160). The play ends with a set of deferred betrothals: Venus eventually tames Mars.[41] From that union, that *discordia concors*, would be born, according to Plutarch, 'the child Harmony'.[42] Shakespeare inscribes the idea in the musical *débat* between Owl and Cuckoo, Winter and Spring at the end of the play. That is a positive strand: equally, however, Amor is a god of death.[43]

ROSALINE   [Cupid] hath been five thousand year a boy.
CATHERINE   Ay, and a shrewd unhappy gallows, too.
ROSALINE   You'll n'er be friends with him, a killed your sister.
CATHERINE   He made her melancholy, sad, and heavy, And so she died.

> (5.2.11–15)

The betrothals are contracted under the shadow of death, the death of the King of France. Cupid's labour may have been lost, and a 'hard reading' of the play might hint that no marriages are in fact going to ensue.

The ambivalence of this Renaissance attitude to sex informed attitudes not just to courtship but to marriage. There is pertinent material in *The Winter's Tale*. We start by thinking of Leontes and Polixenes looking back to a state of innocence when they were 'boy eternal' (1.2.66). Imprinted on this metaphor is, as Hermione makes plain, a dream of Eden from which men were expelled – because of the feminine:

> We were as twinned lambs that did frisk i' th' sun,
> And bleat the one at th'other. What we changed
> Was innocence for innocence. We knew not
> The doctrine of ill-doing, nor dreamed
> That any did. Had we pursued that life,
> And our weak spirits ne'er been higher reared
> With stronger *blood*, we should have answered heaven
> Boldly, 'Not guilty', the imposition cleared Hereditary ours.

HERMIONE   By this we gather
You have tripped since.
POLIXENES   O my most sacred lady,
Temptations have since then been born to's; for
In those unfledged days was my wife a girl.
Your precious self had then not crossed the eyes
Of my young playfellow.
HERMIONE   *Grace* to boot!
Of this make no conclusion, lest you say
Your queen and I are devils.

(*The Winter's Tale*, 1.2.69–84, emphases added)

Here we notice an allusion not only to the fall but to the question of pre-lapsarian marriage. Paradise, for these two men, was a world of masculine friendship, and there woman takes the role not of a Grace but of a serpent. They seem to be explicitly rejecting the largely Protestant notion of paradisal marriage,[44] a notion that had been at the centre of a controversy that had raged a year or so before the play was written between the academic dramatist William Gager[45] and the Revd William Heale who set out his case in *An Apology for Women* (1609). Heale constructs his vindication of women and exposure of the double standard with a goodly number of *sententiae* and *exempla* drawn from a wide range of authors. It ends with a commentary on 'the Eden of felicity',[46] the story of Paradise, in which Heale argues that woman exceeds man because of being made not out of dust but out of man's rib:

And parallel also unto the purity of this golden age was the perfection of man's and woman's soul. For when their bodies were first framed as a picture of wrought wax or an image of hewn stone, God breathed thereunto a lively soul, which he styled the breath of life. And that spirit, being of an aëreal substance and (as it were) angelical essence, defused itself into each part, giving motion, sense, and reason unto the whole.[47]

This suggests a resonance for the statue scene, but I wonder whether Paulina's 're-creation' of Hermione[48] *has* purged Leontes' misogyny. Like everyone I had noticed that Hermione does not speak to Leontes. However, I think I had failed to notice how the implied stage directions suggest that the scene could be played to show Leontes not in the throes of a redemptive joy, but as appalled, even disgusted. He was eager to kiss the 'statue' (5.3.80) but not the living woman. Paulina has to urge Leontes forward:

> Do not shun her
> Until you see her die again, for then
> You kill her double. Nay, present your hand.
> When she was young, you wooed her. Now, in age,
> Is she become the suitor?
>
> (5.3.105–9)

Leontes stays tongue-tied, possibly refusing the implied offer of a hand-fasting or new marriage contract,[49] as his wife seeks to reconjure old emotions:

POLIXENES   She embraces him.
CAMILLO   She hangs about his neck.   (5.3.111–12)

The two do not exchange any dialogue, and most of what Leontes says has to do with procuring a marriage between Camillo and Paulina, as well as asking pardon from his wife and Polixenes.

FREUD

These are some of the Renaissance contexts, anatomical and theological, of misogyny. I now want to turn to various contemporary models. We are thoroughly familiar with the construction of the feminine in Shakespearian texts: 'Sacred and sweet was all I saw in her' says Lucentio of Bianca in *The Taming of the Shrew* (1.1.174). This suggests a strong process of suppression. What was suppressed was below the waist:

> The fitchew nor the soilèd horse goes to't
> With a more riotous appetite. Down from the waist

They're centaurs, though women all above.
But to the girdle do the gods inherit;
Beneath is all the fiend's. There's hell, there's
darkness, there is the sulphurous pit, burning,
scalding, stench, consumption. Fie, fie, fie; pah, pah!
                                    (*Lear*, F 4.5.120–6).

This excess of Lear is obviously pathological, but the equation of hell with
the vagina was a common trope,[50] a Renaissance equivalent to the identification of the Medusa's head with the female genitals made by Freud
and others.[51] How might we explain? In *Much Ado* Claudio wants women
to be sexually inert, to reaffirm their powerlessness in all that they do:

CLAUDIO   You seem to me as Dian in her orb,
           As chaste as is the bud ere it be blown.
           But you are more intemperate in your blood
           Than Venus or those pampered animals
           That rage in savage sensuality.   (4.1.57–61)

Claudio's emotion seems to be in excess of the facts, telling us more
about himself than about Hero. Her nature not her action is the butt
of his pathological indictment of what he takes to be the excessive and
transgressive. The invocation of animals aligns itself with Freud's account
of the way children may displace images of copulating animals into their
fantasies concerning their parents' sexual intercourse. 'They adopt what
may be called *a sadistic view of coition*.'[52] Stories in which humans copulate
with animals may also be reworkings of this 'primal scene' narrative:
Oberon's desire to humiliate Titania by having her fall for an ass is
obviously relevant here.

   Such bestial or sadistic images seem to emerge in Shakespeare as an
index of immature or displaced sexuality. So Iago, who, as Lynda Boose
has demonstrated,[53] is usefully thought of as an Aretinian pornographer
rather than a Machiavellian devil, the 'shadow-side'[54] of the men in
the play, kindles Brabanzio's fury not just by his racist taunts but by
reminding him of how woman brings out the beast in man:

               Even now, now, very now, an old black ram
               Is tupping your white ewe.
                                    (1.1.88–9).

Notice how he calls Desdemona a ewe and not a lamb, suggesting that
she is out to wound Brabanzio's manhood and not just his family honour.
And again:

...you'll have your daughter covered with a Barbary horse, you'll have your nephews neigh to you, you'll have coursers for cousins and jennets for germans... your daughter and the Moor are now making the beast with two backs.[55]   (1.1.113–19)

For Othello he conjures images of bestiality, cunningly getting the Moor to see himself in Cassio's place and so raising 'spirits' that Othello had seemingly methodically suppressed:

> It is impossible you should see this,
> Were they as prime as goats, as hot as monkeys,
> As salt as wolves in pride, and fools as gross
> As ignorance made drunk. But yet I say,
> If imputation, and strong circumstances
> Which lead directly to the door of truth,
> Will give you satisfaction, you might ha't.[56]
>   (3.3.407–13)

Along with bestial fantasies we find a disconcerting sadism in the mental make-up of several of Shakespeare's heroes. It emerges in the 'manliness' of Tullus Aufidius, who eroticizes his enemy Coriolanus:

> Thou hast beat me out
> Twelve several times, and I have nightly since
> Dreamt of encounters 'twixt thyself and me –
> We have been down together in my sleep,
> Unbuckling helms, fisting each other's throat –
> And waked half dead with nothing.
>   (4.5.122–7)

This man's love is not for the 'Other' or woman but for his alter ego, both detested and admired. In *Timon* the hero's command to the whores Phrynia and Timandra, 'Hold up, you sluts, | Your aprons mountant' (4.3.135–6) suggests a metaphorical rape by the gold he pours into their laps, a grotesque parody of what Jove did to Danaë. My point is that misogyny of a particularly sexual kind seems to be apparent in an extraordinarily large number of Shakespearian texts.

THE CONDITION OF WOMEN AND MASCULINE CRISIS

If Freud is right, misogyny may be a function of a well-nigh universal function of childhood fantasies of the primal scene, and I don't know whether I can demonstrate that this sort of thing is what Foucault calls 'a historically singular form of experience'.[57] However, I do not think that it is difficult to demonstrate that there was a condition of woman question in the culture of the English Renaissance. Martin Ingram's work on church courts[58] shows an intense preoccupation with what Natalie Zemon Davis earlier called 'women on top',[59] those whom men considered a threat to the social system, who weren't 'sacred and sweet'.[60]

Perhaps one of the reasons that we have not perceived as clearly that there may have been a 'condition of men' problem is that 'literary' texts, written by men, tend to concern themselves with individual moral and emotional problems, to see women as simply a group that comprises the 'other'. However, whenever there has been any sort of movement for female emancipation we have tended to find group male sexual disorientation.[61] The plethora of cuckolding jokes in comedy may well manifest a fear of female emancipation.[62]

When we turn to a manifestation of this in Shakespeare, I want to start with Othello:

> OTHELLO   I had been happy if the general camp,
> Pioneers and all, had tasted her sweet body,
> So I had nothing known. I, now for ever
> Farewell the tranquil mind, farewell content,
> Farewell the plumèd troops and the big wars
> That makes ambition virtue!
>
> . . .
> Farewell! Othello's occupation's gone.   (3.3.350–62)

The lines are familiar, but that crucial triple sexual pun on 'occupation'[63] – it means role or vocation, as well as designating Desdemona as mere object – remains unglossed in the new Arden (1958) and even the New Cambridge (1984) editions. Othello's social identity entails his sexual identity. He perceives Desdemona's seeming violation of his *ethical* position, his martial honour, mainly as a violation of his *social* reputation, the kind of 'honour' of which Iago speaks. Desdemona had begun by 'deceiving' her father (1.3.293): maybe Othello has begun to believe Brabanzio, and his only reaction to this 'unruliness' may be a more strenuous assertion of what he takes to be his essential maleness, what the text reveals to be simply masculine behaviour.

Another familiar moment, which shows that Othello saw not what doth move:

> OTHELLO   It is the cause, it is the cause, my soul.
> Let me not name it to you, you chaste stars.

> It is the cause. Yet I'll not shed her blood,
> Nor scar that whiter skin of hers than snow,
> And smooth as monumental alabaster.
> Yet she must die, else she'll betray more men.
> . . .
>   When I have
>   plucked thy rose
> I cannot give it vital growth again.
> It needs must wither. I'll smell thee on the tree.
> [*He kisses her*]   (5.2.1–15)

Yet again the masculinity lies in language. Writers have often noted Othello's idealization, not so his bad faith:[64] the Moor refuses to define the cause of his jealousy, he (wilfully?) confuses the final cause *for* which he will kill his wife with the efficient cause *by* which he is driven to kill his wife. Few would now agree with Bradley: 'The deed he is bound to do is no murder, but a sacrifice'.[65] The speech does far more than generate pathos, it makes us acutely uncomfortable. 'When I have plucked thy rose' means, of course, 'when I have taken your maidenhead'.[66] (It is not so glossed in the old or New Cambridge or new Arden editions.) The suggestion is that only by killing Desdemona can Othello meet with Desdemona's sexuality. 'Thy bed, lust-stained, shall with lust's blood be spotted' (5.1.37): this act, moreover, seems to him to be a way of exterminating female sexuality – and his own sexuality. Of Iago he exclaims:

> Ay, 'twas he that told me on her first.
> An honest man he is, and hates the slime
> That sticks on filthy deeds.
>   (5.2.154–6)

The misogyny, based on a pathological aversion to the physical nature of marital copulation, could not be more apparent.

As Eliot made us aware years ago, one of the great questions of the play is whether Othello achieves recognition, sees some shame in motives late revealed, or whether he merely cheers himself up. Othello's 'O blood, blood, blood!' (3.4.455) may indicate some beginnings of awareness: it is a cry of vengeance, a piece of invective against his wife's sexuality, and maybe contains the beginning of recognition that he shares blood with Cassio, that passion will destroy order. At the end he is conspicuously silent about his love. Perhaps this silence betokens a recognition that at last – but too late – he has understood not only the moral innocence but the sexual nature of himself and his wife.

So Lavatch's 'blood', Hamlet's blood-curdled ghost,[67] Othello's 'O, blood, blood, blood!': they all partake of the devil, all generate echoes of the primal scene. They generate the overheated pornographic imagination of Hamlet brooding on reechy kisses and the underheated pornographic imagination of Iago.

VERDICTS

Our so-called patriarchal bard, in a fine frenzy of even-handedness, offers some fierce verdicts on transgressive or excessive masculine sexuality. Men are, as searchers after reputation rather than virtue, perverters of the parable of the talents:

PAROLES   He wears his honour in a box unseen
          That hugs his kicky-wicky here at home,
          Spending his manly marrow in her arms
               . . .   (2.3.276–8)

The taking of maidenheads is an index of virtue, but woman, the owner of maidenhead, causes man to spend, use up, his precious marrow,[68] his semen, his manliness.[69] And, from another sequence in *All's Well*, we hear the disconcerting words:

SECOND LORD DUMAINE
          [Bertram] hath perverted a young gentlewoman
          here in Florence of a most chaste renown, and this
          night he fleshes his will in the spoil of her honour.   (4.3.15–17)

'Fleshes' means to give a first taste of flesh, as to a hawk: here losing virginity is an act of sadism and martial pillage.

Men are in short misogynists, seeking a sexual satisfaction that is endlessly deferred, and, if achieved, achieved only through fantasizing:

HELEN   [*to the Widow*]   O, strange men,
          That can such sweet use make of what they hate,
          When saucy trusting of the cozened thoughts
          Defiles the pitchy night; so lust doth play
          With what it loathes, for that which is away.   (4.4.21–5)

This is a gaming metaphor – although it is not glossed as such in New Cambridge – but the pun on 'play' suggests both faking in bed and sexual molestation. It is a marvellous metaphor for what Freud terms the 'tendency to debasement in love'.[70] (There may also be an echo of an Aristotelian problem: a woman, he averred, 'always loveth the man that hath been the first to receive of her amorous pleasures . . . and contrariwise the man hateth the woman that hath been the first to couple in that wise with him'.[71])

It is all too easy to pluck word crisis out of air, but I do want to suggest that the literary and possibly actual construction of sexuality was at odds with reality.

If we want to construct a historically singular model to account for this deformation we might look to chivalry. It was both a *residual* ideology as it is registered in the archaizing of Spenser, the conspicuously false consciousness of Beaumont and Fletcher,[72] and a *dominant* one as registered in the way Queen Elizabeth turned her chastity to power.[73] Originally chivalry was an ethic for legitimating war: 'as men are valiant, so are they virtuous'[74] – this comes from the sardonic 'Jane Anger'. When mediated through the chivalric epics, the code defines and supports an essentially individualistic ethic. It is a code for knights doing battle against enemies equal to them in rank in the feudal order or against 'paynims', evil others.

As part of a set of residual myths, it imports a set of rituals or metaphors into personal relationships. Manhood was not just a matter of biological age and sex, but became a category of achievement that is acquired only through rites of passage. Youths were invested as squires, then dubbed knights: these central rites of passage from boyhood to manhood, physiological process measured by sexual development, are figured around patterns of war. Margaret Tyler, translator of Ortuñez de Calahorra's *The First Part of the Mirror of . . . Knighthood* (1578), tersely hints at this:

> The chief matter therein contained is of exploits of wars, and the parties therein named are especially renowned for their magnanimity and courage. The author's purpose appeareth to be this, to animate thereby and set on fire the lusty courages of young gentlemen to the advancement of their line by ensuing such like steps.[75]

My hypothesis is that we can show, by a reading of Shakespeare, that chivalry, residual chivalry, affected male sexuality disastrously. Chivalry purports to relate to ethics but in reality it relates to politics. Warlike aims are disguised as service to the female – as we see the idealization of Helen in *Troilus and Cressida* – and turn the consorting of men and women to a hunt for prizes and maidenheads. Chivalry constructs women as passive, as ornaments, and imposes chastity (something that can be owned or taken by a man) as a means of legitimating male power. The condition of women becomes a question of value, women become thereby tokens of exchange, and value is focused on their sexuality, on honesty rather than honour. Men idealize in order to suppress. Courtship is generally courtiership: women's desire is channelled towards their 'servants' or their lords as a way of sustaining dynasty. If the metaphors are not courtly they are martial: power is generated not through courtly negotiation but through 'the vocabulary of gentlemanly combat'.[76] Armed knights are conquered by ladies[77] – that sort of thing.

When, however, a man turns from chivalric warrior to chivalric 'servant' he is in danger of being 'unmanned', made effeminate,[78] and driven to mortal sin by feminine will. Listen to Lear's catechizing of the disguised Edgar:

LEAR What hast thou been?
EDGAR A servingman, proud in heart and mind, that curled my hair, wore gloves in my cap, served the lust of my mistress' heart, and did the act of darkness with her; (Folio text, 3.4.78–82)

'Servingman' seems to me to be a pun here, both the *cavaliere servente* and a servant, the former reduced to the latter. As a loving warrior, Tomalin in Nashe's 'Choice of Valentines' is subject to the power of 'Priapus' who, against the power of his mistress Frances' dildo, is nothing:

> Poor Priapus, [she exalts] whose triumph now must fall,
> Except thou thrust this weakling to the wall;
> Behold how he usurps in bed and bower,
> And undermines thy kingdom every hour.
>
> (247–50)

Book 5 of *The Faerie Queene* begins with a linking of chivalry with justice, and the main quest of the hero is to free Eirena – an idealized feminized figure of Ireland – from the giant Grantorto (the papacy). Proper rule is obviously not only Protestant but masculine. However, one of the most notable victories won by Artegall is that over the Amazon Radigund (5.4.33).[79] Artegall is accompanied by Talus the iron man whose attacks on Radigund are not only violent but wantonly tyrannical:

> And euery while that mighty yron man,
> With his stange weapon, neuer wont in warre,
> Them sorely vext, and courst, and ouerran,
> And broke their bowes, and did their shooting marre.
>
> (V. 4.43)

Artegall is later rescued from the clutches of Radigund by his love Britomart, the incarnation of chastity who, having been granted a vision
in the Temple of Isis or Equity,[80] becomes even more powerful. This all
seems to contain much interest for the cultural historian. For the moment
I should define it as an example of what Freud called 'negation':[81] 'woman
is brought to the surface of social consciousness only to be repudiated'.[82]
Or, as Foucault argued, codes of sexual conduct represent 'an elaboration of masculine conduct carried out from the viewpoint of men in order
to give form to *their* behaviour'.[83] Men come to hate the very paragons
of virtue they have created to save themselves from themselves. Which
may be why a Hamlet, conscious of being like Claudius, prey to desire,
so hates Ophelia.

This investigation is infinitely extendible. I have described four sites,
anatomical, psycho-analytical, social, and ideological, but would be loath
to claim that my descriptions have provided adequate *explanations* for the
misogyny that seems to a modern reader to be a feature of these texts.
Misogyny in most of these contexts seems to be a function of patriarchy,
but the terms in which it is understood form part of a whole series of
signifying systems, not all of which can be attached to historically specific
cultural agendas. I have added some evidence to suggest that the centres
of these texts are inhabited by a number of subjects who see *all* sexuality,
all 'acts of darkness', as shameful and 'adulterous'.[84] Nashe tells in 'The
Choice of Valentines' how Justice Dudgeon-Haft and Crabtree Face
have driven his love Frances from rustic dancing on the town green into
a brothel (21–4). He also writes in the dedicatory sonnet:

> Complaints and praises everyone can write,
> And passion out their pangs in stately rhymes,
> But of love's pleasures none did ever write
> That hath succeeded in these latter times.

True then and, unfortunately, perhaps true now.

First published in *Shakespeare Survey 46* (1994)

NOTES

1 12 February 1992 at the Opera House, Buxton.
2 A prime Renaissance text, often reprinted, is the anonymous *Problems of
   Aristotle*; see also R. Howard Bloch, 'Medieval Misogyny', in R. Howard
   Bloch and Frances Fergusson (eds.), *Misogyny, Misandry, and Misanthropy*
   (Berkeley, 1989), pp. 1–24.
3 *Divinae Institutiones*, 6.

4 George Orwell, 'The Art of Donald McGill' [1942], in *Collected Essays* (London, 1961), p. 175.

5 Sigmund Freud, *Civilization and its Discontents*, The Penguin Freud Library (Harmondsworth, 1985), p. 306.

6 Orwell, p. 178; see Katharine Eiseman Maus, 'Transfer of Title in *Love's Labor's Lost*: Language, Individualism, Gender', in I. Kamps, ed., *Shakespeare Left and Right*, (1991), pp. 205–23.

7 My awareness of these issues was sharpened by a paper given by Ann Thompson at a meeting of the Northern Renaissance Seminar.

8 I concur with Stephen Orgel who writes, 'To take the psychoanalytic paradigm seriously, however, and treat the plays as case histories, is surely to treat them *not* as objective events but as collaborative fantasies and to acknowledge thereby that we, as analysts, are implicated in the fantasy. It is not only the patients who create the shape of their histories, and when Bruno Bettelheim observes that Freud's case histories "read as well as the best novels", he is probably telling more of the truth than he intends' ('Prospero's wife' in Margaret W. Ferguson, Maureen Quilligan and Nancy J. Vickers, eds., *Rewriting the Renaissance: The Discourse of Sexual Difference in Early Modern Europe* (Chicago, 1986), p. 52.

9 The first recorded use of 'misogynist' in *OED* is in the anonymous play *Swetnam the Woman Hater* (1620); of 'misogyny' in 1656; a rehearsal of commonplaces concerning the imperfection of women is to be found in Book 3 of Castiglione's *Book of the Courtier*; see also Constance Jordan, 'Feminism and the Humanists: The Case of Sir Thomas Elyot's *Defence of Good Women*', in Margaret W. Ferguson, pp. 242–58.

10 'Jane Anger her Protection for Women', reprinted in Moira Ferguson, ed., *First Feminists* (Bloomington, N.Y., 1985), p. 66.

11 See Linda Woodbridge, 'The Stage Misogynist' in *Women and the English Renaissance* (Brighton, 1984), pp. 275–99.

12 Orwell, 'The Art', p. 177.

13 Mark Kinkead-Weekes, 'Eros and Metaphor: Sexual Relationship in the Fiction of D. H. Lawrence', *Twentieth Century Studies*, 2 (1969), 3–20, p. 4.

14 Paul Rabinow, ed., *The Foucault Reader* (Harmondsworth, 1986), p. 335.

15 Thomas Laqueur, *Making Sex: Body and Gender from the Greeks to Freud* (Cambridge, Mass., 1990), p. 13.

16 For Jacques Derrida on the way 'man' might be demarcated in terms of gender, see *Spurs: Nietzsche's Styles*, tr. Barbara Harlow, 1979, pp. 59–65, and 103–5.

17 'Satire 2', 48.

18 *OED*, sv. *sb*3, although the passage is not cited there.

19 Tourneur [or Middleton] *The Revenger's Tragedy*, ed. R. A. Foakes (London, 1966), 1.2.47; compare 'he hath fall'n by prompture of the blood' (*Measure*, 2.4.179).

20 See Christopher Ricks, 'The Moral and Poetic Structure of *The Changeling*' *EC* 10 (1960), 290–306; compare Spenser, *The Faerie Queene*, 5.7.9–10 (on the

priests of Isis), and Vittoria in Webster's *The White Devil*, ed. John Russell Brown (London, 1966), 'O my greatest sin lay in my blood. / Now my blood pays for't' (5.6.240–1).

21 *Changeling*, 3.4.126.

22 *Every Man Out of his Humour*, Induction, 103.

23 Compare 'For Hamlet and the trifling of his favour, / Hold it a fashion and a toy in blood, / A violet in the youth of primy nature' (*Hamlet*, 1.3.5–7), and see David S. Berkeley and Donald Keesee, 'Bertram's Blood-Consciousness in *All's Well that Ends Well'*, *Studies in English Literature*, 31 (1991), 247–58; for the way that bleeding was a disgrace for a man, see Gail Kern Paster, ' "In the spirit of men there is no blood": blood as trope of gender in *Julius Caesar*', *SQ*, 40 (1989), 284–98.

24 This is also registered in a line from 'A Lover's Complaint': 'O false blood, thou register of lies' (52).

25 The phrase is from Donne's 'Twicknam Garden', a hymn of hatred for love.

26 See *The Problems of Aristotle* (London, 1597): 'Aristotle doth say that men have small breasts and women little stones' (sig. c6^r); the same text also claims that milk is digested blood (sig. c7^r).

27 Laqueur, *Making Sex*, p. 35; for the implications in *Twelfth Night*, see pp. 114–15.

28 Thomas Vicary, *The Anatomie of the Bodie of Man*, 1577, *Early English Text Society*, Extra Series No 53 (London, 1888), p. 79; cf. *The Problems of Aristotle*: 'The seed ... is white in men by reason of his great heat, and because it is digested better ... The seed of a woman is red ... because the flowers is corrupt, undigested blood' (sig. E3^r).

29 E and T. Tasso, *Of Marriage and Wiving*, tr. R. Tofte (London, 1599), sig c3^r; in *The Problems of Aristotle*, copulation is described as 'purging': 'it doth expell the fume of the seed from the brain, and it doth expell the matter of imposture' (sigs. E1^{r-v} and E2^r).

30 James Grantham Turner, *One Flesh: Paradisal Marriage and Sexual Relations in the Age of Milton* (Oxford, 1987), pp. 40ff.

31 B. Varchi, *The Blazon of Jealousy*, tr. R. Tofte (London, 1615), p. 16; see Michel Foucault, *The Use of Pleasure*, vol. 2 of *The History of Sexuality*, tr. Robert Hurley, 1985, p. 6 for an exploration of the way men become 'the subject of desire'.

32 Compare Gal. 5.24: 'For they that are Christs, have crucified the flesh with the affections and the lusts'.

33 Edgar Wind, *Pagan Mysteries in the Renaissance* (Harmondsworth, 1967), p. 92.

34 F. P. Wilson, ed., *The Batchelars Banquet* (Oxford, 1929).

35 He wrote a poem about his unhappy adventures at a performance of the play; see G. R. Hibbard, ed., *Love's Labour's Lost* (Oxford, 1990), pp. 1–2.

36 4.3.288ff.

37 'Special grace' is glossed by a commentator on Calvin as 'a special endowment of capacity, virtue, or heroism by which a man is fitted to serve the divine purpose in the world, while he himself may remain in the common state of human depravity'. Jean Calvin, *Institutes of the Christian Religion*, tr.

F. L. Battles, 2 vols. (London, 1961), 1, 276n; compare Pierre de la Primaudaye, 'Of Marriage', *The French Academie*, tr. T. B. (London, 1586): '[marriage is necessary] by reason of sin, which came in afterward, except in those to whom God hath granted the special grace of continency, which is as rare a thing as any whatsoever' (pp. 480–1).

38 *Institutes*, 2.3.4, tr. T. Norton (London, 1562).

39 See Boyet's compliment on the grace of the Princess (2.1.9–12); for the Graces, see Spenser, *The Faerie Queene*, 6.8.24, and the Gloss to April in *The Shepheardes Calender*. The Graces, Aglaia, Thalia, and Euphrosyne, were associated with brightness (*splendor*), freshness (*viriditas*), and happiness (*laetitia*) respectively (Wind, p. 269), and it could be that these determine the subjects of the poems to Maria ('. . . fair sun, which on my earth dost shine . . .' [4.3.57 ff.]), Catherine ('. . . Love . . . Spied a blossom passing fair' [4.3.99ff.]), and Rosaline's cheerful witty personality.

40 Wind, *Pagan Mysteries*, pp. 26ff.

41 For the iconology of this figure, see Wind, *Pagan Mysteries*, pp. 89ff.

42 Plutarch, 'Isis and Osiris', *Moralia*, v, 370.

43 Wind, *Pagan Mysteries*, pp. 152ff.

44 See Mary Beth Rose, *The Expense of Spirit* (Ithaca, N.Y., 1988).

45 See Turner, *One Flesh*, pp. 1–2.

46 Heale, *An Apology for Women*, p. 10.

47 Ibid., p. 60.

48 Freud, in 'Mourning and Melancholia', speaks of the way in which 'the loss of a love-object is an excellent opportunity for the ambivalence in love-relationships to make itself effective and come into the open'. *On Metapsychology* (Harmondsworth, 1984), p. 260.

49 This may quote the gesture of Hermione and Polixenes 'paddling palms' in the second scene of the play (1.2.117).

50 See Stephen Booth, ed., *Shakespeare's Sonnets* (New Haven, 1977), pp. 499–500, who cites among other texts Rowland's 15th Epigram from his *The Letting of Humour's Blood in the Head-Vaine* (London, 1600); consider also the designation 'hell' in the game of barley-break (see *The Changeling*, 3.3.165n).

51 Freud, *On Sexuality* (Harmondsworth, 1981), p. 311n.; for an essay that links the image to *Macbeth*, see Marjorie Garber, *Shakespeare's Ghost Writers: Literature as Uncanny Causality* (London, 1987), pp. 97ff.

52 'On the Sexual Theories of Children', *On Sexuality*, p. 198.

53 Lynda E. Boose, ' "Let it be Hid": Renaissance Pornography, Iago, and Audience Response', *Autour d'Othello*, ed. Richard Marienstras and Dominique Goy-Blanquet (Amiens 1987), 135–43.

54 Edward A. Snow, 'Sexual anxiety and the male order of things in *Othello*', *ELR*, 10 (1980), 384–412, p. 409.

55 The figure appears in Rabelais, *Gargantua*, chap. 7, and see M. P. Tilley, *A Dictionary of the Proverbs in England in the Sixteenth and Seventeenth Centuries* (Ann Arbor, 1950), B151.

56 Snow writes, 'In Freudian terms, Iago is alienating Othello from the sexual act by making him participate in it from the place of the superego' (p. 396).

57 Foucault, *Pleasure*, p. 4.

58 Martin Ingram, *Church Courts, Sex and Marriage in England, 1570–1640, Past and Present Publications* (Cambridge, 1987).

59 Natalie Zemon Davis, 'Women on Top: Symbolic Sexual Inversion and Political Disorder in Early Modern Europe', in *The Reversible World*, ed. Barbara A. Babcock (Ithaca, N.Y., 1978).'

60 See also D. E. Underdown, 'The Taming of the Scold' in A. Fletcher and J. Stevenson, eds., *Order and Disorder in Early Modern England* (Cambridge, 1985), pp. 116–36. This may have been itself a symptom of general economic decline as well as of the increasing power of the craft guilds (see Merry E. Wiesner's study of particular German cities, 'Spinsters and Seamstresses: Women in Cloth and Clothing Production', in Ferguson, pp. 191–205.) Doubtless aspects of witch-hunting can be attributed to analogous factors. We might also consider the rule of Elizabeth, the virgin queen (see Peter Stallybrass, 'Patriarchal Territories: The Body Enclosed', in Ferguson, pp. 123–42).

61 See two poems by Lady Mary Wroth, niece to Sir Philip Sidney, 'Love a child is ever crying' and 'Late in the forest I did Cupid see' (in Germaine Greer, *et al.* eds., *Kissing the Rod* (London, 1988), pp. 66–7). These we read, I think, rather differently if we know that they were written by a woman; compare also Lionel Trilling's preface to Henry James's *The Bostonians* (London, 1952).

62 Keith Thomas, 'The Place of Laughter in Tudor and Stuart England', *TLS* (21 January, 1977), 77–81.

63 Eric Partridge, *Shakespeare's Bawdy* (London, 1968), p. 155.

64 A notable exception is provided by Edward A. Snow (see n. 54 above).

65 A. C. Bradley, *Shakespearean Tragedy* (London, 1957 edn), p. 161.

66 Partridge, *Shakespeare's Bawdy*, p. 176.

67 See *Hamlet*, 1.5.69–70.

68 Compare 'Venus and Adonis' where Venus proclaims 'My flesh is soft and plump, my marrow burning' (142).

69 For the economy of semen, see de la Primaudaye, p. 238, Laqueur, *Making Sex*, p. 101.

70 See 'On the Universal Tendency to Debasement in the Sphere of Love' in Freud, *Sexuality*, pp. 247–60.

71 Aristotle, 1 Physics, xviii, cited by Castiglione, *The Book of the Courtier*, tr. Sir Thomas Hoby, Everyman edn, p. 199.

72 See Jonson, *The New Inn*, ed. Michael Hattaway (Manchester, 1984), p. 35.

73 See it mocked in Nashe's *Unfortunate Traveller* (in Salzman, pp. 262ff.)

74 'Jane Anger', in Moira Ferguson, *First Feminists*, p. 70.

75 Reprinted in Moira Ferguson, *First Feminists*, p. 54.

76 See Nancy Vickers, ' "The Blazon of Sweet Beauty's Best": Shakespeare's *Lucrece*', in Patricia Parker and Geoffrey Hartman, eds., *Shakespeare and the Question of Theory* (London, 1985), pp. 105–6.

77 Compare *Pericles*, scene 6, 26.

78 Cf. *Romeo*, 3.1.113–15; on the 'feminizing' of subjects by their princes see Joan Kelly-Gadol, 'Did Women Have a Renaissance?', in Renate Bridenthal and Claudia Koontz, eds., *Becoming Visible: Women in European History* (Boston, 1987), p. 159.

79 See Thomas Healy, *New Latitudes: Theory and English Renaissance Literature* (London, 1992), pp. 94–5.

80 *Faerie Queene*, v.7.

81 'The outcome . . . is a sort of intellectual acceptance of the repressed, while at the same time what is essential to the repression persists'. 'Negation', in *Metapsychology*, p. 438.

82 Dympna Callaghan, *Women and Gender in Renaissance Tragedy* (London, 1989), p. 12.

83 *Use of Pleasure*, pp. 22–3.

84 See Stephen Greenblatt, *Renaissance Self-Fashioning* (Chicago, 1980), pp. 248ff.; compare Snow's conclusion that 'Shakespeare locates the principle of evil and malice at the level of the superego, the agency that enforces civilization on the ego'.

Consummation, custom and law in All's Well That Ends Well

Subha Mukherji

Having wed Helena at the king of Rossillion's behest, Bertram, the king's ward, refuses to bed her and flies to Italy with her dower, leaving a conditional letter for her: 'When thou canst get the ring upon my finger, which never shall come off, and show me a child begotten of thy body that I am father to, then call me husband; but in such a "then" I write a "never" '(*All's Well That Ends Well*, 3.2.57–60).[1]

Bertram's marriage, overseen by king and priest, counts as a solemnized *de praesenti* union for all practical purposes. And as Henry Swinburne confirms in his *Treatise of Spousals*, 'Spousals *de praesenti*, though not consummate, be in truth and substance very Matrimony, and therefore perpetually indissoluble.' This treatise, written around 1600 but published in 1686, is the only systematic exposition of marriage laws and the first handbook of canon law to be written in England.[2] According to Swinburne, the use of long absence as a legal means for escape applied only to *de futuro* spousals.[3]

What, then, is Bertram resisting by refusing to sleep with Helena? What is the status of his apparently impossible condition? This moment in the action has been interpreted by critics as the transformation of a legal possibility into a 'fairy-tale' one, Bertram's stipulation being read as a purely fantastic setting of tasks in the romance mode.[4] But such readings fail to account for Helena's meeting of his terms as though they were an actual legal impediment, and her final securing of him in what is, effectively, a court of law. Bertram's instinctive belief that 'not bed[ding] her' somehow counteracts the effects of 'wed[ding] her' (3.2.21–2) does not stem simply from his own wrong-headedness, but from factors actually present in contemporary English society.

My point of entry into the play's engagement with law will be marital consummation as it figures in Bertram's conduct and Helena's

116

response. I will interpret the concept of consummation in terms of its contrasting roles in Christian marriage and Christian divorce. But the act of sex in the social experience of marriage confounds these two functions, even as it conflates law and customary ritual. Its peculiar status in the play will be shown to hinge on its legal function as evidence. The problems of evidentiary procedure in English church courts provide an important focus for the play's treatment of marriage law. The two main forms of evidence that I will look at are the exchange of rings and pregnancy. My analysis of the ambiguities of evidence will refer to larger theoretical issues of motive and intention that are legally unresolvable but particularly conducive to exploration in drama.

In reconstructing the relevant legal history, I shall use Swinburne's treatise, which I will refer to as *Spousals*. This text represents an attempt to codify as well as interpret the law, since Swinburne was dealing with an area of legislation that was not only supposed to discipline and punish but also to provide moral guidance for social and personal behaviour. *Spousals* seeks to mediate between legal theory and practice, the written word and the spoken, the spoken word and the sign, all of which constituted marriage as social practice. I shall also be drawing upon a draft fragment, preserved in Durham, which follows the completed *Treatise of Spousals* in what seems to be the authorial manuscript. Entitled 'Of the signification of divers woordes importing Matrimonye, etc.', this is, I take it, the beginning of the second part of what Swinburne originally intended to be a three-part treatise on spousals, marriage and divorces. I will refer to it henceforth as *Matrimony*.[5]

My other group of primary materials consists of surviving records of spousal litigation from contemporary church courts, mainly Durham, Chester, Norwich and Canterbury. Together, these two sets of texts provide a comprehensive picture of law as human action, and the contradictions in such action are dramatized in Shakespeare's *All's Well*.

The clue to our understanding of the nature of Bertram's conduct lies in the status of sexual consummation in popular custom, which derived elements from the theology, rituals and attitudes surrounding marriage, and its relationship with law. Among the many factors that constituted the overall sense of the accomplishment of a marriage, consummation had a role of special interest and curious standing. Theologically, a sacramental symbolism and sanctity attached to it, as reflected in *The Book of Common Prayer*: 'For this cause shall a man . . . be joined unto his wife, and they two shall be one flesh. This mystery is great.'[6]

In law, however, intercourse was not strictly a factor in the formation
of marriage in sixteenth- or early seventeenth-century England. The
church, which was in charge of matrimonial litigation, held, from the
twelfth century onwards, that present consent, and not the sexual act,
makes a valid and completed marriage.[7] This position was marked by
Pope Alexander III's promulgation of consent as the basis of the institu-
tion, irrespective of either solemnization or consummation. In England,
where the pre-Tridentine canon law of marriage survived the Reformation and did not change till 1753, informal or private contracts continued
to have claim to legal recognition since consent was still the ultimate and
sole criterion of validity. So, consummation was as irrelevant in 'law'
as solemnization; hence the frequent clubbing together of the two by
contemporary writers such as Swinburne as well as by legal historians in
our own times.[8]

But given the inevitable confusions, uncertainties, and difficulties of
proving consent, unsolemnized marriages were increasingly disapproved
of by state and church. Certain 'legal effects' – property rights and
benefits (*Spousals*, 15) – were made conditional upon solemnization,
and Tudor and early Stuart England floundered through the curious
doubleness of a situation where validity and illicitness could coexist in the
same union.[9] There was tightening pressure from both Protestant and
Catholic reformers to regularize marriage, and one of its manifestations
was an effort to impress on people that ecclesiastical solemnization
alone made sexual union licit.[10] The denunciation of intercourse before
or without the public ceremony implied, firstly, that solemnization
was seen by many as being connected with, indeed, guaranteeing and
sanctioning consummation. Secondly, it suggests the association of
intercourse with the social acceptance of a lawful union. Even among
legal thinkers, there were those who, as Swinburne writes in *Matrimony*
(120–1), made a distinction between 'matrimony initiate' or 'begunne'
and matrimony 'consummate', between 'true' and 'perfect' marriage.
'This word *Nuptiae*, Marriages', he writes in *Spousals*, is not necessarily
used to mean solely 'the Substance and indissoluble knot of Matrimony
only, but doth often signifie the Rites and Ceremonies observed at the
celebration of Matrimony' (*Spousals*, 8–9). It is in terms of a society where
'rites and ceremonies' were an essential constituent of the customary
view and practice of marriage that Bertram's holding out against 'the
great prerogative and rite of love' (2.4.41) has to be understood.

However, though it could not normally constitute a marriage in itself,
there were a few specific circumstances in which sexual consummation

could have a legal function. When a spousal was contracted between infants or between minors, it could be ratified and made into an indissoluble knot by willing cohabitation after attainment of the age of consent.[11] Sexual relations could give *de futuro* spousals between adults the effect of *de praesenti* marriage; they could also turn conditional spousals into matrimony.

If custom and ritual are major contributors to Bertram's perspective, these situations where intercourse has a proof-value form the other, more distinctly legal influence. Indeed, custom itself must have been conditioned by such legal associations. The witness depositions and the personal responses in contract suits of the period communicate a sense of how the specific legal functions of copulation led to a more general and undifferentiating notion of sex as being a factor that could make an otherwise uncertain match conclusive. In a Durham suit of 1570 for restitution of conjugal rights, cohabitation figures centrally in all the depositions. Isabel Walker's witness Richard Bell, keen to stress the validity of her marriage to William Walker and, thereby, *her* claims, says that they 'dwelte in house here in Durham togither, as man and wyfe by the space of one yere, or more'. On the other hand, William's witness emphasizes the finality of Isabel's marriage to her reportedly precontracted husband Robert Stathan; he deposes that 'he hath known . . . [them] . . . dwell to gyther in one house as man and wyfe, as this examinate and neighbours thereabouts dyd take ytt'.[12]

A different legal channel that influenced the way consummation was viewed proceeded from the laws regarding annulment, by which divorce could be obtained by proof of non-consummation in cases of precontract, duress, consanguinity, affinity or impotence. The divorce of Lady Frances Howard from the Earl of Essex came through in 1613 when her allegation of his incompetence was confirmed by his admission that 'he could never know his said wife.'[13] The background to this law lies in the canonical tradition which associated indissolubility with the 'becoming one flesh' of married partners.[14] The question whether a man who, after his betrothal, feels a call to enter religious life was free to do so was met by Pope Alexander III with the answer that he could first marry and then leave off to become a monk if he did not follow up the marriage with carnal coupling. His premise was that the Christian prohibition against putting asunder those whom God had joined applied only to incorporated couples; his precedent, St John's turning to religion from a virginal marriage. But this contradicted the fundamental canonical assumption that consent, not coitus, is the substance – a position he himself upheld. His circumvention of this problem is described by J. T. Noonan as resembling 'a legal trick, . . . a lawyer's way of satisfying contradictory purposes by keeping form and sacrificing substance, of nominally honoring the oath to marry while permitting the actual subversion of the oath'.[15]

One way of reconciling the canonical contradiction is to make, as canon law obviously did, a distinction between the model of Christian divorce, provided by St John, and the example of Christian marriage, provided by Mary and Joseph.[16] The notion that mutual consent was the essence and physical union was the substance of marriage could thus be kept from a direct conflict and be channelled into two separate legal procedures. But this separation proved all too artificial in social practice. For consummation could function both as a constituent of marriage and as a sign of it. Originally, the constitutive function came into play mostly in clandestine or disputed marriages, while the signifying role was predominant in unions accomplished through the full formalities, being, as it were, an ultimate expression of the marriage. In a court of law, however, the two were easily conflated because in both capacities, the fact of consummation was required to establish certainties, to prove a status. Thus, in a Durham case of 1587, the doubts about the reality of the solemnized marriage of Sir Thomas Gray with Lady Catherine Neville arise because they have 'not cohabited continually'. That the marriage emerges as being viable and valid in court is due to the establishment of the fact that since a certain day they have 'nightly laid in one bed, as becometh man and wife'.[17] Anne Yate and George Johnson of Cheshire go through a very different event – a plebeian trothplight match, possibly *de futuro*, contracted through a witnessed handfast, but unsolemnized. But in the legal dispute over it in 1562, as in the previous case, the deponents confirm the marriage with reference to sexual union, and the causal relation suggested by their phrasing indicates the inseparability of consummation as sign of status and as proof of contract. Oliver Foxe asserts that they were 'reputid and taken for man and wief amonge their neighboures' 'for they did lye in one house, and nothinge betwix them but a broken wall and a paintid clothe'. Cecilia Key confirms, 'the neighboures . . . did take them as man and wief, in somuche that they have laine together in bed, and so vsed them selves as man and wief'.[18] Does the importance of consummation here derive from its status as the criterion of indissolubility in the divorce paradigm? Or, from its assimilation into the formalities of making a marriage, and so its association with solemnization instead of consent? It is impossible to tell.

What one can perhaps tell is that the deponents did not pause to work out such distinctions before giving testimony.

Thoughts about marriage and related legal actions covered and intertwined the issues of formation and validation of matrimony, as well as of the making and unmaking of marriage. The status of sexual union continued to be a focus of some of the dualities in marriage law, and Bertram's refusal is both a response to, and an expression of this doubleness. On the one hand, Bertram is holding out against the one formality that is left him to resist, having been rushed through the paraphernalia of 'contract' and 'ceremony'. From this point of view it is a token non-completion of the *ritual* stages of marriage in society. Marital non-cohabitation did draw considerable social attention in early modern England, was on occasions a ground for presentment in court,[19] and could even be disallowed by court decree.[20] A Yorkshire parochial presentment of 1568 states that 'They say all is well saving that John Pennye and his wif lyveth not to geither.'[21]

But on the other hand, the resisted consummation is not, for Bertram, a mere external formality. Given that the legal validity of a marriage depended on mutual consent, he is exploiting the one remaining channel through which he can express his own consent or lack of it. Thus it comes to represent the substance of marriage, the indissolubility that it stands for in the canonical law of divorce. Here is a reconcilement of the apparently opposite standings of intercourse in the marriage and divorce paradigms that is less sophistical and more instinctive than the one offered by Alexander III. If the rationale behind granting importance to copulation is the idea that it expresses volition, the conflict is resolved. Especially in formally solemnized marriages like Bertram's, where the legally constituent elements are taken up in the self-generating momentum of ceremonies, the – contract becomes more clearly an organized event than an expression of individual will; consequently, the post-legal stage of consummation becomes the clearer site of consent. 'I have wedded her, not bedded her, and sworn to make the "not" eternal', he writes to his mother, making a statement about the distinction, in his mind, between what has been achieved by legal form, and a voluntary and meaningful entry into the married state. The duality of the situation is further underlined by Bertram's language; the riddling and the cautious precision in his letters even while at one level he has committed himself – swearing 'to make the "not" eternal' – translates the sense of a lacuna written into the very language of the marriage ritual. The irony remains, of course, that Bertram's very defiance of law takes the form of an action prompted by legal instinct, neither custom nor social attitude being independent of law any more than law can function apart from these.

The transition of 'consummation' from its link with solemnization to its connection with intention is not peculiar to Bertram's psychology. Depositions from the period suggest that men and women did frequently associate the sexual act with 'consent'. The most telling example is that of Mawde Price alias Gregorie whose means of preventing her enforced and solemnized marriage to Henry Price from becoming real was to refuse to let him 'have ... his pleasure apon her', and instead, having regular sexual relations, and two children, with her precontracted husband, Randall Gregorie. This becomes the single focus of each of the depositions in this Chester case of 1562, and is clearly regarded by the witnesses as being directly related to consent. Alice Dood's phrasing actually identifies copulation and matrimonial intention; she says that Henry and Mawde did not 'cohabete voluntarie together, nor did consent together as man and wiff'. Matilda Broke's testimony reinforces this equation; 'verelie they neuer consented together'. To Henry Price himself, Mawde's resistance to sex is a sign of the non-reality of the marriage, and moves him finally to seek judicial annulment. Randall, the precontracted husband, considers Mawde's refusal to have 'carnall dole' with Henry a sure indication of her 'not [accepting] hym as her husband'.[22]

Swinburne stresses the legal weight of 'voluntary Cohabitation' in converting child-marriages into 'true substantial Matrimony' and draws attention to the similarity of this criterion to the one that turns *de futuro* spousals into marriages. He goes on then to distinguish 'other more feeble Conjectures of kissings, ... etc.' from those that 'are evident and urgent, and equivalent to the presumption of Carnal copulation' because it is required 'that this Consent, whereby Spousals are turned into Matrimony, do appear *evidenter*, evidently' (*Spousals*, 40–1). Talking of conditional contracts, he says that if the parties know each other carnally 'before the event of the condition', they are 'deemed to ... yield their mutual Consents to Contract and Consummate pure and perfect Matrimony' (121). Swinburne, we must remember, was a legal practitioner, familiar with custom as well as legal theory. It is significant that his explicit association of consent with consummation is made problematic, if not contradicted, by his resorting to the law of presumption elsewhere. Discussing complicated conditional spousals, he prescribes the 'favourable Presumption' that 'is to be preferred in all doubtful Cases' regarding the purpose of any sexual involvement that may have followed

(219). If a man bound upon oath to marry one of three sisters lies with any one of them, 'he is presumed to have made choice of her as his Wife' (221). The difficulty of ensuring that this presumption is also the truth of intention arises most clearly in the marshalling of proof. The law of evidence, for all its safeguards against getting the intention wrong, can, more than any other legal endeavour, make 'consummation' an absolute tool, disjoined from its motive. So Swinburne says, 'Spousals do become Matrimony by carnal knowledge, albeit the Man were constrained, through *fear of death* to know the Woman' (226).[23] The process by which Bertram's condition is met in *All's Well* dramatizes the way in which the contradiction in Swinburne, which is also a contradiction in law, is produced by the peculiar demands of 'evidence'. This is paradoxical, given that the theoretical importance of sex in marriage law was based so largely on the belief that it could be, potentially, the surest proof of consent.

This is not the only way in which Bertram's instinctive 'use' of law rebounds on him. When, desperate not to let the marriage materialize, but powerless, as a ward, to prove duress, he resolves to 'End ere [he] [does] begin' (2.5.26), he is making a mental demarcation between public ritual and a private counterpart in consummation. Neither Helena nor anyone else has doubts about what law vouches to be hers (2.4.41–2; 2.5.79–82). What Bertram denies is the *relationship* that the contract is presumed to guarantee. He is reclaiming sexual union for the sphere of the personal from the sphere of legal validation. But he does not simply protest through inaction; he further makes consummation the condition for a fuller acknowledgement of the marriage. By himself positing sex as an evidence for Helena to establish the rights of love, he forfeits his rights to a personal scale of criteria. As Helena sets about to realize his condition, consummation becomes more public than ever, and more sharply distinguished from personal consent, by the very virtue of being used as proof, and hence being required 'to appear *evidenter*' in a legal space.

These reversions are the subject of the following section which will also make clear how Helena emerges as a defendant seeking to validate her marriage, while Bertram corresponds to the unenthusiastic party fumblingly attempting a sort of annulment. Seen within this structure, Bertram's preoccupation with non-consummation is entirely appropriate, and fulfils the legal expectation of a divorce suit. Helena's attainment and use of carnal union is equally appropriate to her own legal purpose. The meeting of the two 'causes' demonstrates schematically the coming together of sign and proof, of formation and validation, and with these, of the principles of union and those of annulment in the practised legality of marriage.

The process by which Helena earns the right to be acknowledged by Bertram as his wife is quasi-legal, but by the time it is completed, it looks like a proper legal validation. That is largely because this development is crossed with another, truly legal pattern of events consisting of the interaction between Bertram and Diana, leading to an actual trial where Bertram has to defend himself against Diana's claim of marriage and her allegation of marital disacknowledgement. These legal events, of course, are instrumental to the successful accomplishment of Helena's project, and stems from the plan to use Diana to set the stage for the bed-trick. A Shakespearian creation,[24] Diana stands at the intersection of the legal and the quasi-legal structures, and represents the inextricability of the one from the other. The Bertram–Diana part of the play illuminates the nature of Helena's use of evidence by exploring the ambiguities of proof in a more clear-cut legal framework.

The relationship between Bertram's condition and its fulfilment is also one between a promise and its performance, terms and their enactment, and so, between word and deed. In contract law, a bond, the common device to secure contractual settlements, was finalized by using a 'deed' – the term describing a document under seal. By the beginning of the seventeenth century, the notion of contract had already begun to extend from its original sense of 'a transaction . . . which transferred property or generated a debt' to include the modern sense of a consensual pact, an exchange of promise between individuals – a meaning formerly borne by the word 'covenant'.[25] Such agreements being transient events, the 'deed' is what made them concrete and gave them legal validity.

An examination of the principle underlying this importance of the 'deed', however, reveals its origins in evidentiary problems. In medieval town courts, a contract that had not been observed could be proved by the oath of the plaintiff. This inevitably began to be felt as inadequate: the very need of proof in this matter was prompted by an awareness of the elusive and indeterminate nature of words. This is what led to law's sharp distinction between mere words on the one hand and action or deeds on the other. By 1321 it was legally prescribed that 'the only acceptable evidence of a covenant in the royal courts was a deed'.[26] In its original sense of an exchange of property, a contract had to be executed in order to be effected – there was no notion of sueing an unperformed contract. When its sense expanded, the function of performance was taken on by the act of sealing the document of contract in front of witnesses – something done, and hence a deed. From this, its original meaning in law, the word 'deed' came to be applied by transference to the product of the event – the document itself. Thus, a deed was both what made a contract in the legal sense, and what proved it. As well as being often signified by gestures such as a handclasp, it was itself a sign of the agreement.

The particular relevance of the word-deed hierarchy in marriage law is brought out through the liaison between Diana and Bertram. Persistent in his efforts at overcoming Diana's maidenly resistance, Bertram remonstrates, 'How have I sworn!' (4.2.21). Diana retaliates immediately that his oaths 'are words and poor conditions', and insists on a seal. This is not simply a metaphorical way of disputing Bertram's sincerity but a legal argument; an attempt to steer Bertram's private declarations into a contract that can be proved later in a legal event which, as she knows and he does not, has already been planned.

The explicit use of terms from contract law in connection with professed commitments of love dramatizes an actual link between spousal and contract litigation. Actions against breach of faith that came up as part of the church courts' bulk of marriage litigation were allied in principle to common law actions for breach of contract. Besides, there actually existed a common law action for breach of promise of marriage.[27] Likewise, contract suits formed a sizeable portion of the church courts' business in the sixteenth and seventeenth centuries, and the practice of settling for cash was comparable to the common law action.[28] The law of contract, after all, is essentially the 'law of obligations', as Baker puts it, one that 'governs those expectations of good faith which arise out of particular transactions between individual persons'.[29] This is exactly the issue in many spousal cases surviving from Tudor and Stuart times. Baker goes on to explain that this type of obligation could be dealt with either in terms of 'the right to performance of the contract or of the wrong of breaking the contract and thereby causing loss'. Helena's performance and validation of a conditional contract in the shape of Bertram's letter, and Diana's sueing Bertram for denying marital obligation dramatize these two complementary processes. The demarcation of the spheres of common law and canon law, thus, is among the several polarities that the play breaks down, in representing overlapping spheres of social experience.

When Diana expresses her misgivings about the 'unsealed' nature of a verbal promise, Bertram's reply supplies the possible nature of the deed that can seal it –

> Change it, change it.
> Be not so holy-cruel...
> Stand no more off,
> But give thyself unto my sick desires.
>   (4.2.32–6)

It is the act of sex, tacitly agreed upon thereafter, that Diana refers to when she talks of the need to 'token to the future our past deeds' (64). It is this, again, that Helena has in mind when she anticipates the 'lawful deed' planned for the night.

The marriage contract in Renaissance England can be seen as having consisted of a word component – the expression of present and mutual consent, and a deed component – the physical act of consummation. Like the written document in contract law, then, sexual intercourse is, potentially, what will clinch the private and unwitnessed agreement between Bertram and Diana as well as provide the evidence which Diana cynically suggests will be needed; it will draw his unsealed words into a legal 'deed' and ratify the verbal contract of espousal by performance.

The identification of the promissory and sexual components of a spousal pact with the verbal and the performative respectively, and of these, in turn, with the initial and legalizing aspects of a contract, was an element in the contemporary perception of the legality of marriage. This comes across in such court records as Matilde Price's personal response in the case of Price v. Price discussed earlier:[30] 'necque habuit carnalem copulam cum dicto Henrico, nec quia ex parte sua necque ratificauit hoc matrimonium re aut verbo...' [(she) neither had carnal copulation with the said Henry, nor on her part ratified this marriage by word or fact]. This is a case where the validation of an unsolemnized precontract and the invalidation of a solemnized marriage turn on the establishment of the fact of non-consummation in the latter; where *verba* becomes entirely secondary as the dispute in court diverts all attention to the superior ratifying power of *res*, which in this instance is 'carnal copulation'.[31] One of the meanings of the word 'ratify' in the sixteenth century was in fact 'to consummate' (*OED*, sense 3).

The 'deed' that is accomplished in *All's Well* through Diana's intervention, however, ratifies Bertram's earlier conditional contract with Helena, not his present one with Diana. It is the bed-trick in which all three senses of 'deed' – action, sealed contract and copulation – come together. The instrumentality of the sub-plot for the main plot, and their analogical relation highlight the fact that their distinctness is symptomatic of deeper divisions within the legal action in the main plot. One of the demonstrable instruments of the interlacing of plots is the pair of rings set in circulation by Diana. In serving this function, the rings as tokens of marriage and of intercourse alternate between two configurations in their relation to 'deed'.

While Bertram suggests sex as the seal called for by Diana, Diana demands his ring. This is the first ring to draw the audience's attention. Bertram's giving of it is analogous to a deed or to the signing of a 'deed', either of which can be a seal on an agreement. This takes us right back to Swinburne's discussion of the role of the verbal formula. It is in asserting the assumed function of words in making a marriage that Swinburne is faced with their potential inadequacy, even treacherousness. He does ultimately hold up the validity of the *de praesenti* formula, but in the very process of confirmation, he has to concede that

mortal man cannot otherwise judge of Mens meanings, than by their sayings for the Tongue is the Messenger of the heart; and although it sometimes deliver a false message, yet doth the Law accept it for true, when as the Contrary doth not lawfully appear.   (*Spousals*, 87)

As court records show, the contracting parties were the least likely, especially at the moment of spousal, to be verbally precise, and not sure to be conversant with legal formulae; the witnesses were often uneducated and were mostly reliant on memory. Moreover, spousal disputes brought to court frequently involved secret contracts, with no witnesses to testify.

It is in recognition of such inadequacies or unavailability of the 'word' as evidence that Swinburne offers the exchange of rings as a possible solution (*Spousals*, 86). Moreover, he grants the ring a special position among the non-verbal signs that take on a demonstrative or validating function – deserving to be spoken of 'before all other signs' (207).[32] The giving and receiving of a ring was, indeed, one of the commonest gestures invested with special matrimonial significance in the period. The surviving depositions convey a vivid sense of why rings had such a hold on the popular imagination and how the imperatives of certain actual situations harnessed their symbolic importance to a legal one.[33]

Typically, rings assumed the greatest legal significance in settling disputes concerning unwitnessed and unsolemnized contracts, where material proofs were often the only available evidence.[34] In the case of Thomas Allen *v.* Alice Howling of Norfolk (1562), the determining factor is a 'Ring of gould'. In her personal response to Thomas's claim of matrimonial rights, Alice denies her alleged receipt of this ring 'in the waye of matrimony'. But her attempt at freeing herself is thwarted by John Smith and William Walker, who testify, in almost identical terms, that Thomas gave and Alice accepted the ring as an acknowledged token of present marriage.[35]

The popularly perceived value of ring-giving as a symbolic and integral ceremony in a matrimonial context derived, paradoxically, from its traditional association with solemnized weddings *in facie ecclesiae*; thus it almost lent a semblance of formality to clandestine marriages. The formalizing and mnemonic qualities of the ring come together in George Haydock's deposition about the runaway Sothworth couple of Chester (1565): 'what wordes were spoken betwene the parties, he certenlie cannot declare, biecause he did not marke them well'; what he does remember, though, is that 'gold and silver was put on the boke' and 'a ringe [was] put on her finger'.[36]

In Southern dioceses too, the Puritan challenge does not seem to have revolutionized custom.[37] In the Canterbury case of Wanderton *v.* Wild (1582), the ring clinches a contract – much in the manner prescribed by the pre-Reformation order of matrimony[38] – and gives a *de futuro* spousal the sanctity of present marriage, at least in the eyes of the deponents. After the parties uttered words of pledge to each other which, predictably, 'he remembreth not', Michael Haell, a witness to the contract, said to them, 'If you receaue any such thing as you pretend conclude the matter as it myght to be done els I will not medle in it'. 'Then the said Wanderton took the said Agnes by the handes', and they uttered what was, roughly, the formula of a *de futuro* contract. 'Then they losed ther handes, and Wanderton gaue her a Ring gelt saying to her take this as a token that you have confessed and I the like to you, you to be my wife and I to be your husband [. . .] and she receaued the same Ring thankfully' (176). Haell's claim is that they are well and truly married.[39] This bears out the popular currency, in some places at least, of the legal provision set out but qualified as being practically unsound by Swinburne – that in spousals *de futuro*, 'When as on[e] and above the words, there is an Accumulation of some Act joyned therewithal . . . For example: . . . the Man delivereth to the Woman a Ring . . . hereby the Contract is presumed Matrimonial' (*Spousals*, 71). The delivery of a ring here has the status of an act or deed.

This is the function made to serve by Bertram's 'subarration' to Diana, which, in conjunction with his words, would technically count as a promise of marriage:

> Here, take my ring.
> My house, mine honour, yea my life be thine,
> And I'll be bid by thee.
>
> (4.2.52–4)

We have, here, not only an evocation of the familiar situation of a private contract, and its characteristic method of establishing a formal context, but also the associated possibility of later dispute already present in the inception.

What Diana engineers, however, is an exchange of rings. This accords an altogether more complex set of values to the rings by the time they resurface together at the end, to constitute the comic and legal resolutions. While the course of Bertram's ring gets deflected from its original path through the introduction of Diana, a new ring is imported by her dark promise to Bertram:

> And on your finger in the night I'll put
> Another ring that, what in time proceeds,
> May token to the future our past deeds.
>
> (4.2.62–4)

In its promised exchange with the first ring, it has already become associated with Diana's virginity – 'Mine honour's such a ring. / My chastity's the jewel of our house' (4.2.46–7). This is the jewel Diana pledges in return for Bertram's family jewel. In deed, though, it is Helena's chastity that is going to be its operative but invisible counterpart. The bawdy sense is reinforced by the verbal echo of Bertram's letter to Helena which posited, by linguistic juxtaposition, a cause-and-effect relationship between getting the 'ring upon [his] finger' and showing 'a child begotten of [her] body' (3.2.57–9).

Bertram's language is deliberately rendered ambiguous by Shakespeare to suggest an unmistakeable sexual meaning; 'the ring ... which never shall come off' (3.2.57–8), with its multiple suggestion of a spousal ring with its eternal associations, Bertram's heirloom and the yet uncracked ring of Helena's virginity. It was, in Painter, far more clearly and singly the specific ornament belonging to Beltramo: 'I do purpose to dwell with her, when she shal have this ring (meaning a ring which he wore) vpon her finger, and a sonne in her armes begotten by mee.'[40] The change from 'her finger' to 'my finger' and from 'this ring' to 'the ring ... which never shall come off' not only permits but invites a sexualized reading, and strengthens the syntactical link between the two conditions. It is this metaphorical connection that is taken up by Helena and literalized during the bed-trick.

The literal and bawdy meanings of 'ring' in Bertram's statement of his first condition are, however, taken apart and met separately, even as Helena's agency is divided between herself and Diana. Thus, the actual ring on Bertram's finger that Helena has to get in spite of his resolution that it 'never shall come off' (3.2.58) has already been obtained by Diana. But while its procurement was meant to be a proof of Helena's cohabitation with Bertram, it becomes an alleged token of his marriage to Diana in the scene of arbitration, and a confessed token of his supposed sexual deeds with her. Meanwhile, Helena's pregnancy takes on the role of signifying his actual 'deed' with Helena. This splitting of functions foregrounds the separation between the woman Bertram thinks he sleeps with, and the woman he actually penetrates. His ring gets reconnected with Helena's conception only at the very end, a connection that is explicitly underlined by Helena's words:

> There is your ring.
> And, look you, here's your letter. This it says:
> 'When from my finger you can get this ring,
> And are by me with child', et cetera. This is done.
>   (5.3.312–5)

This is at once a realization and restatement of the implied connection between ring and sex in Bertram's letter, and a reuniting of divided agencies in the figure of Helena – a covering up of the many divisions through which her husband has had to be 'doubly won'.

Meanwhile, the second ring, the actual jewel that Helena has put on Bertram's finger 'in the night', spotted by Lafew as Helena's and by the king as his own gift to her, is defined ultimately as a proof that Bertram 'husbanded [Helena's] bed at Florence', since it is clear that 'this ring was . . . hers' (5.3.126–7). Part of the *raison-d'être* of this ring is its necessary role of providing additional support for Helena's claim of Bertram's paternity of her yet unborn child. Without this token of inter-course between Helena and Bertram, it would be less clear that Helena's conception followed from Bertram's night of pleasure in Florence.

Thus, if the first ring was initially analogous to the action or 'deed' that seals an oral contract, its later use as a sign of Bertram's supposed activities with Diana, and the use of the other ring as a seal and token of his actual congress with Helena, point to yet another relation between ring and deed in the play. 'Deeds', as what the rings, with their spousal and sexual associations, will help make evident, becomes clearly the act or acts of sex. Originally posited as a more reliable expression of intention than words, 'deeds' have now themselves become something to be proved; they, no less than words, are signs to be interpreted.

The special position given to rings by Swinburne and their centrality in the popular perception of marital obligations are borne out by their importance in the final episode. A scene of reconciliation and spousal negotiation quickly darkens into one of arraignment, as the 'amorous token for fair Maudlin' (5.3.69) is recognized by the king as the 'token' by which he would have relieved Helena, and as Bertram stakes all on it:

> If you shall prove
> This ring was ever hers, you shall as easy
> Prove that I husbanded her bed in Florence
> (125–7)

The trial structure of this scene is officially established upon the delivery of Diana's letter. Stating with legal precision her claim of marriage, and clearly setting out the charge against Bertram, this letter takes the place of a libel which is defined by Henry Consett as 'a Writing which containeth the action' in his account of the practice of the church courts in Renaissance England.[41] Here, of course, the court is presided over by the king, instead of a doctor of law, but the royal presence itself is another factor which defines the legality of the space in the disclosure scene.[42] Diana's very phrasing – 'and a poor maid is undone' (141–8) – evokes the ambience of the sex-related litigation of the church courts – recalling numerous pleas by women claiming to be used, deceived or abandoned. The legal situation gets wholly formalized with the king's declaration of his suspicion and the countess's call for 'justice' (152–6).

In this set-up, the rings become the *exhibita* or material objects produced in court to support allegations. Diana's presentation of the first ring – the one given her by Bertram – is clearly accorded a higher truth value than other forms of evidence such as witness testimony. When Bertram casts aspersions on Parolles's personal credibility, the king points out, 'She hath that ring of yours' (212).

The terms in which the characters respond to the rings suggest at least one of the reasons behind their evidentiary impact. The entire drama around the first ring starts when it catches the king's eye – 'for mine eye, / While I was speaking, oft was fastened to 't' (82–3). Bertram's denial that it ever was Helena's is met with the Countess's assertion, 'Son, on my life /

I have seen her wear it' and is corroborated by Lafew's 'I am sure I saw her wear it' (90–2). One remembers depositions like Christabell Andro's, who recounts the contract between William Headley and Agnes Smith, as well as registers its reality entirely in terms of images – 'she . . . *sawe* the parties contract and gyve ther faith and trewth to gither . . . ; and the said William gave the said Agnes one pair of glowes and a bowed grote, and she gave unto . . . William one gold ring'.[43]

It is the impact of 'ocular proof' that Diana exploits when she presents this ring dramatically in court – ' . . . O behold this ring' (5.3.194). The Countess immediately notes, 'he blushes and 'tis hit' (198). But Diana has hit the mark in more senses than one. Everyone else in the assembly reacts as much as Bertram does, and the Countess declares at this point, 'That ring's a thousand proofs' (202). As Swinburne puts it, 'Not to be, and not to appear, is all one in Construction of Law' (*Spousals*, 181). The function of proof, therefore, is to make the truth apparent or visible. *Enargaeia* was defined by Aristotle as an exercise which represents an object before the eyes of the viewers, and the Latin word for *enargaeia*, suggestively, is *evidentia*.[44]

Significantly, however, most of the deponents one encounters do not – and cannot – actually reproduce the incident or the facts they are seeking to ascertain. Rather, they attempt to narrate them vividly. Evidence, thus, involves an exercise in re-presentation and hence, inevitably, a metonymic relation between the truth sought to be proved, and the sign that is meant to evoke it. Even exhibits – be they letters, handkerchiefs, deeds or rings – are legal tokens. The way they make things evident is by symbolically or associatively evoking an entire situation before the eyes of the judge. The necessary translocation involved in evidentiary practice is dictated by the fact that the action or the intention to be proved cannot literally be shown in court, and yet has to be somehow made apparent. The inadequacies and ambiguities of this process gain a specially concise focus in the context of marriage law in which the crucial events and factors to be established were usually private acts and utterances, and very often the specific act of sex. *All's Well's* dramatization of this area of law highlights a condition common to the theatre and the church courts. Both are faced with the task of often having to represent and legislate a realm removed from the public space of the stage or the court. Both, therefore, have to devise their own enargaeic modes to show what must necessarily be absent from this space but what is, at the same time, central to their motives of representation. The ring, here, inscribes this phenomenon, by virtue of its metaphoric valencies and its role as

a 'monumental' token (4.3.18). Legally as well as theatrically it bodies
forth what must lie outside the limits of representation.

This is part of the larger problem of an uneasy relation between intentionality and legal truths revealed by adventitious proofs. When the
king confronts Bertram with the evident truth that Diana 'hath that ring
of [his]', what Bertram denies in self-defence is not the fact that he gave
it to her, nor indeed the implied fact of intercourse, but the matrimonial intention that is assumed and alleged to have informed both these
acts (5.3.213–22). Exactly this argument is given by many defendants
in debates over love tokens, especially rings, in disputed contract suits
from the period. Alice Cotton of Canterbury says she received Thomas
Baxter's gifts as 'mere gift' and not 'in . . . waie of marriage' (1574).[45]
What comes closest to Bertram's disclaimer is perhaps John Smith's distinction between the use of tokens for a sexual contract and for a marital
one in his personal response against Christian Grimsdiche's libel in a
Chester trothplight case of 1562: 'beynge askid, for what intent' he gave
her tokens, 'he sais, because he had, and wold have, to do with her, &
knew her Carnally; & not for that he wold mary her'.[46] Such disputes
highlight the difficulty of assessing the intention of the giver through the
perception of the receiver and of others. From their position of privilege
over the spectators or the judge at a law court, a theatre audience would
have seen enough of Bertram and heard enough from him by the time
he is brought to trial, to be clearly struck by the fallacy of a 'reasonable
inference' of 'Wedlock' from the fact of Diana's possession of his ring.

The 'second' ring – the one that has travelled from the king to Bertram
via Helena and Diana respectively, to surface in court as a proposed gift
for Maudlin – turns out to be no less dubious a proof of intercourse and
identity than the first ring is of spousal subarration. It is, of course, established that this ring was Helena's at one time, something that Bertram
was confident could never be proved; but law's natural conclusion from
this contingency, that Bertram 'husbanded her bed in Florence', completely eschews the question of intention in applying the formula for a
valid marriage. Bertram thinks he sleeps with Diana, and if that act is to
seal any marriage, it is his with her – as indeed it legally would – since
the 'news' of Helena's death, arriving before the bed-trick, has met the
stipulation of Bertram's *de futuro* spousal to Diana (4.2.72–3). The fact
that he is 'quit' (5.3.301) is due to an arbitrary separation of fact and
meant truth in the 'deed of darkness' in Florence.

The connection between this legal fiction and evidentiary law's reliance on what is visible is something Swinburne's *Spousals* is aware

of: 'for proof is not of the Essence of Matrimony' (*Spousals*, 87).[47] But 'although . . . he which is the searcher of the heart doth well know their deceit and defect of mutual Consent', yet the 'judgement of Mortal man' must pronounce them married since 'the contrary doth not lawfully appear' (85). Hence such paradoxes as 'this deceit so lawful' 'Where both not sin, and yet a sinful fact' (*All's Well*, 3.7.38, 47). Hence, too, the irony that though 'not bedding but consent makes marriages' (*Matrimony*, 120), it is the bedding that, in this instance, proves it. The darkness and the silence that are the conditions for the bed-trick come to stand for the limits to the vision of the mortal judge, for what cannot be made evident either visually or by narration in a temporal court of law. Bertram's conditional pledge of love – 'If she, my liege, can make me know this clearly' – touches precisely on the discomfort surrounding the knowledge law brings, but it is immediately forestalled by Helena's assertion – 'If it *appear* not plain and *prove* untrue . . .' (*All's Well*, 5.3.317–19). Helena's answer, in collapsing the gap between cognition and legal certification, articulates the rules that operate in the world of the play, as in law.

The Swinburnian unease around error and the inadequacy of law to accommodate its moral implications lies at the core of the bed-trick. In *Matrimony*, he states clearly and unproblematically that marriage contracted by those who 'doe not consent . . . for that they be . . . seduced by Error mistaking one person for another' 'is of no moment or effect in Lawe' since matrimony must be a 'coniunction of . . . myndes' (121–2). But where the issue is not mere definition but ascertainment of status in the case of a complex human situation, law and its agents have to face a dilemma. Thus, the bed-trick cannot be 'lawful meaning in a lawful act', since the act is joint, and involves two meanings.[48]

The bed-trick is a fictional situation that singles out a potential for fiction in law itself, by which the difference between the singleness of fact and the plurality of truth is collapsed, and a status is presumed. Its likeness to a legal fiction is highlighted by the mendacious means it adopts to achieve an ostensibly ethical end. It is no surprise that Helena, law's most self-aware user, should embody some of the dualities that the play's movement, largely through her energies, seeks to harmonize. To claim the honour that is hers, she has to 'steal' it surreptitiously (2.5.81) by becoming, as it were, a 'girl' of Italy, to make Bertram 'captive' to her service (2.1.21–2). The law trick that is the specific instrument of Helena's design turns on a logic familiar to a Renaissance English audience, but it acquires a specific status by being used in the context of subtle and strategic double-dealing by the heroine at her most 'Machiavellian' in the very land of plots and policies.[49]

But Helena's Italianate plotting does not ultimately create a simply negative sense of unsavoury cunning; nor is law reduced to a sceptic's quarry. Her character is in many senses Machiavellian in a positive way, and, paradoxically, her use of law and its particular literary location, even while they demystify law, result in a configuring of it as a peculiarly human and contingent measure. Her very first soliloquy (1.1.78–97) signals a transition in her attitude to fate, from passive resignation to a belief in the space it allows for individual enterprise – 'The fated sky gives us free scope'. The only hindrance to exploiting such 'scope' – a concept akin to Machiavelli's *occasione*[50] – is our 'slow designs'. Her tough-minded confidence in possibilities and the expedient and inventive effort with which she sets about to achieve these brings her in line with the prudent protagonists – often heroines – of the *novellae*, whose *industria* is usually their main capital.[51]

The dual associations gathered by law in the course of the play lend the ending its distinctively mixed flavour. After the rapid escalation of legal dangers and implications in the final scene, Helena's spectacular entry must seem a relief in the immediate context, indeed some sort of a salvation. Back in Rossillion, Helena has shed her Italian character, and apparently displaces the world of sexual intrigue and precise legal wrangles as she steps into Diana's place to take over the limelight. She is not to be seen as one of those 'clamorous and impudent' women litigants that the likes of Lord Keeper Egerton and Chancery counsel Anthony Benn were, at the time, denouncing and attempting to keep out of the courts.[52] As in the bed-trick, so here, the status of an event is transformed by the replacement of one woman by the other: the lustful defiling of the 'pitchy night' and its legal and obligatory consequences are taken on by the Bertram–Diana sub-plot, while the central relationship of the play is strategically cleansed of its more degrading associations, and prepared for the 'renown' of the 'end'.

The moment that registers this change is when Helena and Bertram are brought to face each other for the first time in the scene, through Bertram's voluntary interposition. In response to the king's wonder at what seems to him an apparition – 'Is't real that I see?' – Helena says,

> No, my good lord,
> 'Tis but the shadow of a wife you see,
> The name and not the thing.
> (5.3.308–10)

Even as the teasing, paradoxical mode of speech gets sublimated here into a medium that brings romance to the verge of anagnorisis, Bertram remonstrates, 'Both, both. O, pardon!' (310). If the bed-trick was the symbolic moment of the split between meaning and action, 'the name' and 'the thing', the present exchange between Bertram and Helena marks, no matter how fleetingly, the healing of these divisions in an act of forgiveness. An appropriate atmosphere is provided by Helena's self-presentation, aided by Diana, which creates an aura of miracle heightened by the regenerative associations of pregnancy. This sense of the wondrous is the main constituent of the romance mode which acts here as an equivalent of the social rituals that transform marriage from a contract into a mystery.

Yet the transition is not seamless. Even while status is attained, the contractual basis of marriage is not let out of sight. The particular instrument for sustaining this awareness is the continued and insistent mooring of the scene in the details of marriage law. Helena's achievement is to have foiled Bertram's attempt at seeking a divorce by establishing the fact of cohabitation: this is the specific significance of her staking 'deadly divorce' on the indisputability of the proofs of having met his terms (320). Thus, in the indistinct but comprehensive area covered between the two, both the marriage and the divorce paradigms behind their 'legal' actions get taken up and pursued till the end of the play where, finally, they are tied together.

Sex having been in *All's Well* the very site of a radical absence of volition, its centrality to the sacramental notion of indissoluble matrimony, which ostensibly contributes to the magic of the final reunion, extends the paradox of the earlier action. Swinburne's explanation of why 'Marriage is that great Mystery' is germane to what the pregnant wife's appearance relies on for its 'miraculous' impact: 'By Marriage the Man and the Woman are made one Flesh, so they are not by Spousals.' It is in the absence of such a union that he declares 'Spousals' to be 'utterly destitute of . . . mystical effect: And . . . Marriage is greater than Spousals . . . ' (*Spousals*, 16). In *All's Well*, 'making one flesh' is in a sense what turns a spousal into matrimony, but the mystery around the incorporation of man and wife is at least partly replaced by consummation as an instrument of law and custom.

As the external symbol and visible outcome of this incorporation, Helena's pregnancy plays a crucial role in foregrounding the contractual basis of the revalidated union. While its procreational and promissory implications introduce a sense of romance quickenings, the function it serves in the resolution of the plot is legal. It is framed as an 'ocular proof' of the sexual consummation stipulated in Bertram's letter: 'one that's dead is quick – / And now behold the meaning!' (5.3.305–6).[53] This is in many senses a scene of remarriage – a familiar scenario, where the fact of intercourse acts as the single validating seal that at once proves and forms matrimony. Bridal pregnancy by itself was common enough in Elizabethan England;[54] and though prenuptial fornication was a punishable offence, in practice, judicial attitudes to it varied according to local custom, and were often quite tolerant where honourable intentions were clear or marriage had already followed.[55] But the remarriage in *All's Well* takes place not in church but in a virtual court. The visual resonances of a pregnant woman turning up in open court would evoke associations of incontinence and fornication – charges often spurred by illicit pregnancy. 'Pregnancies', Ralph Houlbrooke asserts, 'always figured prominently among the presentments made'; and, as he further puts it, 'rather more women than men were normally presented, because a pregnant woman was bound to be more conspicuous than her partner'.[56] As far as Bertram's conscious intention defines the deed that Helena's pregnancy proceeds from, the result is indeed symptomatic of the typical situation; only, it is transformed here by Helena's intention and her triumphant use of 'occasion'. What lends the legal connection of the scene its specific dubiousness is the combination of the marital and the evidentiary purposes behind Helena's action. As often in disputed suits of this kind, what is still at stake, implicitly, is Bertram's agency in the conception. In Shakespeare's time, determination of paternal identity was a troubling legal issue.[57] We have Swinburne's own pronouncement on the matter, in his discussion of why 'wedlock [is] called Matrimonye rather than Patrimonye': 'the mother is alwaies more certein than the father and truthe is stronger than opinion' (*Matrimony*, 118).

It is interesting to note one of Shakespeare's modifications of his source story. In Painter – as in Boccaccio – Giletta was 'brought a bedde of twoo sonnes, which were very like vnto their father . . .'. She enters Beltramo's banquet not pregnant but with these two, their resemblance to their father being posited and accepted as manifest evidence of paternity, strengthening the implication of her possession of his ring: 'for beholde, here in myne armes, not onely one sonne begotten by thee, but twayne, and likewise thy Ryng . . . the Counte hearing this, was greatly astonned, and knewe the Ryng, and the children also, they were so like hym.'[58] If Shakespeare had left this episode unchanged, he would still have had the opportunity to evoke legal associations, for facial similarity has been known to have been a factor in establishing the father's identity in church courts.[59] But pregnancy as a presence in court was

potentially more scandalous because there was an unavoidable uncertainty surrounding paternity and, by implication, a potential for the
use of pregnancy for manipulation. It was not unknown for women to
claim marital rights by offering their conception as proof of cohabitation. The motives could be various – as Martin Ingram puts it, women
resorting to law to pressurize men into marriage could be 'naive, schem-
ing, or . . . desperate'.[60] Among them, pregnant women not only had a
stronger incentive but were 'in a better moral position to attempt coer-
cion' than others.[61] They were also likely to receive local backing, not
least owing to a concern about the threat of bastardy to the poor rates.[62]
In the Salisbury case of Diar *v.* Rogers (1609), Henry Rogers is said to
have promised that 'yf he did beget the said Alice with childe, that he
would marry with her'. The witnesses for the manifestly pregnant plaintiff Alice Diar keep harping on the obligation that her conception has
placed him under; as Alice Tante (?) puts it, it is 'in the respect of the said
Henry Roger's faythfull promise [that] the said Alice offered her selffe
to be begotten with child by . . . Henry'.[63] Even unconfirmed claims of
pregnancy could create enormous pressure and a climate of opinion
hard to cope with.[64] Not only can such a situation, irrespective of the
truth or spirit of the alleged promise, be conducive to enforcement; the
pressures incumbent on the defendant of such a suit are even known to
have tempted women to have 'deliberately sought to become pregnant
to induce the man to marry her'. [65] Such is the lingering sense of uncertainty that Bertram articulates, when he takes a faltering step back from
his spontaneous 'Both, both. O pardon!' to qualify his acceptance of the
situation:

> If she, my liege, can make me know this clearly
> I'll love her dearly, ever ever dearly.
>   (5.3.317–18)

In a play where comic law operates through actual legal means, and
recognition is arrived at through a trial, the incertitude surrounding
the legal knowledge undercuts the absolute nature of the anagnoristic
moment. This marriage, for all that the providential emplotment of
Helena's 'course' suggests, is made not in heaven but in the bawdy court.
Where the king is overwhelmed into a typical romance reaction (307–9),
the audience would be aware that the inevitable outcome of the discovery
has as much to do with legal logic, by which the church court arbiter
would probably order Bertram to take her back and live with her as
married people should.[66]

As ever, though, it is in the figure of Helena, the employer of the legal tricks for the 'miraculous' ending, that the comic energy of the play as well as its use of law acquires a more complex status than mere strategem can lay claim to. In her, policy and genuineness, simulation and sincerity, power and powerlessness have been inextricably compounded from the very beginning: 'I do affect a sorrow indeed, but I have it too' (1.1.51). It is this spirit that she infuses into the final scene. When she appears in court, big with child, her condition – betokening the triumph of her initiative – becomes a means for the strategic adoption of a traditional image of the obedient wife whose pleasure lies in being acted upon by her husband, a calculated evocation of domestic sanctities, so 'that man [can] be at woman's command, and yet no hurt done!'[67] Yet, as with the women 'who', in the words of *The lawes resolutions of women's rights* (1632), could 'shift it well enough' in the legal world of early modern England,[68] this is not simply a camouflaging of Helena's agency. It is also a pointer to her real vulnerability and, in an odd sense, passivity in the emotional transaction contained in the quasi-legal one. When she says, 'O, my good lord, when I was like this maid / I found you wondrous kind', her utterance is a gentle reminder to us that her active plotting has had to be executed through a virtual loss of identity in the act of sex; its humour lies in her acknowledged sexual enjoyment of even this imperfect emotional experience (5.3.311–12). As far as she is concerned, the seamier aspects of what has passed are not simplemindedly forgotten but deliberately put behind: 'This is done', she says, after curtailing her recitation of Bertram's conditional letter with a significant 'et cetera' (315). Peter Hall's 1992 production, appropriately, made Helena tear up the letter – which is also the contract – as she spoke these words.

Through her, then, law is finally felt to acquire a more positive value than merely being a sceptical alternative to either the *vera philosophia* or the perfect science that it was considered to be in some of the most prominent humanist traditions of jurisprudence. It emerges, rather, as an art of the probable, that involves prudence rather than wisdom – a perspective that was actually emerging in the Renaissance, questioning the more idealistic view of law.[69] Law is not in itself a transformative principle, but a pragmatic means of working through the essentially contingent human condition towards achievements that are necessarily provisional. It is for the individual to renounce and go beyond the legal devices to build on the possibilities made available to her by them. Over and above the obvious irony of the play's title, there is a sense in which it is felt to

encapsulate the peculiar and hard-bought wisdom of the play. All one
can begin with, in a sense, is this 'end'. This is not a romance, like *Pericles*
or *The Winter's Tale*, where the children have been born and the regener-
ation has visibly begun. Helena's pregnancy, among its other expressive
functions, suggests the play's projecting of fulfilments in the future. To
take up the possibilities afforded by legal means is what the function of
romance is posited as. Nor need the value of law necessarily lie in the
discovery or assertion of certitudes; probability itself can be its gift to
the human condition, and indeed a positive step towards knowledge.
The king's words, as he accepts Helena's offer of her improbable 'medical' services, capture a perspective which the play ultimately invites the
audience to accommodate:

> More should I question thee, and more I must,
> Though more to know could not be more to
>   trust:
> From whence thou cam'st, how tended on – but
>   rest
> Unquestioned welcome, and undoubted blessed.
>   (2.1.205–8)

Like a promise, marriage, happy endings to stories and happiness itself,
are all, in a sense, absolute and ignorant – like Pascal's wager with God,
a leap of faith.

First published in *Shakespeare Survey 49* (1996)

NOTES

1 Though I use the Oxford Shakespeare, I retain the traditional name for the
   heroine. I should like to thank Ben Griffin for assistance with references.
2 Henry Swinburne, *A Treatise of Spousals, or Matrimonial Contracts*, ed. Randolph
   Trumbach (London, 1985) (hereafter, *Spousals*).
3 For influential examples of the critical opinion that Bertram's resistance is a
   legal escape route, see M. L. Ranald, 'The Betrothals of *All's Well That Ends
   Well*', *Huntington Library Quarterly*, 26 (1962–3), 179–92; p. 186, and Howard
   Cole, *The 'All's Well' Story From Boccaccio to Shakespeare* (Urbana, 1981), passim.
   Enforcement could be a ground for nullification, but only if it was raised by a
   party in court; Bertram's failure to do so at the relevant moment suggests the
   impracticality of this provision in a situation of authority and dependence.
   The one technically permissible objection a ward could raise – that against
   disparagement – is brought up by him but not sustained. On wardship,
   see Joel Hurstfield, *The Queen's Wards: Wardship and Marriage under Elizabeth I*
   (London, 1958).

4 See Madeleine Doran, *Endeavors of Art: A Study of Form in Elizabethan Drama* (Madison, 1954), pp. 251–2, and W. W. Lawrence, *Shakespeare's Problem Comedies* (New York, 1960), pp. 32–77.

5 Durham University Library, Palace Green, Mickleton and Spearman Manuscript 4, fol. 115–124. I am indebted to Sheila Doyle of the Durham University Law Library for drawing my attention to this manuscript volume.

6 *The Book of Common Prayer 1559: The Elizabethan Prayer Book*, ed. by John E. Booty (Charlottesville, 1976), p. 297. Though, by this time, both the reformers and the bishops were clear that scripture did not provide sanction for the sacramental status of marriage, its desacramentalization remained largely a matter of theological definition in England. To prevent it from being divested of dignity and solemnity in popular perception – an effect that was distinctly possible, and would threaten exactly the regularization sought by the reformers – the service was made to stress that marriage was a 'holy ordinance', and further, was coupled with the receiving of Holy Communion, at the same time as the sacramental language and claim were dropped. This was enough to preserve the sacramental sanctity of marriage for the common people, who did not pause to work out the technical distinctions of the reformers. See Eric Joseph Carlson, *Marriage and the English Reformation* (Oxford, 1994), pp. 36–49.

7 On church courts, see Ralph Houlbrooke, *Church Courts and the People during the English Reformation 1520–1570* (Oxford, 1979). For accounts focusing on marriage litigation, see Martin Ingram, *Church Courts, Sex and Marriage in England 1570–1640* (Cambridge, 1987); R. H. Helmholz, *Marriage Litigation in Medieval England* (Cambridge, 1974); *Marriage*, and Carlson, pp. 142–180.

8 See, for example, Helmholz, *Marriage Litigation*, p. 27; Martin Ingram, 'Spousal Litigation in the English Ecclesiastical Courts, *c.* 1350–1640' in R. B. Outhwaite, ed., *Marriage and Society: Studies in the Social History of Marriage* (London, 1981), pp. 35–57; pp. 37, 45; *Spousals*, p. 14.

9 See G. E. Howard, *The History of Matrimonial Institutions chiefly in England and the United States* (Chicago, 1904), 3 vols., vol. 1, p. 339. The interplay of attitudes to Claudio and Juliet's sexual involvement in *Measure for Measure* turns exactly on this duality. For an incisive exposition of this point, see A. D. Nuttall's '*Measure for Measure*: The bed-trick' in Nuttall, *The Stoic in Love* (London, 1989), pp. 41–8.

10 See James A. Brundage, *Law, Sex and Christian Society in Medieval Europe* (Chicago, 1987), pp. 551–574.

11 See *Spousals*, pp. 21, 36–41; Sir Edward Coke, *The First Institute of the Lawes of England* (London, 1628), section 104.

12 James Raine, *Depositions and other Ecclesiastical Proceedings from the Courts of Durham, extending from 1311 to the Reign of Elizabeth* (London, 1845), pp. 218–26.

13 See J. O. Halliwell, ed., *The Autobiography and Correspondence of Sir Simonds D'Ewes* (London, 1845), vol. 1, pp. 87–9.

14 See James A. Coriden, *The Indissolubility Added to Christian Marriage by*

Consummation: A Historical Study from the End of the Patristic Period of the Death of Pope Innocent III (Rome, 1961), pp. 7–23.

15 J. T. Noonan, *Power to Dissolve: Lawyers and Marriages in the Courts of the Roman Curia* (Cambridge, Massachusetts, 1972), p. 80.

16 For Swinburne's reference to the marriage of Mary and Joseph as the authority behind the notion that 'carnall knowledge' is not essential for 'perfect matrimony', see *Matrimony*, p. 120.

17 Raine, *Depositions*, pp. 322–6.

18 Furnivall, *Child-Marriages, Divorces, and Ratifications, &c. In the Diocese of Chester, A.D. 1561–6* (London, 1897), p. 58.

19 See, for example, the 1623 case against John Cocke of Tillington and his wife, cited in P. Hair, ed., *Before the Bawdy Court: Selections from church courts and other records relating to the correction of moral offences in England, Scotland and New England, 1300–1800* (London, 1972), p. 107, or the Yorkshire presentment cited in n. 21 below.

20 See E. D. Stone and B. Cozens-Hardy, eds., *Norwich Consistory Court Depositions 1499–1512 and 1518–1530*, Norfolk Record Society 10 (1938), no. 90.

21 See T. M. Fallow, 'Some Elizabethan Visitations of the Churches belonging to the Peculiar of the Dean of York', *Yorkshire Archaeological Journal*, 18 (1905), 197–232.

22 Furnivall, *Child-Marriages*, pp. 76–9.

23 See also *Spousals*, p. 225.

24 See Joseph Jacobs, ed., *The Palace of Pleasure: Elizabethan Versions of Italian and French Novels From Boccaccio, Bandello, Cinthio, Straparola, Queen Margaret of Navarre, And Others, Done into English by William Painter* (New York, 1966) (hereafter, Painter), 'The thirty-Eigth Nouell' – Shakespeare's immediate source for the story of *All's Well*.

25 J. H. Baker, *The Legal Profession and the Common Law* (London, 1986), pp. 153–69; p. 360. See also pp. 361 and 375.

26 Ibid., p. 362.

27 See S. F. C. Milsom, *Historical Foundations of the Common Law* (London, 1983), pp. 88–90 and 289.

28 Ingram, 'Spousal', p. 52. On the reciprocal influence between common law, and canon law as practised in the church courts, see R. H. Helmholz, *Canon Law and English Common Law*, Selden Society Lecture, 1982 (London, 1983), esp. pp. 15–19.

29 Baker, *The Legal Profession*, p. 360.

30 See p. 122 above.

31 Cp. Humphrey Winstanley *v.* Alice Worsley, a 1561 divorce suit from Chester, Furnivall, *Child-Marriages*, pp. 2–4.

32 See also *Spousals*, pp. 71, 101, 206–12.

33 On the various symbolisms of the ring, see *Spousals*, pp. 207–9; A. H. Bullen, *An English Garner: Some Shorter Elizabethan Poems* (Westminster, 1903), p. 296, posy no. 15; J. E. Cirlot, *A Dictionary of Symbols and Imagery*, tr. J. Sage (London, 1971), p. 273; G. F. Kunz, *Rings for the Finger* (Philadelphia, 1917), pp. 193–248; Shirley Bury, *An Introduction to Rings* (London, 1948), pp. 15–17;

Stith Thompson, *Motif-Index of Folk Literature* (Copenhagen, 1958), vol. 6, pp. 650–1.

34 See Houlbrooke, *Church Courts*, 58, esp. n. 14; Peter Rushton, 'The Testaments of Gifts: Marriage Tokens and Disputed Contracts in North-East England, 1560–1630', *Folk Life* 24 (1985–6), 25–31. See also *Spousals*, Sections XII–XV.

35 Norfolk and Norwich Record Office diocesan records (hereafter, NNRO), DN/DEP (deposition books of the consistory court) 9, bk. 8, 158v, 162–3v; DN/ACT (Act books) 9, bk. 10.

36 Furnivall, *Child-Marriages*, pp. 65–6.

37 For attacks on the ring in Puritan writing, see Anthony Gilby, *A Pleasaunte dialogue, Betweene a Souldier of Barwicke, and an English Chaplaine* (Middleburg, 1581), M5r; Dudley Fenner, *Certain Learned and Godly Treatises* (Edinburgh, 1952), p. 96; Andrew Kingsmill, *A View of Mans Estate* (London, 1576), sig. K2r. Also, Donald McGinn, *The Admonition Controversy* (New Brunswick, 1949), pp. 218–19; Richard L. Greaves, *Society and Religion in Elizabethan England* (Minneapolis, 1981), pp. 184–5.

38 *The Sarum Missal*, tr. A. H. Pearson (London, 1844), p. 552. See also 'The Form of Solemnization of Matrimony' as given in *The Book of Common Prayer*, pp. 290–3.

39 Canterbury Cathedral Archives (hereafter, CCA), X.10.20, 173–6.

40 Painter, p. 174.

41 Henry Consett, *The Practice of the Spiritual or Ecclesiastical Courts* (London, 1685), p. 76.

42 On the relation between the definition of a 'court' of law and the presence of the monarch, see Baker, *The Legal Profession*.

43 Raine, *Depositions*, pp. 238–40. See also Furnivall, *Child-Marriages*, pp. 187–96 (Edmund v. Bird) and pp. 65–7 (Sothworth v. Sothworth); Raine, *Depositions*, p. 243 (Grynwill v. Groundye).

44 *Rhetoric*, 3.11.1, 3.11.4, and 3.10.6, in *The Rhetoric and Poetics of Aristotle*, tr. W. Rhys Roberts and Ingram Bywater, ed. Friedrich Solmsen (New York, 1954). The potential of the image for being an instrument of proof is a well established concept in Aristotle and emerges from a collateral reading of the *De Anima* and *Nichomachean Ethics*. On the provenance of this notion in Renaissance England, see Kathy Eden, *Poetic and Legal Fictions in the Aristotelian Tradition* (Princeton, 1986), pp. 69–111.

45 CCA, X.10.17, 152v. See also ibid., X.10.12, 182–v.

46 Furnivall, *Child-Marriages*, p. 57.

47 'Legal fiction' may be roughly defined as a lie perpetrated with official or institutional authorization, in the interest of the commonweal. On 'legal fiction', see Ian Maclean, *Meaning and Interpretation in the Renaissance: The Case of Law* (Cambridge, 1992), pp. 138–42.

48 On Swinburne's upholding of legal presumption in 'such a favourable matter' as marriage, see *Spousals*, pp. 88, 98, 103 and 149.

49 On the contemporary English stereotype of Italy, see Roger Ascham's interpolation at the end of the first part of his *Scholemaster* (*c.* 1570), quoted in

Jacobs's introduction to Painter, p. xix. See also Thomas Nashe, *The Unfor-*
tunate Traveller in R. B. McKerrow, ed., *The Works of Thomas Nashe* (Oxford,
1958), vol. II, pp. 301–2.

50 See Quentin Skinner and Russell Price, ed., *Machiavelli: 'The Prince'*
(Cambridge, 1988) (hereafter, *The Prince*), Chap. XXVII for the discussion
of Caesar Borgia's prudence and ability (*prudentia* and *virtu*) manifested by
his alertness to *occasione*, i.e. his recognition of the right opportunity and his
acting upon it. See also Chap. XXI. Also relevant to this discussion is Machiavelli's stress on flexibility and adaptability to a particular circumstance or
fortuna with all its limitations – see *The Prince*, Chap. XXV, pp. 85–7. This
recipe for success is exactly what Helena's compromises are based on. Its
link with prudence in Machiavelli, as stated in Chap. XV, is also an element
in Helena's personality.

51 See Cole, *The 'All's Well' Story*, chap. II, esp. pp. 19–20, on the honour ac-
corded to human effort, ability, and ingenuity in Boccaccio. See also Lorna
Hutson, 'Fortunate Travelers: Reading for the Plot in Sixteenth-Century
England', *Representations*, 41 (1993), 83–103, on the 'transformative virtues'
of prudence, enterprise and pursuit of occasion in Italian *novellae* and in
Machiavelli, esp. pp. 88–90, 97, 99.

52 See W. Baildon, *Les Reportes del Cases in Camera Stellata 1593–1609* (1849), pp.
39 and 161; Bedfordshire Record Office, L28/46. See also W. R. Prest, 'Law
and Women's Rights in Early Modern England', *The Seventeenth Century*, 6
(1991), 169–87; 182.

53 Cp. the function of Juliet's 'plenteous womb' in *Measure for Measure*, which
'expresseth [Claudio's] full tilth and husbandry' to the public gaze (1.4.42–3).

54 See Ingram, *Church Courts*, pp. 219–23, esp. p. 219.

55 Ibid., 223–6.

56 Houlbrooke,*Church Courts*, p. 76.

57 See L. A. Montrose, ' "Shaping Fantasies": Figurations of Gender and Power
in Elizabethan Culture', *Representations* 1:2, Spring, 1983, 61–94 (72–3). For
a historical study of the evolution of embryology, see J. Cole, *Early Theories
of Sexual Generation* (Oxford, 1930).

58 Painter, vol. I, pp. 178–9.

59 See NNRO Dep. 4B, 30v; Dep. 5B, 173v; both cited in Houlbrooke, *Church
Courts*, p. 77 (n. 74).

60 Ingram, 'Spousals', p. 47.

61 Ibid., p. 210.

62 Ibid., 210–11. See also G. R. Quaife, *Wanton Wenches and Wayward Wives:
Peasants and Illicit Sex in Early Seventeenth-Century England* (London, 1979),
pp. 218–20.

63 Salisbury Diocesan Records, deposition books preserved in the Wiltshire
Record Office (hereafter, WRO), D1/26, 136v–137v; 140r–141v.

64 See, for instance, J. T. Fowler, ed., *Acts of Chapter of the Collegiate Church
of St. Peter and Wilfred, Ripon, 1452–1506*, Surtees Society 64, 1875,
p. 31 ff.

65 Ingram, *Church Courts*, p. 225. See, for example, Office v. Rowden, WRO (1612), AS/ABO 11; and Office v. Greene (1621), WRO, AW/ABO 5.

66 See W. Hale Hale, *A series of precedents and proceedings in criminal causes extending from the year 1475 to 1640; extracted from act-books of ecclesiatical courts in the diocese of London* (1847), p. 44; Stone and Cozens-Hardy, *Norwich*, p. 90.

67 *All's Well*, 1.3.90–1.

68 T. E., *The lawes resolution of women's rights: or, the lawes provision for women* (London, 1632), p. 4.

69 On the jurisprudential debate on whether law was a science or an art, the conflicting visions of the status of law, and the argument for law emerging as an 'unphilosophical mixture of the necessary and the contingent in jurisprudence' that was 'in fact superior to that of philosophy', see Maclean, *Meaning*, pp. 20–9. See also Donald Kelley, 'Vera Philosophia. The Philosophical Significance of Renaissance Jurisprudence', in *History, Law and the Human Sciences: Medieval and Renaissance Perspectives* (London, 1984), pp. 267–79. On the history of the idea of probability, see Ian Hacking, *The Emergence of Probability: a Philosphical Study of Early Ideas about Probability, Introduction and Statistical Inference* (Cambridge, 1975), and Douglas Lane Patey, *Probability and Literacy Form: Philosophic Theory and Literary Practice in the Augustan Age* (Cambridge, 1984), esp. pp. 3–74.

The scandal of Shakespeare's Sonnets

Margreta de Grazia

Of all the many defences against the scandal of Shakespeare's Sonnets –
Platonism, for example, or the Renaissance ideal of friendship – John
Benson's is undoubtedly the most radical. In order to cover up the fact
that the first 126 of the Sonnets were written to a male, Benson in his
1640 *Poems: Written by Wil Shake-speare. Gent.* changed masculine pronouns
to feminine and introduced titles which directed sonnets to the young
man to a mistress. By these simple editorial interventions, he succeeded
in converting a shameful homosexual love to an acceptable heterosexual one, a conversion reproduced in the numerous reprintings of the
1640 *Poems* up through the eighteenth century. The source for this account is Hyder E. Rollins's authoritative 1944 variorum Sonnets, the first
edition to detail Benson's pronominal changes and titular insertions.[1]
Subsequent editions have reproduced his conclusions, for example John
Kerrigan's 1986 edition which faults Benson for inflicting on the Sonnets 'a series of unforgivable injuries', above all 'a single recurring revision: he emended the masculine pronouns used of the friend in 1 to
126 to "her", "hers", and "she" '.[2] With varying degrees of indignation and amusement, critical works on the Sonnets have repeated the
charge.

The charge, however, is wrong. Benson did not attempt to convert a
male beloved to a female. To begin with, the number of his alterations
has been greatly exaggerated. Of the seventy-five titles Benson assigned
to Shakespeare's sonnets, only three of them direct sonnets from the
first group of the 1609 Quarto (sonnets 1–126) to a woman.[3] Furthermore, because none of the sonnets in question specifies the gender of the
beloved, Benson had no reason to believe a male addressee was intended.
As for the pronominal changes, Rollins himself within nine pages of his
own commentary multiplies the number of sonnets 'with verbal changes
designed to make the verses apply to a woman instead of a man' from
'*some*' to '*many*'.[4] Rollins gives three examples as if there were countless

146

others, but three is all there are and those three appear to have been made to avoid solecism rather than homoeroticism. In only one sonnet are pronouns altered, though even there not uniformly.

In Benson's printing of sonnet 101, masculine pronouns are altered to feminine in lines 11 and 14, but masculine (or neutral) pronouns are retained in lines 6 and 9. The alteration may have been made to distinguish the personification 'Truth' from the person of the beloved. In sonnet 104, 'friend' is emended to the more conventional 'fair love', apparently for consistency: the 'fair love' of sonnet 104 corresponds to the twice repeated 'my love' of 105, the sonnet with which it is grouped (along with sonnet 106) to form a single poem entitled 'Constant Affection'. The only other alteration may also have been for the sake of consistency: the emendation of sonnet 108's nonce 'boy' to 'love' avoids the anomaly of a single sonnet addressed to a boy.[5]

Indeed the 1640 collection hardly seems concerned with covering up amatory poems to males. The very first fourteen lines printed in the 1640 *Poems* contain eleven male pronouns, more than any other sonnet, in celebrating an emphatically male beauty. If Benson had wished to censure homoerotic love, why did he not omit the notoriously titillating master–mistress sonnet (20)? Or emend the glamorizing sonnet 106 that praises the beloved – in blazon style, part by part – as the 'master' of beauty? Or the sexually loaded sonnet 110 that apologizes to a specifically male 'god in love' for promiscuity of a decidedly 'preposterous' cast?[6] The same question applies to the numerous sonnets in which references to a male beloved as 'my love', 'sweet love', 'lover', and 'rose' are retained.

It is not Shakespeare's text, then, that has been falsified by Benson but rather Benson's edition that has been falsified by the modern tradition.[7] The question is, why has so patent an error not been challenged before? Certainly it is not for scarcity of copies: while only twelve copies exist of the original 1609 Sonnets, there are that many of the 1640 *Poems* in the Folger Library alone.

I wish to propose that modern treatments of the Sonnets have displaced onto Benson a singularly modern dilemma: what to do with the inadmissible secret of Shakespeare's deviant sexuality?[8] Benson is described as having put an end to that dark secret in the most radical way imaginable, by altering the sex of the beloved and thereby converting an ignominious homosexual passion into a respectable (albeit still adulterous) heterosexual one. In attributing such an act and motive to Benson, modern criticism curiously assumes – indeed posits – the secret it then reviles Benson for concealing. Quite simply, Benson's alleged act

of editorial suppression presupposes something in need of suppression:
there *must* be something horrible at the heart of the sonnets – the first
126 of them – to compel such a dire editorial manoeuvre.

I have dwelled on Benson only parenthetically to set the factual record
straight. My real interest is not in factual error but in the kinds of cultural
imperatives that motivate such errors. I see Benson's error as a glaring
instance of the need to bury a shameful secret deep within the Sonnets.
The need was not Shakespeare's. It has been rather that of Shakespeare
criticism which for the past two centuries has been repeating variants of
the repression it obsessively ascribes to Benson. This repression has, as
I will proceed to argue, produced the very scandal it would deny. At the
same time, it has overlooked the scandal that *is* there, not deep within
the text but right on its surface.

I

This has been the case from the time the Sonnets were first edited: by
Edmond Malone in his 1780 edition.[9] Or, to be more precise, from the
time the Sonnets were first *not* edited: by George Steevens who reprinted
the 1609 Sonnets in a collection of early quartos in 1766 but refused to
edit them for his 1793 edition of Shakespeare's complete works. While
he could justify their publication as documents, he refused to honour
them with an editorial apparatus, the trappings of a classic.[10] Though he
maintained that it was their literary defects that disqualified them, his response to sonnet 20 points to something more visceral: 'It is impossible to
read [it] without an equal mixture of disgust and indignation.'[11] Surely it
is this kind of aversion that prompted his condemnation of Malone's de-
cision to edit them: Malone's 'implements of criticism, like the ivory rake
and golden spade in Prudentius, are on this occasion disgraced by the
objects of their culture'. For Steevens, Malone's attempt to cultivate such
soiled objects as the Sonnets defiled the tools of editing. It was Steevens
then and not Benson who first attempted to conceal the scandal of
Shakespeare's dirty sexuality, not by changing pronouns but by reproducing the Sonnets in the form of a dusty document rather than of a lofty
classic.

Malone, by providing the Sonnets with a textual apparatus in 1780
and then by including them in the canon proper in his 1790 edition of
Shakespeare's Plays and Poems achieved precisely what Steevens had
dreaded: he elevated the Sonnets to the status of literature. But the filth
that embarrassed Steevens remained – remained to be covered up. In
fact, as we shall see, Malone's major editorial ambition in regard to

the Sonnets – to establish the connection between the first person and Shakespeare[12] – made the cover-up all the more urgent: if the Sonnets were in Shakespeare's own voice, what was to be done with the fact that the majority of them expressed desire for a young male?

Malone's driving project of identifying the experience of the Sonnets with Shakespeare's own is evident in all his major editorial interventions. Unlike Benson who expanded their contents to accommodate the experience of all lovers by giving them generic titles, Malone limited them so that they applied exclusively to Shakespeare.[13] His first step was to restrict the Sonnets to two addressees by introducing a division after sonnet 126. With only two beloveds, the task of identifying particulars could begin. First the young man was identified on the assumption that he was the same as the dedication's Mr W. H. Other identifications followed suit: of persons, time, things, circumstances. The dedicator's T. T. was Thomas Thorpe, Spenser was the rival poet, the 'now' of the sonnets was early in Shakespeare's career, the gift referred to in 122 was a table-book given to Shakespeare by his friend, sonnet 111's 'publick means, which publick manners breeds', referred to Shakespeare's own lamentable ties to the theatre, the unfaithful lover of sonnet 93 was Shakespeare's own wife. All of these efforts to give particularity to the Sonnets contributed to Malone's project of personalizing them. His attempts to identify their abundant deictics, what Benveniste has called 'egocentric markers' – their hes and shes, thous and yous, this's and thats, heres and theres – fastened the Sonnets around Shakespeare's 'I'.[14] Thus the experience they recorded could be recognized as that which Shakespeare lived.

The identification proved, as might be anticipated, highly problematic, for there was one connection that could not be allowed: as Malone's own division emphasized, most of the sonnets were addressed to a male. At each of the three points where Malone insisted upon the division at 126, circumlocutions betrayed his unease: although he referred to the addressee of the second group as a 'lady' and 'female', the addressee of the first group was no man or male, but rather 'this person', the majority of the sonnets are '*not* addressed to a female'.[15] The unspeakable, that 126 sonnets were addressed to a *male*, remained literally unspoken; at the same time, the basic division according to the beloved's gender proclaimed it.

Within the text too, Malone had to dodge the implications of his own specification, indeed whenever any of the first 126 sonnets were explicitly erotic or amatory. Footnotes then must strain to distance Shakespeare from their content, as did the note to the notorious sonnet 20: 'such addresses to men, however indelicate, were customary in our author's time, and neither imported criminality, nor were esteemed indeco-rous' (p. 207). Even more belaboured was Malone's rationalization of Shakespeare's references to himself as the 'lover' of the male youth. Here, too, it is not Shakespeare who offends, but rather the custom of his age: and the customary offence was even then not at the level of conduct but at the level of speech. It was 'Such *addresses* to men', '*expressions* of this kind', as well as 'the general *tenour* of the greater part of them' that were 'common in Shakespeare's time, and . . . not thought indecorous' [my emphasis] (pp. 219–20). For Malone, nothing separated his present from Shakespeare's past more than the 'strange' custom among men of *speaking* of other men as their 'lovers'.[16] The offence was linguistic and literary and not behavioural; to censure the Sonnets would, therefore, be as 'unreasonable' as faulting the plays for violating Aristotle's *Poetics* – an anachronistic *literary* judgement (p. 207). Thus for Malone the greatest difference between his late eighteenth-century and Shakespeare's late sixteenth-century was that in Shakespeare's time, male/male desire was a manner of speaking and not doing, whereas in Malone's more en-lightened time it was neither: not done, not even spoken of (hence his repeated euphemisms and circumlocutions).

There is another remarkable instance of how Malone embroils himself in his own editorial commitments. While wanting to read the Sonnets as personal poems, he must impersonalize what his edition foregrounds as their most salient feature: that most of them are addressed to a young male. His longest footnote stretching across six pages pertains to sonnet 93, 'So shall I live supposing thou art true', a sonnet on sexual jealousy. He fastened on this sonnet in full conviction that Shakespeare, in the Sonnets as well as in the plays, wrote with particular intensity on the subject of jealousy because he himself had experienced it; it was his 'in-timate knowledge' of jealousy that enabled him to write on the subject 'more immediately *from the heart*' (p. 266). Malone avoids the scandal that Shakespeare experienced sexual jealousy for a boy by a 'Bensonian' changing of Shakespeare's *boy* to Shakespeare's *wife*, thereby violating his own ascription of the first 126 sonnets to a male, or rather 'not a female'. This weird displacement freed Malone to talk comfortably about Shakespeare's sexual experience – in heterosexual (Shakespeare as cuckold) rather than homosexual terms (Shakespeare as pederast). A digression on his wife's infidelity provided the additional benefit of justi-fying the adulterous liaison that the second group of sonnets recorded – Shakespeare was unfaithful to his wife because she had first been unfaith-ful to him. Realizing the danger of such inferences, Steevens (in the notes he contributed to Malone's edition) attempted to block it by insisting that the poem reflected not Shakespeare's *experience* but his *observation*, an impersonal rather than a personal relation (pp. 266–8). Malone stuck fast to his position, finding grounds for Shakespeare's experience of jealousy in documents, anecdotes, and the plays themselves.

James Boswell the younger, when he completed Malone's edition of *The Plays and Poems* in 1821, sided with Steevens, ruling Malone's conviction as 'uncomfortable conjecture'.[17] The judgement was unusual for Boswell, for throughout the twenty-one volume edition he rarely contradicted his friend and mentor. Yet his comments on the Sonnets opposed Malone with astonishing frequency. Indeed it would be fair to say that Boswell dismantled all of the connections Malone had worked so hard to forge between the Sonnets and Shakespeare's experience. The reason is clear: Boswell wanted to counteract the impression that Malone's 1780 edition, reissued in 1790, had produced: it is 'generally admitted that the poet speaks in his own person' (p. 219). Boswell, in the preliminary and concluding remarks with which he bracketed Malone's edition, as well as in scattered internal notes, attempted to stifle all autobiographical possibilities, beginning with Malone's opening identification of 'the individual to whom they were principally addressed, and the circumstances under which they were written'. The Sonnets could not have been addressed to any real nobleman for none, according to Boswell, would have tolerated such effeminizing verse. Any 'distinguished nobleman' would have taken offence at the 'encomiums on his beauty, and the fondling expressions' appropriate only to a 'cocker'd silken wanton' (p. 219). Thus such amorous language could not have been 'customary' between men in Shakespeare's time, as Malone had insisted, for it would have implied that men were effeminate. For Boswell, male desire for males could not have been an acceptable way of even speaking, even back then. For him, male/male desire existed nowhere (in England anyway), not in Shakespeare's past, not in his own present; not in language, not in deed. It was sheer make-believe: what Boswell terms, not unsalaciously, 'effusions of fancy . . . for the amusement of a private circle' (p. 220).

To establish their status as 'fancy', Boswell must sever all the connections Malone had forged between the Sonnets and Shakespeare's life. And so he does, one by one: Shakespeare was as young as thirty-four or at most forty-five when writing the sonnets so how could it be he who is represented as old and decrepit in several sonnets? Of course, it is not the association with old age (or with the theatre) that disturbed Boswell, but the logical extension of *any* connection: 'If Shakespeare was speaking of himself in this passage, it would follow that he is equally pointed at upon other occasions' (p. 220). More specifically, if it was Shakespeare who was old then it was also he who was 'grossly and notoriously profligate', the perpetrator of ' "harmful deeds" ', whose ' "name had received a brand" ', and whose reputation suffered from the ' "impression which vulgar scandal stamped upon his brow" '. Such identifications were, Boswell insisted, absurd, for among the extant biographical materials 'not the slightest imputation [was] cast upon his character'. This is not surprising, for Malone and Boswell in their *New Life of Shakespeare* had rejected as factually inaccurate the numerous scandalous anecdotes that had cast him in the shady roles of poacher, adulterer, and carouser.[18]

If Boswell found any fault at all in Shakespeare, it was for his 'selection of topics', his representation in any form of male/male desire. But Boswell legitimized this choice by attributing it to Shakespeare's altogether admirable 'fondness for classical imitation' (p. 221). Boswell now is at last able to name the unspeakable topic, though only in simultaneously disavowing it: and not in his own words, but in words properly removed from his own by quotation marks and from standard English by sixteenth-century old spelling. The quotation is from Webbe's *Discourse of English Poetrie* that defends Virgil's second eclogue by insisting that the poet 'doth not meane … any disordered loue, or the filthy lust of deuillish Pederastice' (p. 221).[19] Boswell keeps a clean distance from the 'filthy' object as if afraid of dirtying his ivory rake and golden spade. Having dismantled all of Malone's connections, Boswell can conclude with a discussion of the Sonnets' literary merits, the only relevant consideration after they have been wrenched from toxic reality and consigned to innocuous fancy.

I have discussed the Malone (1780, 1790) and the Malone/Boswell (1821) editions because it is with them that the modern history of the Sonnets begins, and since no full edition of the 1609 Quarto was printed prior to Malone's, that belated history can be considered their *only* history.[20] They have the further importance of having established the two critical approaches that have repeated themselves for two centuries now – sometimes ingeniously, sometimes hysterically: (1) Malone's – the Sonnets are about Shakespeare but not as a lover of young men or, (2) Boswell's – the Sonnets are not about Shakespeare or anything else, especially not about Shakespeare as a lover of young men. Though these approaches are antithetical and mutually exclusive, it must be stressed that both are motivated by the same urgency to deny Shakespeare's desire for a male.

In this regard the history of the Sonnets' reception provides a stunning example of the phenomenon Jonathan Dollimore has recently identified: the centrality of homosexuality in a culture that denounces it.[21] The denial of homosexuality in the Sonnets has produced the two polarized approaches by which they have been traditionally read for two centuries. Furthermore, what has been denied (by evasions, displacements, circumlocutions, suppressions, abstractions, etc.) has slipped into the text itself producing (as if from the Sonnets themselves) an hermeneutical interior capable of concealing a sin, a crime, a pathology. The unspeakable of Sonnets criticism has thus become the unspoken of the Sonnets – to the exclusion of, as has yet to be seen, what they quite forthrightly say.

II

I now wish to turn to one of Malone's major editorial acts, his division of the sonnets into two gendered groups, 126 to a young man, the remaining twenty-eight to a woman. The division has been generally accepted. It seems, after all, quite obvious: none of the first 126 sonnets are addressed explicitly to a woman and none of the remaining twenty-eight are addressed explicitly to a male. *Explicitly* is the key word, for what Malone's clear-cut division has obscured is the astonishing number of sonnets that do *not* make the gender of the addressee explicit.[22] Shakespeare is exceptional among the English sonneteers (Sidney, Spenser, and Daniel, for example) in leaving the beloved's gender unspecified in so many of the sonnets: about five-sixths of them in the first 126 and just less than that in the collection entire. The uncertainty of the beloved's gender is sustained by other types of ambiguity, most notoriously in the 'master-mistress' sonnet 20, but also in sonnet 53 in which the youth is described as a paragon of both masculine and feminine beauty, of both Adonis and Helen; similarly, a variety of epithets recur that apply to either sex: rose, friend, love, lover, sweet, fair.

The little evidence we have of how the Sonnets were read before Malone strongly suggests that the first 126 sonnets were not read as being exclusively to a male. Benson assumed that the sonnets were to a female unless otherwise specified, as the titles he assigned to his groupings indicate.[23] So too did the numerous eighteenth-century editors who reprinted Benson: Gildon (1723) referred to them as 'being most to his Mistress' and Sewell (1725) believed them to have been inspired by 'a real, or an imaginary Lady'.[24] Independent of Benson, there is further and earlier evidence. Gary Taylor has discussed five manuscript versions of sonnet 2 from the early decades of the seventeenth century with the title 'To one that would die a maid';[25] there is also a 1711 reprint of the 1609 quarto that describes the collection as '154 Sonnets all of them in Praise of his Mistress.'[26] The eighteenth-century antiquarian William Oldys who possessed a copy of the quarto assumed that some of the first 126 sonnets were addressed to a female, and George Steevens defended his logic: 'From the complaints of *inconstancy*, and the praises of *beauty*, contained in them, [the Sonnets] should seem at first sight to be addressed by an inamorato to a mistress'.[27] Malone's preliminary note announcing the division at 126 literally prevented such a 'first sight', precluding the possibility open to earlier readers of assuming the ungendered sonnets to a female.

This is not, however, to say that Malone got it wrong: clearly no sonnets are addressed to a female in the first 126 and none to a male (except Cupid) in the subsequent twenty-eight. Just as clearly, the poet abandons the young man in 126 and declares his allegiance to a mistress in 127 and the formal irregularities (twelve pentameter lines in couplets) may punctuate that shift.[28] Nor is there any reason not to take 144's announcement – 'Two loves I have': 'a man right fair' and 'a woman, colour'd ill' – at face value. Some kind of binary division appears to be at work.[29] The question is whether that division is best described in terms – or *only* in terms – of gender difference: in terms, that is, of the object choices that have lent themselves so readily to the modern distinction between homosexuality and heterosexuality.[30]

For that construction of desire – as Foucault's expansive history of sexuality as well as Alan Bray's concentration on the Renaissance have demonstrated[31] – depended on a construal of the body and of the psyche that postdated Shakespeare, like Malone's edition itself, by about two centuries. It may then be that Malone's overly emphatic division of the Sonnets into male/female appears more in keeping with the cultural preoccupations at the turn of the eighteenth century than of the sixteenth. It may be symptomatic of a much later emphasis on sexual differentiation, one that has been fully charted out recently in Thomas Laqueur's *Making Sex: Body and Gender from the Greeks to Freud*.[32]

According to Laqueur, 'Sometime in the eighteenth century, sex as we know it was invented.'[33] What he means by this bold pronouncement is that until then there was essentially one sex rather than two. According to the classical or Galenic model, the female possessed an inverted, interior, and inferior version of male genitalia; as countless anatomical drawings attest, the uterus was imagined as an inverted scrotum, the vagina an inverted penis, the vulva an inverted foreskin. Reproductive processes as well as parts were also on par, so that conception required orgasm from both male and female. Not until the eighteenth century were male and female typically divided into two discrete sexes with distinct reproductive parts and processes: hence the invention of 'sex as we know it'. The shift is reflected in an array of verbal and graphic representations: the construction of a different skeleton for women than for men; anatomical drawings representing incommensurate reproductive structures rather than homologous ones; the division of formerly shared nomenclature into male and female so that once ungendered sperm, testicles, and stones are gendered male and differentiated from female eggs and ovaries. In short, a reproductive biology was constructed based on *absolute* rather than *relative* difference. It is only then, Laqueur notes, that the expression 'opposites attract' is coined, suggesting that 'natural' sexual attraction is between unlikes rather than likes.[34]

As Laqueur points out, this reconstrual removed sexuality from a vast system of metaphysical correspondences based, like society itself, on hierarchical order and situated it firmly in the body or 'nature'. That a woman was previously imagined to possess less perfected versions of male genitalia legitimized her subordination to man. Biology thus upheld social hierarchy. Once difference was grounded in the body rather than in metaphysics, once male and female anatomy was perceived as incommensurate rather than homologous, then sexuality lost its 'social' bearings and became instead a matter of 'nature'. As Laqueur insists repeatedly, and as his characterization of the shift as an *invention* rather than as a *discovery* suggests, the change represents no empirical or scientific advance – 'No discovery or group of discoveries dictated the rise of the two-sex model'[35] – but rather a cultural and political reorientation. Malone's division of the Sonnets may best be understood in the context of this reorientation.

There is another shift that strangely corresponds to both Malone's twofold division and biology's two-sex model, and it occurs at roughly the same point in time. In eighteenth-century grammars and discussions of grammar, a new attention to linguistic gender binaries appears. The hierarchy preserved in the one-sex model had also applied in questions of grammatical agreement: male gender prevailed over female because it was the 'more worthy' gender. In his popular rhetoric (1553), Thomas Wilson considered natural order violated when women preceded men in a syntactic construction, since man was clearly the dominant gender. In his official Latin Grammar (1567), William Lyly assumed the same

principle in explaining that an adjective describing both a male and female noun must agree with the male ('Rex et Regina Beati') because
'The masculine gender is more worthy than the feminine.'[36] In the eighteenth century, however, this ontological and grammatical hierarchy has
ceased to be self-evident. And the reason appears to be that grammar
now looks to biology rather than to metaphysics for its lead. New discoveries in biology are brought to bear on grammar, so that it is maintained that the discovery that plants have sexes introduced inconsistency
into classical grammar's classification of plants as neuter.[37] In highly
gendered languages like German, a general rethinking of conventional
grammatical gender occurs. In English that possesses no conventional
grammatical gendering, the problem took a more focused form. Towards
the end of the eighteenth century, the first call for an epicene or gender-
neutral pronoun is heard, in response to what is only then perceived as
a problem: what to do with constructions like '*everyone* should go to *his*
place' where a female and male antecedent is represented by the male
'his'.[38] As in biology, grammar can no longer assume an hierarchical
relation between male and female to justify the predominance of male
gender.

It is not only in relation to the third person that hierarchy disappears;
in English, it had also by the start of the eighteenth century disappeared
from the second person. In standard English, *thee/thou* had been dropped
in favour of *you*, collapsing the complexly nuanced range of distinctions
based on class relations. It is curious that Malone, who took great pride in
noting philological difference in Shakespeare's age, ignored the second
person pronoun while focusing on the third. Several recent critics, however, have discussed it, noting that the first 126 sonnets vacillate between
you and *thou*, while the second twenty-eight consistently stick to *thou*.[39]
Their explanations have been varied, contradictory and incomplete; the
highly complex code remains unbroken. What can be ventured, however, is that the unwritten rules governing second person usage in the
Renaissance were social and hierarchic.[40] They originated in social rank,
though clearly complicated by a calculus of differentials that included
age, gender, education, experience, race, ethical worth, emotional stake,
etc.[41]

This is not to propose a new division, the first 126 to 'you/thou' the
next twenty-eight to 'thou'[42] – but rather to suggest that gender difference is not the *only* way to differentiate the Sonnets' 'Two loves'. There
are other forms of otherness that the Malonean or modern tradition
has ignored. Sexual difference is only one differential category in these

poems, class is another, so is age, reputation, marital status, moral pro-
bity, even physical availability. In each of these categories, the poet is
more like the mistress than like the youth; love of like would, therefore,
incline him more to the mistress than the boy. It is because Joel Fineman's awesome *Shakespeare's Perjured Eye: The Invention of Poetic Subjectivity
in the Sonnets* limits difference to sexual difference that its argument is
so troubling. Far more relentlessly and consequentially than any one
since Malone, Fineman has emphasized the distinction between male
and female; indeed, it is fundamental to his Lacanian account of the
constitution of subjectivity. The rupturing transition required by this account occurs, for Fineman, in the move from homosexual love of the
same to heterosexual love of the other, from the ideal specularity of the
youth to the false linguistics of the mistress, a move that readily translates into the Lacanian break from the imaginary into the symbolic. In
short, Fineman bases what may be the vastest claim ever made for the
Sonnets – that they invent poetic subjectivity for the western tradition –
on sexual difference, on that rupturing but constitutive transition from
a like and admired object to an unlike and loathed one.[43] Yet in light
of the biological and grammatical phenomena we have been attending,
Fineman's construal of sexual difference is premature. The 'Invention of
Poetic Subjectivity' he attributes to Shakespeare must await 'the invention of sex' Laqueur sees as an eighteenth-century phenomenon. Until
male and female can be seen as two discrete sexes rather than variants
on one sex, how can subjectivity be constituted in the break between the
two?

It is because Fineman overstresses the gender division at sonnet 126
that his study might be seen as the culmination of the Malonean tradition.
Focus on male/female difference lends itself too readily to a psychosexu-
ality that excludes the psychosocial. If social distinctions like class or even
age were introduced, for example, the entire Lacanian progression would
be turned on its head, for the poet would experience the youth's aristocratic otherness *before* the mistress's bourgeois sameness, his extreme
junior *before* his approximate peer. How, then, would it be possible to
make the transition Lacanian subjectivity requires from imaginary identification to symbolic dislocation? I've put the burden of two centuries of
criticism on Fineman's massively difficult book in order to make a very
simple point: tradition has postulated (and concealed) in the Sonnets a
sexual scandal that is based in the personal abstracted from the social,
on a biology of two-sexes rather than on an epistemology of one-sex, on
a division according to a gendered third person rather than a ranked

second person. As I will show in the remainder of this paper by turning –
at long last – to the Sonnets themselves, this has been a mistake . . . so *big*
a mistake that the real scandal has been passed over.

III

The ideological force of the imperious first line of the Sonnets has gone
virtually unnoticed: 'From fairest creatures we desire increase.'[44] In the
first seventeen poems which have traditionally (and rather preciously)
been titled the procreation sonnets, there can be no pretence of *fair* being either an abstract value like the Platonic Good or a disinterested one
like the Kantian Beautiful. *Fair* is the distinguishing attribute of the dominant class, not unlike Bourdieu's *taste* that serves both to distinguish the
dominant class and, by distinguishing it, to keep it dominant.[45] The first
seventeen sonnets urging the fair youth to marry and beget a son have an
open and explicit social function: to reproduce, like an Althusserian state
apparatus, the *status quo* by reproducing a fair young man, ideally 'ten for
one' (6). The preservation of the youth preserves his aristocratic family
line, dynasty or 'house': 'Who lets so faire a house fall to decay?' (13). If
such houses are allowed to deteriorate, the social formation would itself
be at risk: hence the general (and conservative) desire to increase 'fairest
creatures' and to convince those privileged creatures that the repair of
their 'beautious roofe' should be their 'chiefe desire' (10). Were these
houses and roofs *un*fair, there would be no cultural imperative to maintain them, just as there is none to reproduce *un*fair (homely) persons:
'Let those whom nature hath not made for store, / Harsh featurelesse,
and rude, barrenly perish' (11); while the youth is 'much too faire, /
To be deaths conquest and make wormes thine heire,' (6) the 'Harsh,
featureless, and rude' can return to dust unlamented. 'Increase' is to be
desired only from those whom Nature has 'best indow'd' with 'boun-
tious guift' (11); and those gifts are not simply physical or spiritual riches
but the social and material ones that structure society from the top. For
this reason, it is only the fair lineaments of fair lineages that should be
reproduced for posterity – 'Thou shouldst print more, not let that coppy
die.'
   Underscoring the social concerns of this first group is their origin in
pedagogical materials designed to cultivate fair young men. As has long
been noted, these sonnets derive from Erasmus' 'Epistle to persuade a
young gentleman to marriage', Englished in Thomas Wilson's widely influential 1553 *The Arte of Rhetorique*.[46] The treatise was used in schools as

a rhetorical exercise in persuasion. Languet repeated it in a letter to the young Sidney and Sidney in turn echoed it in his *Arcadia*, that consummate expression of aristocratic ethos. The treatise's tropes and arguments attained commonplace status, as is suggested by the seventeenth-century popularity of the sonnet that deploys the most of them, sonnet 2, copies of which survive in twelve early manuscripts.[47] It seems likely, then, that these opening sonnets would have evoked the pedagogical context which prepared fair young men to assume the social position to which high birth entitled them. The 'private friends' among whom according to Francis Meres these sonnets circulated as well as the patron to whom the collection is ostensibly dedicated can be assumed to have recognized this rhetoric as a blueprint for reproducing the fair values of the dominant class.[48]

Shakespeare's 'Two loves' relate to this opening set piece quite explicitly: after sonnet 17, it is through his own poetic *lines* rather than the youth's generational *loins* that fair's lineaments are to be reproduced, fair's lineage extended.[49] The fair line ends, however, at 127 with the shocking declaration that 'now is blacke beauties successive heire'. As if a black child had been born of a fair parent, a miscegenating successor is announced, one who razes fair's lineage ('And Beautie slandered with a bastard shame') and seizes fair's language ('beauty hath no name') – genealogy and etymology. Desire inverts its object at this breaking point: from an embodiment of a social ideal to an embodiment of a social atrocity. In praising the youth's fair lineaments, social distinction had been maintained; in praising the mistress's dark colours, social distinction is confounded. This reverses the modern ranking of the 'Two loves' that has found one unspeakable and the other simply regrettable. For the love of the youth 'right fair' which tradition has deemed scandalous promotes a social programme while the love for the mistress 'collour'd ill' which tradition has allowed threatens to annihilate it.

This is a sign, I think, that there is something misleading about the male/female categories by which Malone divided the collection: they too easily slip into the post-Enlightenment categories of homosexual and heterosexual which provoke responses that are precisely the inverse of what the Sonnets themselves call for. I would like to propose instead that the two groups be reconsidered under rubrics available in the period, appearing in E. K.'s note to the *Shepherdes Calendar* defending Hobbinol's passion for young Colin Clout on the grounds that 'paederastice [is] much to be preferred before *gyne*rastice, that is the love that inflameth men with lust toward womankind'.[50] Unlike homosexual and heterosexual, the terms better correspond with Shakespeare's 'better' and 'worser' loves, his pederastic love of a boy ('my lovely Boy', 126) and gynerastic love of a womb (the irresistible 'waste of shame', 129).[51] As E. K. specifies, pederastic love is 'much to be preferred' over gynerastic, and the Sonnets demonstrate why: because it does not imperil social distinction.

Indeed the poet's main task in the first group is to protect those distinctions, a task that takes the specific form of preserving the youth's lineaments from Time's disfigurations. Shakespeare's 'pupill pen' is in contest with 'Times pensel' (16). In his own verse lines, he would transcribe the youth's fair features before 'confounding Age' unfairs them by cross-hatching his physiognomic lineaments with 'lines and wrincles' (63), cancelling or deleting the youth's fair copy, rendering him thereby 'featurelesse' like those consigned to perish barrenly – as if to make him indistinguishable from the 'Harsh' and 'rude'. In the gynerastic group, however, it is not Time but Lust that threatens distinction. Lust mars not through the sharp incisions of Time's stylus – its pen-knife – but through the obscuring adulterations of 'a woman colour'd ill'. While Time's deadly scriptings disfigure what is seen, Lust's murky adulterations confound what is known. Once a black mistress preempts the fair youth, a whole range of epistemological distinctions collapse: between black and fair (131, 132) to be sure, but also between truth and lies (138); private and public (137); first person and second, first person and third (135–6); past, present, and future (129); is and is not (147), worst and best (150), angel and friend (144). In the first group, though aging himself ('Beated and chopt with tand antiquitie' (62)), the poet sets himself up as Time's adversary, his own glamourizing lines counteracting Time's disfiguring marks; in the second group, however, Lust and Will are familiars rather than adversaries, so much so that Will is literally synonymous with Lust in 135 and 136, and Lust personified blurs into Will's person in 129. Pederasty's 'Pupil Pen' reinscribes the pedagogical ideal with which the Sonnets begin; while the gynerastic 'waste of shame' adulterates even the most black and white distinctions.

This is not to say that love of the youth is altogether 'of comfort'. The majority of the sonnets to him register intense longing, humiliation, loss felt and anticipated, betrayal, and even worse, self-betrayal – all the result, perhaps, of a cultural overinvestment in 'fairest creatures'. Yet the cost is nothing in comparison with what gynerasty exacts.[52] As the promiscuous womb threatens social order, so too gynerasty threatens psychic stability. Will himself takes on the hysterical attributes of the womb that obsesses him, in the breathlessly frantic copulatives of 129, in the semantic confusions listed above which in sonnet 147 he calls 'mad mans' discourse. There could be no more shocking manifestation of his hysteria than sonnet 136 in which every word could be said to signal his desire, homonymically or synonymically.[53] This maniacal repetition is audible in '*Will*, will fulfill the treasure of thy loue, / I fill it full with wils, and my will one', but it is present in all the sonnet's phonetic variables as well, reducing their signification to the tautological deadlock of 'Will wills will'. Nor is Will ever released from this uterine obsession; like all men in sonnet 129, he does not know how to avoid the sulphuric pit (144), how 'To shun the heauen that leads men to this hell' (129); hence the fatal return in the final two Anacreontics to his mistress's genital 'eye', her inflammatory and unquenchable 'Well'.[54]

But the real horror of gynerasty is social and general rather than personal and particular. Edgar in *Lear* contemns Goneril's royal womb adulterated by the bastard Edmund as 'indinguish'd [*sic*] space of Womans will'.[55] It is precisely this failure of discrimination that characterizes the dark lady's sexual capacity, as is evidenced by her indiscrete admission of Wills. In these sonnets it is not only common names that lose distinction, but also proper. Men named Will are indistinguishable: Will Shakespeare would be among them, and perhaps Will of the dedication's Mr W. H., and perhaps the mistress's husband is also Will, but what difference does it make when Will like *Homo* (like 'sausie Iackes' too) is a common name to all?[56] Repeatedly in these sonnets the indiscriminate womb is contrasted with that exclusive treasured 'place' or 'viall' (6) in which the youth's purely aristocratic seed would be antiseptically distilled or 'pent in walls of glasse' (5). The 'large and spacious' place that is the focus of desire in the second group is no such discerning 'seuerall plot': it is 'the wide worlds common place' (137) and primarily an incontinently liquid one – 'the baye where all men ride' (137) and 'sea all water, [that] yet receiues raine still' (135) – in which all distinctions of blood bleed into one another.

As the law itself under Elizabeth confirmed by more severely prosecuting fornication between men and women than between men, nothing threatens a patriarchal and hierarchic social formation more than a promiscuous womb. By commingling blood-lines, it has the potential to destroy the social fabric itself. The gynecrasty of the Sonnets, then, needs to be considered in terms of the range of sexual practices Alan Bray has foregrounded (among them, bestiality, adultery, rape, and prostitution) that were in the period termed 'sodomy' and associated with such crimes against the state as sorcery, heresy, and treason.[57] There is good reason, therefore, to credit Jonathan Goldberg's recent suggestion that in Renaissance terms, it is Shakespeare's sonnets to the dark lady rather than those to the young man that are sodomitic.[58]

The dark lady's indiscriminate womb images social anarchy no less than Lear's invocation of cosmic cataclysm: 'all germains spill at once'.[59] The germains spill serially in the mistress rather than all 'at once', but with the same helter-skelter randomness, *including those of the fair youth*, so that his noble seed is intermixed with that of common 'sausie Iackes' (128) and of unnumbered intercoursing 'Wills'.[60] The patriarchal dream of producing fair young men turns into the patriarchal nightmare of a social melting pot, made all the more horrific by the fact that the mistress's *black* is the antithesis not just of fair but of *white*. Tradition has been ever slower to entertain the possibility that these poems express desire for a black woman rather than desire for a boy. But the important work that is being done on England's contact with Africa and on its cultural representations of that contact is making it increasingly difficult to dissociate in this period blackness from racial blackness – black from blackamoor – promiscuity from miscegenation, especially in a work that begins by arguing for the perpetuation of pure fair blood.[61]

This paper began with one traditional error and ends with another. The first was minor, an erroneous representation of Benson's publishing efforts. The last, however, is quite major. The scandal in the Sonnets had been misidentified. It is not Shakespeare's desire for a boy; for in upholding social distinctions, that desire proves quite conservative and safe. It is Shakespeare's gynerastic longings for a black mistress that are perverse and menacing, precisely because they threaten to raze the very distinctions his poems to the fair boy strain to preserve. As with the Benson falsification, it is the motive behind the error that is worth thinking about. And I will end by doing so.

Since the eighteenth century, sexuality has been seen in biological and psychological terms rather than social.[62] Perversion, therefore, is seen as pathological rather than subversive. But in a period in which the distribution of power and property depended on orderly sexuality, it remained imperative that sexuality be understood and judged in social terms. The social consequences of sexual arrangements (whether male–female marriages or male–male alliances) and derangements (male–female adultery or male–male sodomy) was too basic to allow them to become merely personal matters – to become, that is, what they have become in modern sexual discourse: the precondition of personal identity. Modern readings of the Sonnets (the only kind we have) have skewed the relation of

Shakespeare's 'Two loves' to conform with this classification. The result is quite topsy-turvy: readings of the young man sonnets have concealed a personal scandal that was never there; and readings of dark mistress sonnets have been blank to the shocking social peril they promulgate. A category mistake lies at the bottom of this odd hermeneutic: the Sonnets' 'Two loves' have been misclassified, the 'love of comfort' avoided as abnormal and unnatural and the 'love of despaire' countenanced as normal and natural. This essay has argued that a reclassification is in order according to a different system altogether, one that would replace the personal categories of normalcy and abnormalcy with the social ones of hierarchy and anarchy – of desired generation and abhorred miscegenation.

First published in *Shakespeare Survey 46* (1994)

NOTES

1 *A New Variorum Edition of Shakespeare: The Sonnets*, 2 vols. (Philadelphia, Pa. and London, 1944), vol. 2, p. 20, n. 1. Sidney Lee in his introduction to a 1905 facsimile of the Sonnets noted Benson's changes but without itemizing them or speculating on Benson's motives: *Shakespeare Sonnets: Being a Reproduction in Facsimile of the First Edition* (Oxford, 1905), pp. 57–8.

2 *The Sonnets and A Lover's Complaint* (Middlesex and New York, 1986), p. 46.

3 Benson gives the title 'Selfe flattery of her beautie' to sonnets 113–15, 'Upon receit of a Table Booke from his Mistris' to sonnet 122, 'An intreatie for her acceptance' to sonnet 125. See Rollins, *The Sonnets*, vol. 2, pp. 20–1 for a list of Benson's titles.

4 Cf. Rollins, *The Sonnets*, pp. 20 and 29.

5 Benson alters the pronoun from male to female only in the last four lines of the sonnet: 'To make *her* much out-live a gilded tombe'; 'To make *her* seeme, long hence, as *she* showes now' (emphasis added). The masculine pronoun is retained in lines 6 and 9: 'Truth needs no colour with his colour fix'd'; 'Because he needs no praise wilt thou be dumbe?'). Benson, *Poems: Written by Wil. Shake-speare. Gent.* (London, 1640), Ev.

6 See Stephen Booth's gloss to sonnet 110, lines 9–12, pp. 356–7 as well as to sonnet 109, lines 9, 10, 13, 14, pp. 352–3 in *Shakespeare's Sonnets* (New Haven, Conn. and London, 1977).

7 For accounts of how Benson's printing-house and editorial practices have also been maligned, see Josephine Waters Bennett, 'Benson's Alleged Piracy of *Shakespeares Sonnets* and of Some of Jonson's Works', *Studies in Bibliography*, 21 (1968), 235–48. See also Margreta de Grazia, *Shakespeare Verbatim: The Reproduction of Authenticity and the 1790 Apparatus* (Oxford, 1991), p. 49, n. 1, pp. 163–73.

8 On the hysterical response to this problem in modern readings of the Sonnets, see Peter Stallybrass, 'Editing as Cultural Formation: The Sexing

of Shakespeare's Sonnets', *Modern Language Quarterly*, 54 (March, 1993), 91–103.

9 *Supplement to the Edition of Shakespeare's Plays Published in 1778 by Samuel Johnson and George Steevens*, 2 vols. (1780), vol. 2.

10 *Twenty of the Plays of Shakespeare*, 4 vols., ed. George Steevens (1766).

11 Quoted by Rollins, *New Variorum Edition*, vol. 1, p. 55.

12 See de Grazia, *Shakespeare Verbatim*, p. 154.

13 See Ibid., pp. 155–6.

14 For the profusion of deictics in the Sonnets, see Joel Fineman, *Shakespeare's Perjured Eye: The Invention of Poetic Subjectivity in the Sonnets* (Berkeley, Los Angeles, London, 1986), pp. 8–9, pp. 311, n. 6.

15 *The Plays and Poems of William Shakspeare*, 10 vols. (1790; facs. rpt, New York, 1968), vol. 10, pp. 191, 265, 294. Subsequent references to this volume will appear in the text.

16 On 'lover', see Booth, *Shakespeare's Sonnets*, p. 432.

17 *The Plays and Poems of William Shakspeare* (1821; facs. rpt, New York, 1966), vol. 20, p. 309. Page references to this volume will henceforth appear parenthetically in text.

18 For Malone's invalidation of the inculpatory anecdotes, see de Grazia, *Shakespeare Verbatim*, pp. 104–7, pp. 135–41.

19 Boswell corrects Webbe for referring to the eclogue as the sixth ('by a slip of memory, or the printer's mistake') when it should be the fourth (p. 221). Bruce R. Smith situates this eclogue in Renaissance pastoral in 'The Passionate Shepherd', *Homosexual Desire in Shakespeare's England: A Cultural Poetics* (Chicago and London, 1991), pp. 79–115.

20 The 1609 Sonnets were reprinted but without an apparatus by Bernard Lintott in 1711 and by George Steevens in 1766.

21 *Sexual Dissidence: Augustine to Wilde, Freud to Foucault* (Oxford, 1991).

22 See Booth's scrupulous account of the division, p. 430.

23 Rollins aligns the 1640 titles with the 1609 sonnet numbers, vol. 2, pp. 21–2.

24 See de Grazia, *Shakespeare Verbatim*, p. 155, n. 57.

25 'Some Manuscripts of Shakespeare's Sonnets', *Bulletin of The John Rylands University Library*, 68, 1 (1985), 217.

26 Bernard Lintott, *A Collection of poems in Two Volumes . . . Being all the Miscellanies of Mr William Shakespeare, which were Publish'd by himself in the Year 1609 . . .*, 2 vols.

27 Malone and Boswell, *Sonnets*, p. 306.

28 In the 1609 quarto, the irregularity is rendered typographically conspicuous by two sets of empty brackets in place of the final couplet.

29 On the possibility that the Sonnets were organized according to a tripartite structure (152 Sonnets, 2 Anacreontics, a Complaint) based on generic rather than gender difference following the model of Daniel, Spenser, Lodge, and others, see Kerrigan's Introduction to *Sonnets*, pp. 13–14 and the bibliographic references on p. 66.

30 On the taxonomy of 'homo' and 'hetero', see Eve Kosofsky Sedgwick, *The Epistemology of the Closet* (Berkeley and Los Angeles, 1990).

31 Michel Foucault, *The History of Sexuality*, vol. 1: *An Introduction*, trans., Robert Hurley (New York, 1978) and Alan Bray, *Homosexuality in Renaissance England* (London, 1982).

32 (Cambridge, Mass, and London, 1990).

33 p. 149. Laqueur notes the agreement of Michel Foucault, Lawrence Stone, and Ivan Illich in identifying the late eighteenth century as the point at which human sexuality was reconceptualized, p. 5 and n. 14.

34 Laqueur, *Making Sex*, 152.

35 Ibid., 153.

36 *A short Introduction of Grammar* (London, 1530), p. 47.

37 See Dennis Barron, *Grammar and Gender* (New Haven, Conn., 1986) p. 35.

38 Ibid., pp. 190–1.

39 See G. P. Jones, 'You, Thou, He or She? The Master–Mistress in Shakespearian and Elizabethan Sonnet Sequences', *Cahiers Elisabéthains* 19 (1981), 73–84 and Andrew Gurr, 'You and Thou in Shakespeare's Sonnets', *Essays in Criticism*, 32 (1982), 9–25. Arthur F. Marotti is sensitive to the tonal effects of such positionalities in his discussion of how Shakespeare's artistry can compensate for his inferior social rank, in '*Love is not Love*: Elizabethan Sonnet Sequences and The Social Order', *English Literary History*, 49 (1982), 413–16.

40 On the origins of the distinction between *tu/vos* in Latin and *thou/you* in English, see R. Brown and A. Gilman, 'The Pronouns of Power and Solidarity', in T. A. Sebeok, ed., *Style in Language* (Amherst, Mass., 1960), pp. 253–76.

41 The same perplexing instability of address characterizes another male/male couple divided by rank, not to mention age, experience, and size: Falstaff and Hal, who shift constantly from one form to the other as they uneasily jockey for position in a relationship characterized by jockeying, a relationship in which male/male erotic desire is, as Jonathan Goldberg has recently argued, not entirely absent, 'Hal's Desire, Shakespeare's Idaho', in *Henry IV Part One and Two*, ed. Nigel Wood (Philadelphia, 1995), pp. 145–75.

42 Sonnet 145 is the sole exception; it substitutes 'you' for 'thou', in the interest of preserving rhyme: 'I hate, from hate away she threw, / And sau'd my life saying not you'.

43 The book's overinvestment in gender binaries raises troubling political and hermeneutic questions. Its argument that subjectivity is attained through the renunciation of the imaginary realm of homosexual sameness bears a disturbing resemblance to a pseudo-Freudianism that perceives homosexuality as stunted or incomplete development. It also requires that sonnets 1–126 be read as univocal and 127–52 as equivocal, though Fineman later revises this programme by maintaining that equivocation is present in both groups, though only latently in the first.

44 The Sonnets will henceforth be quoted from the facsimile of the 1609
    Shake-speares Sonnets printed in Stephen Booth's edition. Lars Engle has
    recently discussed this first line as inaugurating the Sonnets' concern with
    'human value in time', but without noting the specific class inflection of this
    value, 'Afloat in Thick Deeps: Shakespeare's Sonnets on Certainty', *Publica-
    tions of the Modern Language Association*, 104 (1989), 832–43.

45 Pierre Bourdieu, *Distinction: A Social Critique of the Judgement of Taste*, trans.
    Richard Nice (Cambridge, Mass., 1984).

46 For the influence of this epistle on Shakespeare and others, see Rollins,
    Variorum 1, p. 7 and 11, p. 192, T. W. Baldwin, *The Literary Genetics of Shake-
    speare's Poems and Sonnets* (Urbana, Ill., 1950), pp. 183–5, and Katharine M.
    Wilson, *Shakespeare's Sugared Sonnets* (London and N.Y., 1974), pp. 146–67.

47 See Taylor, 'Some Manuscripts', pp. 210–46.

48 This is not to say that the Sonnets unequivocally reproduce aristocratic value.
    As Thomas M. Greene points out, the thrift and husbandry urged upon the
    young man in the first seventeen sonnets is decidedly bourgeois ('Pitiful
    Thrivers: Failed Husbandry in the Sonnets', *Shakespeare and the Question of
    Theory*, ed. Patricia Parker and Geoffrey Hartman (N. Y. and London, 1985,
    pp. 230–44)). Furthermore, the socially inferior poet (sonnets 25 and 110)
    by taking on the youth's responsibility for reproducing fair in effect assumes
    aristocracy's genetic privilege: his inky poetic lines preempt the youth's fair
    genealogical ones: 'His beautie shall in these blacke lines be seene' (63).

49 For the semantic and homonymic connections between lines and lineaments,
    see William Empson, *Seven Types of Ambiguity* (New York, 1947), pp. 54–5,
    cited by Booth, *Shake-speare's Sonnets*, p. xiii. For the line/loin resonances, see
    Additional Notes to Booth's 1978 edition, p. 579.

50 Kerrigan brings E. K.'s gloss to bear on the Sonnets to conclude that the
    Sonnets register a 'profound homosexual attachment of a scarcely sensual,
    almost unrealized kind', p. 51; Stephen Orgel comments briefly on the
    psychological and legal advantages of 'paederastice' over 'gynerastice' in
    'The Boys in the Back Room: Shakespeare's Apprentices and the Economics
    of Theater', unpublished manuscript. See also Smith's discussion of the
    quote in relation to Virgil and Spenser, (Bruce Smith, *Homosexual Desire in
    Shakespeare's England* (Chicago, 1991)), pp. 95–8.

51 On the identification of woman with womb, see Richard Verstegan: 'And
    as Homo in Latin doth signifie both man and woman, so in our toung the
    feminyne creature also hath as we see the same of man, but more aptly in
    that it is for due distinction composed with womb, *she being that kynde of mann
    that is wombed*, or hath the womb of conception, which the man of the male
    kynd hath not', *The Restitution of Decayed Intelligence* (Antwerp, 1605), p. 194.

52 Stephen Orgel, in commenting on the 'all but axiomatic' love of men for
    boys in the period, refers to the Sonnets as evidence that 'the problem
    of sex between men involves a good deal less anxiety' than between men
    and women, 'Call me Ganymede', *Impersonations: The Performance of Gender in
    Shakespeare's England* (Cambridge, 1996), p. 71.

53 No special case has to be made for 'loue' or 'loue-sute' as synonyms for will, and Booth's commentary supports the equivalence of the sonnet's other nouns ('soule', 'things of great receit', 'stores account', 'treasure', 'number', 'one', 'nothing', and 'none'), pp. 469–73. Verbs also relate to lust: 'come' to climax; 'check' to its deferral; 'knows', 'prooue', 'reckon'd' to forms of carnal knowing; 'fullfill' and 'fill' to orgasm; 'is admitted' and 'hold' to sexual entry. Adjectives express sexual desirables – 'sweet', 'great', 'blind' – and adverbs modify the sexual act, 'so neere', 'thus farre', 'with ease'.

54 On eye as vulva, see Booth, *Shake-speare's Sonnets*, p. 521.

55 *The Tragedie of King Lear*, The Norton Facsimile *The First Folio of Shakespeare*, prepared by Charlton Hinman (New York, 1968), TLN 2724.

56 Paul Ramsey notes that $22\frac{1}{2}$ per cent of all Englishmen were named Will at the end of the sixteenth century, *The Fickle Glass: A Study of Shakespeare's Sonnets* (New York, 1979), p. 23.

57 See Smith, *Homosexual Desire*, esp. pp. 41–53 and Jonathan Goldberg, *Sodometries: Renaissance Texts, Modern Sexualities* (Berkeley, 1992), pp. 18–23.

58 'Hal's Desire, Shakespeare's Idaho', p. 41.

59 *The Tragedie of King Lear*, TLN 1663.

60 The promiscuous dark lady is not unlike Spenser's miscegenating Acrasia ('bad mixture') who razes the estates of her noble lovers in *FQ*, Bk. II, 12.

61 On the racial inflections of fair/dark and black/white in the early modern period, see Ania Loomba, *Gender, Race, Renaissance Drama* (Manchester and New York, 1989), pp. 42–5 and Kim Hall, *Things of Darkness: Economies of Race and Gender in Early Modern England* (Ithaca and London, 1995), pp. 6–15.

62 This paragraph owes much to Dollimore, *Sexual Dissidence*, pp. 236–40 et passim.

Representing sexuality in Shakespeare's plays

John Russell Brown

For the first four decades of the seventeenth century, Robert Burton, scholar, priest, dramatist (in Latin), and bachelor, investigated as best he could the varieties of mental and bodily disorders in people who are driven by desire for another person. His account of 'Love Melancholy', capacious and capricious – and sometimes very shrewd – mixes quotations from authorities of different persuasions with statements based on his own observation and reasoning. Both types of evidence are used to support his view that 'This love is the cause of all good conceits, ... plays, elegancies ... and all the sweetness of our life.' In the words of his own recital of pleasures, love is the reason for making 'all our feasts almost, masques, mummings ... plays, comedies ... etc.' 'Danaus, the son of Belus', he goes on, had 'at his daughter's wedding at Argos, instituted the first plays (some say) that ever were heard of'. Theatre, he concluded, had been invented for love's sake and to give pleasure to lovers.[1]

Theatre's association with love and sexual pleasure was taken for granted among most of Burton's contemporaries, whether they approved of the alliance or not. *Romeo and Juliet* was used as a source of effective phrases to be recycled in pursuit of one's own love.[2] The young John Donne was said to be 'a great visitor of ladies, a great frequenter of plays, a great writer of conceited verses',[3] as if writing the early love poems had satisfied the same nature in much the same way as female company and repeated visits to the theatres. In performance, actors could appear to be sexually driven and their audiences would respond similarly. Jonson's Volpone, preparing to seduce Celia, boasts that

> I am, now, as fresh,
> As hot, as high, and in as jovial plight
> As when in that so celebrated scene
> At recitation of our comedy,
> For entertainment of the great Valois,
> I acted young Antinous, and attracted

The eyes and ears of all the ladies present,
T' admire each graceful gesture, note, and footing.
                                    (*Volpone* 3.7.157–64)

In Chapman's *Widow's Tears* (1605), Hylus, when rehearsing to play
Hymen, 'ravishes all the young wenches in the palace'; at the subsequent performance, one young woman believes he 'does become it most
enflamingly ... he is enamor'd too', and another cries out, 'O, would
himself descend, and me command' (3.2.19–20, and 83, 88, and 107).

Shakespeare's plays are full of sexually arousing incidents. Sexual passion drives the plot of many of them, notably the comedies, early and
late, and *Romeo and Juliet*, *Othello*, and *Antony and Cleopatra*. In *Measure for
Measure*, against his expectation, Angelo gives his 'sensual race the rein'
(2.4.160) and so breaks habits of a life-time. At the very centre of this play
is 'sharp appetite', 'prompture of the blood', 'a pond as deep as hell';
on its surface 'a momentary trick', 'dark deeds', 'a game of tick-tack'
(2.4.161 and 178; 3.1.95 and 115; 3.2.167; 1.1.184–5). This comedy,
alone, could demonstrate that Shakespeare expected his actors to show
the effects of sexual arousal in their performances.

Even in the histories, the same currents must run strongly: the Lady
Margaret, soon to be Queen, is 'enthrall'd' to the Earl of Suffolk
(*1 Henry VI* 5.3.101); Lady Anne forgets her undying hatred and repulsion
in the presence of Richard III; the Princess of France seems to have a
'witchcraft' in her lips that can charm Henry V silent and render him
complaisant (*Henry V* 5.2.175). Sexual passion is not central to *Hamlet*,
Lear, or *Macbeth*, but none of these will be credible unless the audience
senses the force of sexual attraction and appetite as it contributes to the
course of each play's action. So many plays deal outright with sexual
desire and gender difference that anyone wishing to study or stage them
needs to ask how Shakespeare dealt with these subjects and the means
he expected to be used to enact them.

SILENT SEXUALITY

The presentation of sexual passion has very special difficulties for a
dramatist, especially at a time when plays were performed on open stages
almost surrounded by a potentially unruly audience, and usually in day-
light. Words and the activities of public life were the chief means at an
author's disposal in Elizabethan and Jacobean theatres, not a simulation
of the more intimate happenings of real life. Speaking a speech was then
the appropriate way for an actor to demonstrate his quality.

Yet while sexual encounter was not easy to present in such a theatre, Shakespeare did so in a variety of ways, coping with the difficulties as if he took pleasure in overcoming the obstacles. Perhaps his most noteworthy device, in comparison with the practice of his contemporaries, was to draw attention to the inadequacies of words and so make the audience notice a tongue-tied sexual involvement. 'Silence is the perfectest herald of joy', says the enraptured Claudio in *Much Ado About Nothing* when forced to speak: 'I were but little happy if I could say how much' (2.1.275–6).

Silence also grips Orlando when Rosalind approaches him at their first meeting in *As You Like It*: and only after she has left the stage can he speak of the 'passion [that] hangs these weights upon my tongue' (1.2.224–67). Sometimes two lovers are held still, gazing at one another while the words have been given to others: 'at first sight / They have chang'd eyes', says Prospero in one of the silences which mark Ferdinand and Miranda's meeting in *The Tempest* (1.2.110–11). And sometimes a silent exchange involves more than the eyes, as when Goneril, drawn by desire, gives 'strange oeillades and most speaking looks / To noble Edmund' (*Lear* 4.5.25–6).

The first meeting of Isabella and Angelo in *Measure for Measure* has a sequence of silences which grow in length and strangeness until the sexual content of the scene seems to become almost unbearably stifled. Lucio fills in the gaps with comments on the progress of the encounter, and twice Angelo manages to do so, briefly and with amazement as if in a trance. Although not speaking directly of his overwhelming desires, he also manages to address Isabella, but again so briefly that it seems as if he is struggling to hide his feelings. The awkwardness of the encounter grows until everyone has left the stage, saying very little – and then Angelo acknowledges what has happened, at first using short exclamations and bitter questions. The very inadequacies of speech here suggest the resistless force of his sexual arousal: Angelo hardly knows what he does or what he is. He becomes more coherent in speech only as he tries to dismiss all that has happened as if it were a dream (see, especially, 2.2.173, 179).

Silent encounters are not always so tense. In *Troilus and Cressida*, outward signs of the heroine's sexual arousal are described just before she meets Troilus: 'she fetches her breath', says Pandarus, 'as short as a new-ta'en sparrow' (3.2.32–3). When she comes on stage she says nothing, while in her presence Troilus is also 'bereft of all words' until, after a time, he is able to hold her close to him with a kiss. When they do start to talk together, it is to acknowledge their stumbling folly: 'the abruption' of what they say and the 'monstruosity' of their love (3.2.39–95).

Later in the play, when she has been taken off to the Greek camp, Cressida tantalizes her hosts with enticing words, but to the watching Ulysses what she does and what she is are still more provocative:

> There's language in her eye, her cheek, her lip,
> Nay, her foot speaks; her wanton spirits look out
> At every joint and motive of her body.
>
> (4.5.55–7)

In *As You Like It*, sexual desire is said to be sudden and reckless on both sides, like a 'fight of two rams', and its effect brutal and overwhelming, like Julius Caesar conquering Gaul – 'I came, saw, and overcame' (5.2.28–31) – but on this occasion Shakespeare kept the actual encounter offstage and left others to speak of it subsequently.

PREVARICATION AND PASSION

Silence given some definition by either description or later acknowledgement did not solve all Shakespeare's problems when he wished to present sexually driven behaviour. He was to become progressively more skilled at finding the words whereby their speaker could show the processes and the growth of desire. Words sometimes suggest sexual passions by what they do *not* say, rather than by what they do. Prevarications, lies, evasions, hesitations, repetitions, exclamations, clumsy words, and nonsenses can all be more revealing than direct and would-be truthful speeches. An early example of a verbal reaction that reveals hidden desire while trying to hide it is Julia's repetitive and furious words to Lucetta which lead her to tear a letter sent from Proteus, when all the time she is longing to see and read, and ultimately to kiss, that letter (*Two Gentlemen* 1.2.33–140).

In the Nunnery Scene, stumbling and lurching prevarications show the frightening effects of Hamlet's inward passion when he is in the sexually attractive presence of Ophelia. For him, she is either unattainable or else hopelessly corrupt, and so speech becomes repetitive, contradictory, and evasive; it strains, buckles, and breaks down into silence. Choice is difficult between the various readings which have found their way from Shakespeare's manuscripts into the original editions:

OPHELIA   How does your honour for this many a day?
HAMLET   I humbly thank you, well.
       or Thank you, well, well, well.

OPHELIA   My lord, I have remembrances of yours
   That I have longed long to redeliver.
   I pray you now receive them.
     or I pray you now, receive them.
     or I pray you, now receive them.
HAMLET   No, not I.
     or No, no.
   I never gave you aught.
OPHELIA   My honour'd lord, you know right well you did, . . .
     or I know right well you did, . . .   (*Hamlet* 3.1.92–7)

Such talk, torn into fragments, stumbling and then rushing forwards, driven by the force of deep sexual frustration, does not provide the punctuation and smooth transitions with which editors or compositors feel comfortable – or readers or actors either. Its effect in performance is to make the action appear to take place at that level of consciousness where thoughts cross and feelings collide.

In *Othello*, terrible disjunctions of sexually driven speech render words almost useless even as they are being used. They lead on to an epileptic fit, but not before Othello knows that his passion is beyond rational speech: 'It is not words that shakes me thus – pish! – noses, ears, and lips. / Is't possible? Confess! Handkerchief! O devil!' (4.1.41–3).

Verbal reiteration can show terrible sufferings caused by sexual longings and fears, as in Lady Macbeth's calling her husband to bed in her guilt-ridden sleep-walking or the staggering and driving rush into jealousy of Leontes in the very first act of *The Winter's Tale*. In this play, the progress of sexual feeling is towards rather than away from simplicity and silence, as seen at last when Hermione, restored to life, 'hangs about [Leontes'] neck' (5.3.112).

In an opposite and lighter vein, Rosalind recognizes very early on that love can make speech wayward and lunatic, and then proceeds to exemplify this with all the happy wonder of sudden discovery (*As You Like It* 4.1.144; 3.2.370–5). Consciousness of sexuality's madness recurs many times in the comedies: the lovers of *A Midsummer's Night's Dream* know themselves to be 'wode [mad] within this wood' (2.1.192); in *Twelfth Night*, Sebastian argues that 'I am mad / Or else the lady's mad' (4.3.15–16); in *Much Ado*, Benedict finds he can remember only stupid babbling rhymes to express his feelings (5.2.22–37). Perhaps Petruchio and Katharine both learn the truth in what her sister says: 'being mad herself, she's madly mated' (*Taming of the Shrew* 3.2.240).

USES OF BAWDY — AND PERSONIFICATION

When a character is motivated by sexual instincts, a run of *doubles entendres* in his or her words will frequently show what is happening and where the mind is going. In *Much Ado About Nothing*, when Benedict and Beatrice spar with each other about warfare or wit, or about their views of themselves and other people, sexual allusion gallops ahead as if both speakers are willing riders of their most libidinous desires even while they are pretending to be at crossed purposes with each other.

When Rosalind talks about love to Orlando, or to Celia or Touchstone, this bawdiness seems to come unbidden; and so it does between Viola and Feste talking about Orsino, or between Hamlet and almost anyone, talking about almost anything. In Hamlet desire so mixes with fear that in Ophelia's presence at the performance of *The Mousetrap* his obscenities seem a calculated and public affront, or a revulsion so deep that it turns into heedless aggression. Yet bawdiness in Shakespeare's dialogue can also seem benign, an easing of other troubles, as in the 'sweetest morsel of the night' that Doll Tearsheet and Falstaff are about to share or in the teasing wordplay between Katharine of France and Alice and, later, the warlike Henry himself. Between Florizel and Perdita, both dressed as shepherds at a pastoral feast in *The Winter's Tale*, bawdy references slide easily into tenderness and reverence (4.4.127–53).

More directly, words can also bring a heightening of sexual expectation when they are used to call as witnesses the gods, lovers or monsters of Renaissance myth, or to summon memories of fabled dangers or pleasures to evoke an appropriate context. Prospero thus creates for Miranda's betrothal a masque of goddesses who represent female power, harvest riches, and unashamed beauty, and so enacts the 'present fancies' of a loving and apprehensive father for his only child and daughter (*Tempest* 4.1.122).

Almost all the lovers in Shakespeare's plays seem to have such personifications present and alive in their thoughts and talk about them to show the excitement caused by sexual arousal. In the last act of *The Merchant of Venice*, Jessica and Lorenzo, alone at night and at ease on the beautiful hillside of Belmont, play a quiet and teasing game together, calling on great lovers from mythology to identify the feelings of their love and their instinctive fear, in counterpoint to the fuller harmony of music.

Such mythological references have very little to do with book-learning or pedantry, although scholarly notes in modern editions may give that impression. Sometimes an abundance or curiosity of thought indicates mental as well as sensual excitement, but mythological names and stories are commonly used by Shakespeare to represent the boundlessness of sexual fantasies, outstripping ordinary events, and the ever-present sense of sexually attractive bodies which haunt the minds of lovers.

For Perdita, they come almost tumbling out of her memory, as if she is possessed by mythological personages even more than by the delicate sweetness of nature. She responds to these stories as to her own fears and tender feelings:

> O Proserpina,
> For the flower now that, frighted, thou let'st fall
> From Dis's waggon! – daffodils,
> That come before the swallow dares, and take
> The winds of March with beauty; violets, dim
> But sweeter than the lids of Juno's eyes
> Or Cytherea's breath; pale primroses,
> That die unmarried ere they can behold
> Bright Phoebus in his strength – a malady
> Most incident to maids.
>
> (4.1.116–25)

And in *A Midsummer Night's Dream* Helena moves from mythology to fabled beasts and on to generalized abstractions which bite more deeply because of the context that has been provided for them:

> Run when you will; the story shall be chang'd:
> Apollo flies, and Daphne holds the chase;
> The dove pursues the griffin; the mild hind
> Makes speed to catch the tiger – bootless speed,
> When cowardice pursues and valour flies.
>
> (2.1.230–4)

For some characters, the supernatural world of holy scripture serves in much the same way as a carrier of their thoughts. Olivia, intent on possessing Cesario, calls it up in an instant:

> Well, come again to-morrow. Fare thee well;
> A fiend like thee might bear my soul to hell.
>
> (*Twelfth Night* 3.4.206–7)

SEXUALITY AND ACTUALITY

Perhaps Shakespeare's most extraordinary use of words to express sexual desire is the introduction, through metaphor and simile, of references to the everyday procedures of living. These give a tactile actuality to the strange fantasies of sexual desire, a visual clarity, a shift from unmanageable abstractions to direct sensation and the ordinary business of life. By such means the drama is presented in terms – not exclusive to book-learning, wealthy privilege, or rare opportunity – that everyone in the audience will have experienced. Examples are everywhere, from the early *Henry VI* plays to the very latest innovations in Shakespeare's style and dramatic structure. A suckling child comes to the thoughts of the Earl of Suffolk when parting from the Queen, his mistress:

> Here could I breathe my soul into the air
> As mild and gentle as the cradle-babe
> Dying with mother's dug between its lips . . .
> *(2 Henry VI* 3.2.391–3)

Olivia sees Cesario's lip, and her mind at once races on to think of a guilty criminal, night-time and noon, roses and spring-time, and only then comes to the heart of her message:

> O, what a deal of scorn look beautiful
> In the contempt and anger of his lip!
> A murd'rous guilt shows not itself more soon
> Than love that would seem hid: love's night is noon.
> Cesario, by the roses of the spring,
> By maidhood, honour, truth, and every thing,
> I love thee so . . .
> *(Twelfth Night* 3.1.142–7)

Seeing the youth to whom she is attracted, it is her references to everyday experience that give a 'body' to her speech that an audience is able to feel,[4] and by doing so make her strange predicament more accessible to an audience in the theatre.

In *Antony and Cleopatra*, the lovers on their first entry speak with an exaggeration and airy playfulness which could be taken as signs of mere weakness and triviality, and the Roman soldiers so interpret them. Yet their mundane references to boundaries of land, beggars, and bills of reckoning (as in a shop or tavern) are all immediately recognizable, and neither grandiose nor exotic as might be expected. These words are not explicitly sexual but they ground the sexual content of this moment in everyday actuality. The reference to a new heaven and earth is to some degree mythic, but will also remind an audience of that new-found world across the Atlantic from which most people present must have seen a trophy taken at one time or another:

CLEOPATRA   If it be love indeed, tell me how much.
ANTONY   There's beggary in the love that can be reckon'd.
CLEOPATRA   I'll set a bourn how far to be belov'd.
ANTONY   Then must thou needs find out new heaven, new earth.

(1.1.14–17)

Ordinary tactile images are often linked in Shakespeare's plays to the strangest and most unsettling experiences of sexual arousal, as when a lover vows 'to weep seas, live in fire, eat rocks, tame tigers . . .' (*Troilus and Cressida* 3.2.76–7).

THE MUSIC OF SEXUAL SPEECH

A further use of words to express sexual realities does not rely on their meanings, references, or allusions, or on their obvious evasions, their lies or incapacities. The very sound or 'music' of utterance speaks directly to the senses of a hearer, and Shakespeare skilfully used this to evoke the moods and rhythms of sexual activity. The effect is both mysterious, because it is never talked about, and compelling, because members of an audience are mostly unaware of this influence upon them and so do little to prevent its operation.

As the sound of performance changes, according to the sound of individual words and the on-going beat of iambic pentameters, so does the pulse of the audience and its attentiveness. In some scenes this music has a strong and heavy beat; in others all is slow and unforced, or uncertain and yet unhurried. In yet others, the variations of syntax, requiring certain pauses and certain extensions of phrasing, together with the metre, requiring certain emphases, build up a complex rhythm over a considerable period of time.

Such effects are not merely verbal and auditory. In the person of the actor, the 'music' of speech may be created by crucial changes of breath and nervous tension. Change of posture may also be necessary. No one can speak without making some bodily actions, and the more demanding the words spoken – in phrasing, metre, texture, reference and so on – the more complicated and impressive those actions that make speech possible. In effect, the actor's body must take part in a kind of dance which is the physical concomitant of speech, necessarily responsive to it as well as its cause. When sexual activity is a central fact of the drama, performance can become like a combination of dance and opera, so musical does utterance become and so poised and defined its physical enactment.

Without skilled actors and a full audience to demonstrate, this is not an easy matter to prove, so the effect is often missed by readers and critics. Yet the importance of verbal music and its physical enactment as a means of quickening the audience's response can hardly be overestimated. The best proof of this power will always be skilled productions of the plays in a full theatre, but these conditions for research do not come on demand. Lacking this resource, the best alternative would be to read some suitable passage aloud, with an attentive ear and a watchfulness for the physical accompaniments of speech.

To realize the full effect of a speech in performance, any activity called for by the story of the play should also be taken into account. Consider, as an example, the occasion when Cleopatra and her ladies, overcoming earlier fears, are hauling the dying Antony up into the monument in 4.15: the repeated exertion of all their strength and the quick eagerness of Cleopatra's kisses mingle with the effects of speech, its *doubles entendres*, repetitions, emphases, delays, exclamations, its changing sentence structures, the metre's occasionally strong beat and its rests. All this, and the presence of anxieties about death, make up a complex dramatic moment in which the strength of sexual attraction can seem to find its breath as appetite strains for satisfaction.

These strategies in writing for performance have one common characterisic: all rely, to some degree, on the audience making good what is only partially achieved on the stage. Each member is invited to complete the illusion of sexual activity in his or her own mind, and left free to do so according to individual prejudices and predilections. Shakespeare's representation of gender and sexuality is given its full sense of immediacy in the audience's active imagination when the drama is re-created according to each member's innermost feelings and desires. The very incompleteness of his depiction of sexual activity was one of the means whereby this particular subject could be given such a large role in the plays and the reason why it carries conviction in such variety and gives such widespread pleasure.

MODES OF IMAGINATION

In the last resort, all good theatre thrives by what happens in the minds of its audience and not by what happens on stage, but this may never be such a crucial factor in success as in its treatment of sexuality. For this subject, talk is never enough and words have comparatively little direct effect. Nor are actors capable of pleasing everyone in these matters, or of attempting to do so night after night and promptly on cue.

For this subject, theatre is quite unlike other arts that depict the circumstances of our lives. In painting, sculpture, and especially film and photography, the artist can get his or her chosen effect, as fully as possible, once and for all: but in theatre, one performance is seldom sufficient. One person in an audience does not see from the same viewpoint as another, and nothing can be made fixed and reliable. As if Shakespeare realized all this, sexuality and gender-difference in his writing are consistently suggestive and not definitive.

The task of arousing the private sexual fantasies of his audience and then giving them free play was a challenge Shakespeare undertook repeatedly and with seemingly endless invention. As actor-sharer in the theatre company, as well as dramatist, he must have felt the extraordinary power of this kind of audience response, its spontaneity and recklessness, its occasional intensity and multiple particularity. The actors would act the better for this stimulus so that the performance of an entire play might be kicked into more compelling life. In this theatre, the portrayal of slow or brooding sexual encounter was hardly practicable, but a whole world of suggestion was entirely possible, and was Shakespeare's means of awakening the audience's imaginations.

The use of young male actors to play the women's roles is an Elizabethan theatre practice that fits well with this way of writing, because their lack of a woman's sexuality could be supplied, along with much else, by the audience. Too many actresses have triumphed in the female roles for us to believe that this practice limited Shakespeare's imaginative input or that modern productions should follow Elizabethan precedent in this matter, but the texts of these plays are so dependent on suggestion for giving an illusion of sexual encounter that an audience will always be drawn to contribute, even if the female actor supplies more in some ways than a young male could ever do.

It might even be argued that in their day the 'boy actors' would have been more effective than actresses because their audience was not accustomed to public display of female bodies – as we have become through seeing innumerable advertisements, films, television entertainments, and theatre shows – all of which are frequently explicit sexually, and can depict the most intimate of occasions.

The use of 'boy actors' has been studied in many ways in recent years, so that Stephen Orgel, in his *Impersonations: the Performance of Gender in Shakespeare's England* (1996), can draw together much earlier research on this and related topics: about medical thinking in continental Europe by Stephen Greenblatt; about responses to public performance by Peter Stallybrass; about attitudes of audiences by Lisa Jardine and Jean Howard; about sexual anxieties by Valerie Traub; about the sexual attractiveness of young male bodies and what reactions might have been to this in Shakespeare's day by Eve Sedgwick and Alan Bray.

Orgel adds to this swell of scholarship by careful study of particular women who acted in some ways like men in real life at this time, but he makes his most useful addition to the debate by pointing out that the convention of using 'boy actors' was not a necessity forced on the theatres.[5] Women – even James I's own Queen – did act in amateur and provincial performances, while actresses who were permanent members of professional companies in other European countries continued to perform publicly when on tour in England. Scholars have been given a new question to consider: not only, 'How did boy actors serve the plays?', but, 'Why did all professional companies in London continue to rely on them?'

One answer to Stephen Orgel's second question must be obvious: that the young male actors pleased their audiences, and so the companies continued to use them. As to *why* they were successful, this review of some of Shakespeare's sexually driven scenes suggests that their shortcomings in imitating women suited the way in which the plays were written. The audience would complete the suggestions emanating from the stage – and for this, in view of the extremely personal nature of sexuality, the absence of too strong a physical statement had special advantages.

While some members of the audience might keep the real young man present in their minds as they viewed him imitating a woman, many others would have had no desire and, usually, no need to do so. Each spectator would complete the image of life that was half-created on the stage for his or her own pleasure, and would do so according to individual tastes and instincts. In this respect, the mirror held up to nature presented an image that anyone could enter into and complete, with a sense of wonder and achievement as well as recognition.

It might be objected that such imaginative collusion is too sophisticated a mental activity to have a place in the truly popular Shakespearian theatre which attracted so wide a range of audience in terms of class, wealth, and education. But the fact is that many other equally popular theatres have used all-male casts and a considerable number of them continue to do so at the present time in competition with the mixed casts (and greater accessibility) of film and television.

In India, the Jatra Theatres of Bengal and Orissa, the Kathakali of southern Kerala and Theyam of northern Kerala, and numerous other old forms of theatre have traditions of all-male casts and have always been hugely popular. In Japan, Kabuki was once a popular form and has retained the Onnagata performers even though a great many other features of production have been modernized. In the casts of Beijing Opera, women are now fully established and whole operas have been written for performance by star actresses, but the popularity of the form, especially among younger audiences, has not been increased by this innovation.

An ability to fantasize about sex is not a rare gift and it need not be a sophisticated one: rather, this is a potential in everyone and popular theatre can readily exploit it. By doing so, it gives very reliable pleasures which audiences pay back with enthusiasm and applause.

AROUSAL THROUGH THE IMAGINATION

Shakespeare and many of his contemporaries knew well enough the power of fantasy in the sexual part of anyone's life. Benedict in *Much Ado About Nothing*, having been tricked into thinking Beatrice loves him, has to face her when she is in a very black mood, saying nothing to indicate any affection or any interest in him of any sort, but the facts of the matter have little to do with what he sees or hears: 'I do spy some marks of love in her', he announces before she has had a chance to speak. And after she has spoken, he sees double meanings that express hidden yearning in the least suggestive parts of her brief communication – in words that are as plainly *un*loving as might well be invented. Orlando, in *As You Like It*, can speak fervently to 'her that is not here, nor doth not hear' (5.1.101); in fact, she *is* there, in front of him, but his words and her reaction to them indicate that his thoughts are not concerned with that bodily presence.

Robert Burton, in the course of his investigations, discovered a lover who would rave about his mistress when she was absent with the same passion and particularity as when she was present, and so become strongly aroused by his imagination alone:

Her sweet face, eyes, actions, gestures, hands, feet, speech, length, breadth, height, depth, and the rest of her dimensions, are so surveyed, measured, and taken by the astrolabe of fantasy, and that so violently sometimes, with such earnestness and eagerness, such continuance, so strong an imagination, that at length he thinks he sees her indeed, he talks with her, he embraceth her ... Be she present or absent, all is one.[6]

Elsewhere he wrote of a rich young man who became 'far in love' merely by hearing talk and 'common rumour' about a certain fair woman: he was 'so much incensed, that he would needs have her to be his wife'. Among numerous cases of love induced by fantasy, when 'we see with the eyes of our understanding', Burton quoted Lucian about one who said he never read about a certain woman 'but I am as much affected as if I were present with her'.[7]

All this fits well with modern knowledge, although Shakespeare's contemporaries are unlikely to have understood as fully as we do exactly how such sexual fantasies can be awakened and an audience be tempted to indulge them. We realize that while the new media can manipulate powerful images that directly and blatantly assault the senses, they continue to use suggestion as the major instrument for sexual arousal.

While outright and unambiguous sexual statements are common today, a kind of stealth is employed when playing on fears and desires. Images are constructed so that they remain incomplete, understated, or unbalanced, and will thereby create in the mind of a viewer not satisfaction, but rather a wish to complete the impression and so think about the possession of some as yet unobtained object, to fantasize with some hope of enjoyment.

Jon Stratton's *The Desirable Body: Cultural Fetishism and the Erotics of Consumption* (1996) describes some techniques of suggestion which belong to present-day society and economy but work on our minds in much the same ways as those used by Shakespeare for the depiction of sexuality. This recent book would be a more valuable guide about how to read the plays than some of those studied by modern scholars – diatribes by puritan writers who attacked the theatre's practices in Shakespeare's day without enjoying any of its performances, or books of arcane knowledge about the natural world which bears little relationship to what we now know to be the facts, or accounts of a few exceptional people who were ill at ease with the world in which they found themselves.

Because the perennial power of suggestion plays such a large part in the treatment of sex in Shakespeare's plays, two rules may be formulated for readers and for actors and directors. The first is that words cannot always be trusted in this matter and can seldom be pinned down to a single or precise meaning. The second is that the whole truth is seldom presented on the stage: what is placed there is intended to awaken an imaginative response, not to create moments of actuality. Not only are characters given speeches that conceal or evade, but, when sexuality is most important for the drama, a full realization of what is happening has been left to the imaginations of individual members of the audience – it had to be this way, and it was effective and compelling this way.

ⓒ John Russell Brown, 1997. First published in *New Theatre Quarterly*, 13, number 51.

NOTES

1　*The Anatomy of Melancholy* (1651 ed.), Partition 2.3.3; 1932 edn, 3.181.
2　See *2 Parnassus* (*c.* 1599), 3.1.1006–55. When Gullio begins to woo a lady, Ingenioso predicts, correctly, 'We shall have nothing but pure Shakespeare and shreds of poetry that he hath gathered at the theatre.'
3　Sir Richard Baker, quoted in R. C. Bald, *John Donne: A Life* (Oxford, 1970), p. 72.
4　The phrase is adapted from *All's Well* 1.1.169–70.
5　Orgel, Introduction, and p. 35: 'Why, then, if boys in women's dress are so threatening, did the English maintain a transvestite theatre?'
6　Burton, *The Anatomy of Melancholy*, 3.148.
7　Ibid., 3.65.

Nude Shakespeare in film and nineties popular feminism

Celia R. Daileader

> The thought beneath so slight a film –
> Is more distinctly seen –
> As laces just reveal the surge –
> Or mists – the Apennine
>> Emily Dickinson

When I first decided to write about nudity in Shakespeare films, I thought I would approach the topic with the premise that nudity, particularly in the heterosexual erotic vein, is essentially not 'Shakespearian', and that the trend licensing interpolated love scenes begun by Franco Zeffirelli's 1968 *Romeo and Juliet* amounts to additional evidence of the lengths to which modern directors must go in 'selling' Shakespeare to mass audiences. But after thinking through the theoretics of film nudity, the formula of 'more nudity equals less Shakespeare' struck me as somewhat facile. After all, nudity on stage and nudity on screen constitute drastically different performative phenomena. Nudity on stage comes across as 'real' in a way that film nudity does not: viewers are looking at breathing bodies in real space, with all the psychological impact that entails. Reactions may involve shock, titillation, or the more detached aesthetic assessment of the connoisseur – but on the whole these reactions will differ from those of the movie audience forewarned (in America) by an 'R' (restricted) rating that a film will contain nudity. I distinctly recall, for instance, worrying about the welfare – not moral, but physical – of a young actress playing the precocious school-girl heroine of *The Prime of Miss Jean Brodie*, when she was required, in the scene wherein she models for her artist teacher/lover, to stand topless for a painfully extended period of time in London's brutally air-conditioned National Theatre. For me this was meta-theatre at its least comfortable. Film would have allowed a less visceral reaction.

183

By contrast to nudity in theatre, filmic nudity is patently 'unreal', even potentially surreal; simultaneously flattened and magnified, reduced to two dimensions while blown into larger-than-life proportions, there is something non-human about the filmic nude, and that non-human quality may disturb as often as it delights – or, worse still, it may simply alienate or bore its viewers. Nudity, after all, is as prone to cliché as any other cinematic device; this is particularly the case in mainstream films, with their investment in heterosexual erotic narratives involving bodies which meet certain predictable standards. Moreover, most viewers now know that filmic nudity may not even involve the 'real' body of the actor: where Shakespeare's theatre used boy actors, modern mainstream films often use body-doubles. And this prompts me to revise my initial premise: there is, paradoxically, something a bit more 'Shakespearian' about cinematic as opposed to stage nudity. Across four hundred years and the virtual reinvention of art through the eye of the camera, the two media within their respective socio-historico contexts echo one another in their central ontological limitations: that of not offering 'the real thing' when it comes to the erotic body. [1]

On the other hand, is the question 'how Shakespearian is it?' a valid one? Richard Burt contends that 'the present mass mediatization of academia is putting an end to the Shakespearean', for in mass cultural appropriations of Shakespeare, 'the very identity of Shakespeare as author/author function is called into question'. [2] Burt also questions the way in which cultural critics, particularly feminists, evaluate Shakespeare in film by assuming 'an intelligent, if not authentic, Shakespeare against which adaptations could be distinguished as more or less Shakespearean', a binary system which 'uncritically reproduces the same old hierarchies of (humanizing, unique) literature above (dehumanizing, standardized) mass media'. [3] I agree with Burt that such high/low binaries must be handled with caution, and this is a particularly crucial point to make in relation to feminist critics, who have a strong investment in uprooting hierarchies generally. But I don't see how Renaissance scholars and consumers and critics of all things 'Shakespearean' can possibly relinquish this label, even if (or especially if) we wish to read as feminists our culture's deployment of Shakespeare's authority, and determine whether this usage furthers conservative or progressive ends. I do not share Burt's apocalyptic vision of 'the end to the Shakespearean': after all, decades have passed since Roland Barthes declared 'The Death of the Author' – but authorship, in my eyes, looks healthier than ever. And despite the begrudging amount of attention paid to critiques of the canon[4] bardolatry is alive and well–perhaps nowhere more so than in film.

What ultimately interests me most, however, is not the attribution to certain films of an essential 'Shakespearian-ness' – although I do intend to distinguish (tentatively) between elements that approach this ideal and those that do not – but the question of what a particular 'Shakespearianism' *tells us about ourselves*. In particular, I would ask of the late twentieth century: what does nudity in Shakespeare *mean?* The list is considerable, encompassing Zeffirelli's post-coital teenagers, the nude somnambulance of Roman Polanski's Lady Macbeth, the bedroom visions of Oliver Parker's *Othello*, Ophelia's 'flashbacks' in Kenneth Branagh's *Hamlet*, the sheet games between Luhrmann's Romeo and Juliet, and the shimmering skin-splendour of Hoffman's *A Midsummer Night's Dream*, to say nothing of Peter Greenaway's oddly anti-erotic pubic pageant in *Prospero's Books*. And what are we to do with that most stupefying surprise in American popular culture, the academy-awarded, quasi-soft-porn sensation of *Shakespeare in Love*, a film which is as false to Shakespeare as it is true to Hollywood's Shakes-fantasies?

Burt takes as one of his central concerns the 'dumbing down' of Shakespeare and literary studies in general, borrowing the phrase from the rhetoric of conservative culture critics such as Harold Bloom. And although Burt takes issue with the traditionalist viewpoint, critiquing the notion of 'a (mythic) decline from [the] familiar Shakespeare'[5] of Bloom's generation, the argumentative thrust and overall tone of his book has the effect of reinforcing, rather than challenging, the very nostalgia he discredits in traditional Shakespeare studies. With its channel-surfing feel, its barrage of televisual anecdotes, its saturation with the idiomatics of teen culture (deployed in ruthlessly witty chapter headings like 'My So-Called Shakespeare' or 'Loser Criticism, Part Duh'), with its focus on the rise of the 'loser' and his (it does tend to be 'he') existential malaise and cultivated, 'cool' stupidity, the book ultimately offers most of its readers no attractive replacement for time-worn notions of Shakespeare's universality. I expect this to be especially true of feminist readers, who are bound to resist the image of hyper-adolescent, disaffected masculinity embodied in the loser, and who have, we must admit, more at stake in the valuation of intelligence, which is, after all, what got us out of the kitchen. Nonetheless, Burt is right in emphasizing that what popular culture 'does' with Shakespeare often has little to do with Shakespeare at all. Yet not all popular Shakespeare is the same: *Shakespeare in Love* was indisputably 'dumber' about the author than was the *Midsummer Night's*

Dream which followed on its heels, although the two movies were similar in their target audiences, content, and casting profiles.

Is nude Shakespeare a kind of 'dumbing down', a cheapening, a reduction of the essential Shakespeare analogous to the cutting of the text? Does the trend begun by Zeffirelli constitute the stripping that will lead to the flogging that will lead to the crucifixion of a literary icon? Not necessarily. After all, when we 'do' nude Shakespeare we are adding something specifically post-modern: we are, in a sense, dressing him up. And in material terms, there is nothing 'naked', and certainly nothing of 'the naked truth', about filmic nudity, anyway. Even aside from the rarity of 'real' actor nudity – even aside from body-doubles and coyly hidden crotch-pads – the semiotic system of cinema transforms 'flesh' to one hue in the spectrum. Illuminated, enlarged, framed, cropped, airbrushed, digitally altered – the actor's flesh becomes pure artifice. Deprived of its volume in real space, skin becomes primarily *texture*. The cinematic nude is sex in its Sunday best.

Not all film nudity, of course, is designed to signify sexually (witness the nude witches in Polanski's *Macbeth*) – and even when it is, it assuredly will not meet every viewer's definition of 'sexy'. Most of the love scenes to be discussed in this essay are, by virtue of belonging to mass culture, calculated to please the average, middle-class, usually white, heterosexual movie-goer. Nonetheless, viewers who do not fit this profile may find a way to subvert the film's normalizing framework; both Zeffirelli's and Luhrmann's versions of *Romeo and Juliet* have produced compelling queer readings.[6] (This will merit further comment.) In any case, one can safely generalize that popular cinematic discourse encodes nudity *as* erotic – particularly when the body on display bears the marks of the conventionally romantic protagonist. Thus, nudity of the hetero-romantic sort may be used as an index in tracing the evolution in Shakespearian cinema of a distinctly nineties' erotic sensibility. And insofar as nineties' hetero-eroticism ideally involves some attempt at gender parity – thanks to demographic changes and political shifts I will optimistically label 'post-backlash' – we may also look to these nude scenes for evidence of a director's feminist sympathies, or lack thereof.

Early feminist film criticism dwelled on the primacy of 'the male gaze' and the corresponding objectification of the female screen star.[7] Now, with sex-positive, popular (as opposed to academic) feminism being marketed in women's magazines like *Cosmopolitan*, *New Woman*, *Jane*, and *Elle*,[8] mainstream film shows some signs of incorporating the *female* erotic gaze. This essay will proceed from the assumption that one might find more and less 'feministic' (as opposed to avowedly feminist) variations on the rather tired conventions of cinematic nudity, and will examine recent Shakespeare films – particularly Parker's *Othello*, Luhrmann's *Romeo*, and Hoffman's *Midsummer Night's Dream*[9] – in light of the pressure put on cinema by an increasingly educated, increasingly sexually confident, and increasingly salaried female audience. From this critical perspective, we may find that the much-touted 'return of the Bard' owes more to Shakespeare's sister(s) than to Shakespeare as protector of the western canon. Whether this turn itself can be deemed truly Shakespearian – or, conversely, true to feminism as a political movement – remains, nonetheless, to be seen.

Anything wrong and everything right with the recent Shakespeare films should be blamed on Zeffirelli. His 1968 *Romeo and Juliet* in many ways provided the prototype for a genre which, after an odd dormancy in the seventies and early eighties, has since come into its own. This genre which I will call the 'period romance' lent itself well to Shakespeare's love stories, and has its apotheosis in *Shakespeare in Love*. I will later return to the relationship between this filmic tradition and the romance novels which seemed to inspire it, as well as the relationship of both traditions to the Shakespearian precedent.[10] Here I wish only to set down some observations about Zeffirelli's construction of eroticism, in order to measure his influence on directors in the nineties.

One of the trademarks of the period romance is a certain visual opulence, epitomized in Zeffirelli's Capulet ball. The historical setting alone need not require such extravagance of costume, such numbers of extras, such heavily ornamented goblets and flagons, such over-laden tables of food. Yet, while critics faulted the director for this visual excess, audiences clearly loved it.[11] And, as I have elsewhere argued, the lavish costumes in particular play a crucial role in setting the stage for the erotic unveiling in the dawn-parting scene.[12] Romeo's peek-a-boo game with his mask in the dancing sequence epitomizes the film's specularity, its construction of the erotic body as that which is to-be-uncovered. According to Roland Barthes, this is what constitutes eroticism generally: 'the staging of an appearance-as-disappearance'.[13] But not all approaches to erotic undressing are alike; the effect of a nude-shot featuring a previously over-dressed body will differ dramatically from the effect of a more gradual revelation of skin.

And Zeffirelli's lovers do seem especially covered-up during the ball scene. The sensuality of the dance sequence is conveyed by the more subtle means of facial expression and gesture. Olivia Hussey's touch to her lips, her soft guttural noises during the kiss and after, and that ineffable, almost drugged quality of her gaze, more effectively connote the surprise of adolescent sexual discovery – itself a strange combination of the infantile and the precocious – than any amount of groping. (Luhrmann's Juliet does not approach this aura of erotic surrender: Claire Danes is too controlled and, ironically, too mature.) The fact that it is Juliet rather than Romeo whose erotic aura deserves comment here should not surprise anybody; the play has always been, to some degree, *about* Juliet, and this quality is only strengthened by what Peter S. Donaldson calls the '(bi-)sexual gaze' of Zeffirelli's camera. The focus on Juliet's sexual response in the ball scene anticipates the privileging of her gaze in the dawn-parting scene.[14]

But we were talking about undressing, and before we plunge into the naked feast of 3.1 we should touch upon the glimpse of Juliet's cleavage in the balcony scene. Another important component of the period romance is the heroine's corset. Although Olivia Hussey's Juliet is arguably less corseted than subsequent romantic heroines, in this scene it is very hard to ignore the contraption which makes a spectacle of her pubescent bust, strategically targeted by the camera as she leans over the balcony. Setting aside for the moment my feminist distaste for the implement – which will be addressed later, in the context of the corset's continuing appeal in the motion picture industry – what stands out is its pertinence to the notion of nudity-as-construct. The corset is technically an item of clothing, yet it *creates* a kind of nudity; in its redesigning of the female figure, the corset winds up offering more cleavage to the eye than might be available when a woman is naked. When the corset-wearer in question is scarcely a woman at all, like the fifteen-year-old Hussey, this enhancement effect becomes even more striking.

Romeo's voyeurism in the balcony scene is, of course, true to Shakespeare's text, and thus the focus on Juliet's breasts is hardly surprising. Far less true to the source is the scene which Shakespeare intended as its twin: the dawn parting at Juliet's balcony. In discussing Zeffirelli's version of 3.1 it is easy to lose sight of the impact it had on its original audiences; indeed, by the time Luhrmann began his version of the play, the bedroom interior had become a tradition of its own as the setting for Shakespeare's aubade. I have written at length about this scene elsewhere,[15] so I will simply summarize for the sake of future comparison. First, a pillow-shot: the two profiles, asleep. The camera pans back to show the bed: Juliet, on her back, her breasts covered by her hair and Romeo's arm, the sheets wrapped around her from the stomach down; Romeo, on his stomach and, by contrast, wholly uncovered (the frame exposes him to the calves). He wakes, goes to the window and stands framed in the sheer white curtains, back, buttocks and thighs in focus. Cut to Juliet stirring, pulling the sheet up to her neck; cut back to nude Romeo; cut to Juliet, now waking fully and looking at him; cut back to Romeo, as he bends to put on his hose. During the 'jocund day' discussion, he slowly dresses, but at 'Let me be taken' he throws his shirt aside and begins nuzzling her. At 'It is the lark', she leaps out of the bed, allowing a flash of her chest; then she is in her smock, and he finishes dressing.

Although Parker's *Othello* (1995) is chronologically the first nineties' film in our list, a more natural transition would be to Luhrmann's 1996 *Romeo*, providing a direct post-modern comment on Zeffirelli's classic.[16] Contrasts between the two films are, of course, too numerous to detail in the space of this overview; what interests me are the points of intersection in the ball scene, the balcony scene, and the dawn parting. First, however, there is the matter of genre; Luhrmann's film is not a period romance as defined above – indeed, to compete with Zeffirelli's film, it could *not* be. Luhrmann's brilliance lies in his borrowing of certain 'period' elements and superimposing them on a darkly post-modern urban setting. The ball scene in particular reworks Zeffirelli's in self-conscious, even dryly ironic ways: all of the opulence is there, the circular dances replaced and out-done by the fireworks blossoming above the revellers' heads. The Capulet mansion is architecturally pre-modern. Also, many of the costumes at the ball are historical, most notably Romeo's suit of armour and Juliet's Renaissance-angel costume; indeed, the white gown is strikingly reminiscent of Hussey's in the balcony scene, and although Juliet's costume doesn't require a corset, her mother's 'Egyptian' costume (anachronistically) does.

The film's erotic texture is, however, quite different from that of Zeffirelli's film. From the beginning, there is more skin on view, generally male chests airing in the heat of 'Verona Beach' (Romeo habitually leaves his Hawaiian shirts open); the effect of this display is, however, to de-eroticize, or at least to normalize, a certain amount of nudity, requiring other devices to convey the sexuality of the young lovers. Hence, Luhrmann's use of water imagery – from the fish-tank obscuring the lovers' first mutual gaze, to the pool in which they declare their love, to the storm on the night of their nuptials.[17] And indeed, for an audience as jaded as nineties' middle-class teenagers, simple nudity might not have done the job. Nor, I think, would the indignity of Hussey's corset have worked on the sophisticated 'girl power' icon, Danes, whose equally willowy figure would have required as much cleavage-building rigour.[18] Thus, in lieu of Romeo's moonlit voyeurism, we witness a late-night swim in the pool conveniently placed under Juliet's window. The effect is remarkable. Wet skin, even clothed (especially clothed, with some fabrics) is automatically sexier: wetness is more 'naked' or nakedly sexual in suggesting the sweat and fluids of coitus, and yet it is also curiously ornamental, its luminosity transforming the banal facts of biology. One need not talk about the pornographic convention of the wet tee-shirt to get this point across – though I'm sure that some viewers were dismayed by the stubborn opacity of Danes' drenched bodice.

More is owed to Zeffirelli in the dawn-parting scene – here broken into a night arrival, followed by a speeded-up and relatively chaste morning-after. Romeo is soaked with rain and also bleeding as he arrives at Juliet's window; the two start undressing one another, keeping Juliet's back to the camera; the same bare back is featured in the above-the-bed sunrise shot, a virtual replica of Zeffirelli's but with Romeo on his back and covered to the waist. You can see a sliver – almost nothing – of Juliet's left breast from this angle. Romeo slides out of bed, revealing nothing, and coyly pulls on his boxers under a corner of sheet. He gets his shirt halfway on and interrupts himself – like Zeffirelli's Romeo – for more cuddling at 'let me be taken'; however, his shirt stays more or less in place as he dives under the sheets for some adorable, if not highly erotic, horse-play. Next the camera takes us under the sheets with a shot of Romeo from below – the tent of linen behind his head creating a kind of halo effect – then, a reverse-shot of Juliet's face, smiling, framed by the pillow. In semiotic terms, these shots go farther than Zeffirelli in opening up the diegetic space of Shakespeare's offstage bedroom; rather than peering up at a balcony or even down at a couple in bed, here the viewer is placed *in* the bed, sharing the intimacy of this moment (significantly, this shot/reverse-shot features in the 'flash-backs' after the dual suicide). The camera then exits the bed and shows the lovers upright and cocooned in the sheets. Again, the moment is both tender and curiously innocent; as in the 'tent' shot of Romeo, cloth creates intimacy. But it is brief; the nurse interrupts. Romeo cutely struggles into his pants, and an instantly robed Juliet rushes him out of the window. Despite the borrowings from Zeffirelli, the scene has its own flavour: more sweet than sexy and considerably less solemn.

Parker's *Othello* is deservedly advertised as an 'erotic thriller'. Again, though, the materials of which Parker composed this eroticism differ strikingly from Zeffirelli's. This movie is the only one in our list which includes simulated intercourse – though these instances actually involve no nudity, just the suggestion of minimally parted clothing. During the wedding-night sequence, an anonymous pair copulate in a cart under which Iago and Roderigo sit, discussing Desdemona's sexual habits; the rhythmic creaking and grunting appropriately punctuate the conversation, as does Iago's rude lunge (for emphasis, I presume) at Roderigo's crotch. Later, Iago mounts Emilia – in reward for her obtaining the handkerchief – and addresses the camera about 'trifles light as air' as he begins the sex act.

More intriguing than these clothed but sordid moments, however, is the love-scene between Desdemona and Othello, involving a ritualized undressing to the vaguely African-sounding music of the festivities continuing outside the bridal chamber. The camera lingers on Othello's naked chest and then moves to a close-up of his belt as he undoes his buckle; cut to Desdemona, backing off timidly and then beginning to undo the laces of her dress from behind (and yes, she wears a corset). Another cut, and we see her from far across the room, quickly dropping her dress and diving behind the sheer curtains of the bed. The full-frontal shot lasts a fraction of a second, and hereafter she is obscured – to great effect – by the gossamer curtains, as she crawls provocatively across the bed. The inside-the-bed sequence involves little sustained nudity – just a bit of breast in profile – but manages to signify all the stages of coitus by way of clever attention to Desdemona's hands and feet. We see her foot climb up the back of Othello's leg and curl around his thigh; from the angle, one can tell (at least I could when I pressed 'pause' on my VCR) that she is positioned for sexual intromission. A close-up of her hand clutching the sheets suggests her climax; as his hand closes over hers, the act is complete.

The wedding night sequence sets the stage for the movie's most creative bit of eroticism: Othello's jealous fantasies of Desdemona and Cassio, in the nuptial bed. The first of these (which follows, appropriately, the aforementioned bedroom scene with Iago and Emilia) appears to be a nightmare, the second Othello's vision during the 'trance'. Both make effective use of the curtains enclosing the bed. In the dream, Othello approaches the bed bare-chested or perhaps nude, and sees, through the curtains, the alleged lovers entangled in sex-play; Desdemona is on top, half-draped in a red sheet; she giggles and throws a mocking look over her shoulder. The wedding-night hand-shot is then repeated, with Cassio's (white) hand enclosing Desdemona's. Othello wakes in a sweat. The second sequence is the sexiest in the film. There is a pillow-shot of

Cassio, a piece of Desdemona's shoulder or head in the corner of the frame; she moves down, then up, while Cassio makes orgasmic faces. We cut back to Othello as his fit comes on; cut to Desdemona's eyes, smiling; her thigh hooked over Cassio's, his hand on her thigh; a French kiss; her thigh and his hand again; back again to Othello; then a rapid sequence amounting to a pornographic blur, which can only be detailed and analysed on a VCR with the help of 'pause' and 'rewind'. The segment is brilliant in that it technically contains nothing obscene and yet conveys, through increasing tempo (underscored by the soundtrack), some of the steamiest sex an 'R' rating can afford. Her thigh, draped over his waist or hip; her mouth as she bites her lower lip; their hands overlapped; a hand on skin. As the tempo increases once more, we are shown her open mouth, and a sequence of hand-on-skin shots too fast to follow (even with 'pause'); the body-parts at this point are ambiguous and very erogenous-seeming (more thigh, definitely, and maybe a belly-button), plus open mouths and a tongue against skin. The film cuts back to Othello, and returns to the bed for a final shot of Desdemona's look over her shoulder.

There is a distinct contrast, thus, between Parker's rendering of Shakespeare's offstage bedroom and the precedent set by Zeffirelli. The latter made use of a few lengthy looks at Leonard Whiting's buttocks from across a softly lit bedroom; this eroticism is built, in a sense, out of distance, both temporal and spatial. (There is, of course, the blink-and-you-miss-it shot of Hussey's breasts, but the film invests far more in male nudity than female.[19]) By contrast to Zeffirelli's slow-paced eroticism and his reliance on panning and perspective, Parker makes use of speed and rhythm, and favours close-ups which fill the screen with skin. In respect to these differences, it appears as though Zeffirelli's eroticism, not surprisingly, is more 'classic', that is, closer to the humanist aesthetic tradition with its ideals about nature and beauty – a fitting mode in which to present Shakespeare's young idealists. Parker, on the other hand, employs certain devices which happen to be central to pornography: the close-up, the pastiche of body-parts, repetition and over-saturation of erotic reference. Yet his method, too, seems suited to the text, with its focus on the obscene.

The three directors discussed above have not, however, exhausted the possibilities for nude Shakespeare. This is evident in Michael Hoffman's *A Midsummer Night's Dream*, which, though a period romance *par excellence*, is also the most contemporary in its erotic sensibilities. The film announces its concern with costume in an opening inscription explaining the setting: turn-of-the-century rural Italy, where 'necklines are high' and 'parents are rigid'. The reference to high necklines is much needed, as the erotic trajectory of the film will require a gradual stripping of the two central, 'mortal' couples, with particular attention paid to the males. While human society is set up as sartorially 'Victorian', however, the fairy kingdom is presented, early in the film, as quintessentially quasi-nude, with the visually compelling difference that fairy attire tends to be translucent and fairy skin dusted with glitter – that is, the categories of 'clothed' and 'nude' are harder to distinguish. The first shot of Michelle Pfeiffer's Titania encapsulates this effect: we see her through the gossamer curtains of her litter; when the visual barrier is removed, we note the gold dust which etherealizes her flesh, and the long, glittering tresses which obscure the mechanics of her seemingly negligible garment. Oberon, played by Rupert Everett, that perfect specimen of the woman-maddening gay,[20] displays much of his oiled torso and assumes a reclining, *Playgirl* pose through much of the movie. All together, the oil and glitter of the fairy-world result in something similar to Luhrmann's erotic wetness; light is reflected in aesthetically intriguing ways, and nude corporeality is both heightened and transformed. (This also applies to those topless nymphs shown chest-deep in a stream.)

Nudity among the mortal characters is approached differently. When Lysander and Hermia bed down in the forest, he strips completely, she only to her smock and corset (which made me wonder, why bother?). In his thwarted seduction, he handles the inflated upper hemisphere of her corseted breast, but also offers to view the profile of his naked back and buttocks. In rebuffing him, Hermia briefly notes his exposed penis (below the frame), which she quickly covers with her wadded-up dress. From this point forth, the woman's garment becomes a comic loin-cloth for Lysander; its precariousness and its skirt-like appearance render him sexy, silly, and somewhat cross-dressed as he runs about – or, even more goofily, pedals about – the forest. Needless, to say, this is not Hollywood's usual boy-flesh fare.

While the weight of male nudity seems a clear indication of the film's hetero-female target audience, Hoffman tries to balance things by having the as-yet-more-clothed women play out their rivalry in a mud-wrestling scene. Hermia has retained the corset, simultaneously a symbol of her sexual repression (and Lysander's nude magnificence makes it hard to sympathize with her not-till-the-wedding-night prudery) and a fetishized accessory, allowing the film a loop-hole in the high neckline rule. But things take a decidedly *Penthouse* turn once the two women start flailing about in the mud – another lubricating, naked-making agent, like Luhrmann's swimming-pool. Despite its reminiscences of tacky porn, the scene is irresistibly funny; much clothing is lost in the process, and both women wind up head-to-toe in black gloss, exoticized in earth just as the fairies are etherealized in glitter.

Another aspect of the film which suggests a female-oriented eroticism is the Titania/Bottom sub-plot. Casting Kevin Klein as Bottom somewhat diminished the fairy Queen's humiliation by Oberon: Klein is an effective comedian and good at a kind of endearing foolishness, but he is also not unpleasant to look at. Moreover, Hoffman made a point of leaving Bottom more or less intact after the metamorphosis, substituting a pair of ears and some extra facial hair for the usual ass-head – while also brilliantly implying, by way of amused onlookers during his first kiss with Titania, the impressive size of his presumably equine penis. When Oberon observes him in his wife's bower, asleep and curled up in her limbs, his look of jealousy is justified, if not particularly true to the text.

Nowhere is the pro-female slant more evident than in the final scene in the forest. Thanks to Puck's magic, the two couples are discovered asleep in the nude and draped over one another as in post-coital exhaustion; flowers and loose hair veil the taboo body-parts. The arriving company peruse this erotic tableau – the camera pauses on it – before startling them awake. Again, it is the men who – oddly enough – wind up more naked here; the women, for some reason, have an easier time finding their clothes, while the men scramble to cover their groins. Then, just to drive the point home, we get a look at the group from behind and see the men's exposed backsides. The scene is typical of the film's pattern of irresistible erotic interpolations – irresistible not only because amusing and lovely to look at, but more importantly because they are narratively unobtrusive (unlike Branagh's in *Hamlet*, which re-write the play) as well as true to the spirit, if not the letter of the text. Moreover, this nude awakening, if you will, appeals to modern sensibilities by giving the patriarchal social system of the play and the Victorian prudery of the film's chosen setting ('necklines are high') the come-uppance it deserves: the audience knows that the four have been chaste, despite all – but the arriving party, in Hoffman's pseudo-Shakespearian fiction, assume they are dealing with a sexual revolution. So much for Hermia's corset. So much for the Christian Coalition.

One of the functions of the period romance seems to be just that: setting up a repressive social context in order to give (particularly) women the opportunity to rebel. I have not yet figured out whether this is a good thing. On the one hand, it seems to foster a feministic, 'go girl!' response in its audiences, but on the other hand, it offers a debased definition of female empowerment – namely, marrying the man you want – and thereby induces complacency about opportunities for women today. The political implications are further complicated in the Shakespearian sub-genre, which by definition reinforces the authority of a four-centuries dead male author. For even when that authority is deployed for progressive political purposes – subtly discrediting, for instance, the pro-chastity movement in American fundamentalism – the film may indeed be obscuring the repressive ideology which underwrites the original literary source. This is a Catch-22, I realize – and perhaps the fairest approach to this feministic Shakesperotica is to look at the way it deconstructs the fad for Bardolatry in contemporary right-wing rhetoric such as that spewed forth in Bloom's *Shakespeare: The Invention of the Human*. It is a way of saying to Bloom and his comrades, 'You want Shakespeare? We'll give you Shakespeare!' It is a disarmament tactic.

Or maybe not. It is noteworthy how many conservative commentators have pointed to this rash of new films in re-iterating their complaints about 'political correctness' in the academy. In fact, one point often made in pro-canon propaganda is that Shakespeare is 'sexy'.[21] The dilemma is perhaps nowhere more apparent than in *Shakespeare In Love*, a film I have avoided here for its flagrantly non-Shakespearian character. Yet it now seems that this very quality needs to be addressed. The film meets all the requirements for a period romance – a corseted but spirited aristocratic heroine, an arranged marriage, a forbidden love – with the added cleverness of having Shakespeare himself as the hero, and the heroine the 'biographical' inspiration for Juliet. From here the movie proceeds to re-tell *Romeo and Juliet*, and does so without compunction, as the whole point is that 'it really happened' to Shakespeare. Now, watch the director pull a rabbit out of a historical hat, so that a woman plays Juliet on the English Renaissance stage. She wants to be an actor, so she (unconvincingly) cross-dresses and auditions before the playwright himself; she is chosen to play Romeo. Now, I might have believed her without the faux moustache, as a boy auditioning for the part of Juliet, but that would have sacrificed the final plot-twist, which lands the two lovers on stage in the appropriately gendered roles. Of course it does not take long for the young Shakespeare to discover the actor's true identity and fall in love; the remainder of the movie consists of rehearsals on stage and in bed, with the Bard speaking Juliet's lines to his mistress' Romeo. The appeal of these love-scenes lies in the patent reversal of both the play's and the Renaissance theatre's gender politics. The nudity clinches the deal. Much attention is paid to Gwyneth Paltrow's breasts, which the hero must dotingly unbind for her when they make love; I counted eight frames in which you could see a nipple. Disappointingly, Joseph Fiennes displayed nothing but chest and back. Hetero males: eight. Females: zero.

Perhaps this is why the film's eroticism left me cold. I'd grown used to the way Shakespeare films courted the hetero female gaze (and perhaps, surreptitiously, the gay male gaze). I also sensed something insidiously political in all the chest-shots of Paltrow – not to say the conceit of the film, its effect that of redeeming the writer of the 'master–mistress' sonnets for heteronormativity. It was as if the film expected us not only to *buy* the cross-dressing, but to recoil at the shot of a moustached 'boy' lunging for a kiss from the absurdly obtuse, safely straight, guy's guy 'Will'. And that is a rather patronizing move, considering how many of us have seen *The Crying Game* (or *Tootsie*, or *The Bird Cage*, or *Priscilla, Queen of the Desert*, or *Victor / Victoria* . . .).

On the other hand, the cross-dressing plot itself has its feministic appeal, in much the way that Shakespeare's own cross-dressed heroines do; at least the heroine is allowed a career of sorts. She even gets credit for some of Shakespeare's lines. Correspondingly, the film somewhat counters Bardolatry by emphasizing Marlowe's greater popularity and Shakespeare's resulting jealousy. These elements equalize things, upholding the heroine as the creative power behind the authorial throne. But this is done at the expense of historical accuracy, effacing the Bard's own ambiguous sexuality, and that quality of his love-stories that my students like to call 'heterophobia'. What is the solution? The interests of popular, sex-positive feminism and that of queer-identified historicism – or good scholarship in general – seem on a collision course here.

The problem may have its roots in the politically ambivalent nature of the period romance genre. Both utopian and dystopian – what fun to dress like that; what a nuisance to have to dress like that. A place where women in corsets get to run around, roll in the mud, and flout their fathers' rules; a place where women might do all these things, but must do them wearing corsets. And let's face it: it's easy to be a 'spirited heroine' when you're wearing that get-up; a short jog up a hill and you're panting like a marathon-runner, drawing all that attention to your 'heaving bosom'. Who needs a law degree, a promotion, pay equity, or the ERA – when you can look that good without liposuction, and bed Joseph Fiennes to boot? Forgive the sarcasm. It's just that the corsets do seem to be multiplying on screen these days. I understand the allure of the past, and perhaps it is an accident that the perfect balance between the alien and the antiquated resides in the reign of the corset. But is it not somewhat suspicious that as soon as anorexia went out of fashion in Hollywood, the corset reappeared? I will stop the feministical paranoia here, since, after all, it is women who read and write 'bodice-rippers', and women who prefer period romance (and for that matter, it was women who put women in corsets, for about three centuries). If romance is 'pornography for women',[22] it seems that the genre should be afforded the same lattitude by feminists who, like myself, fall on the free-speech side of the pornography debate. One scholar writes that pornography 'may be false to the spirit of everything we believe about men and women, love and even lust. But porn is true to fantasy. And fantasy is not fair'.[23]

It is my perhaps unproveable contention that the 'return of the Bard' in popular culture owes as much to the vogue for period romance and therefore to female consumers as anything going on in the academy (since when does Hollywood care about academics?). Zeffirelli's *Romeo and Juliet* was quite successful, but the genre faded for almost three decades, to be resuscitated in 1995 not by Shakespeare, but Jane Austen, when *Sense and Sensibility* and *Persuasion* (together with the modernized re-telling of *Emma* in *Clueless*) competed for audiences with Parker's *Othello*. The motion picture industry is almost out of Austen novels, but the Bard can reasonably be expected to go on providing material for period romance well into the twenty-first century. As to whether these films will remain recognizably 'Shakespearian' – or whether Burt's prophecies will prove true – only time will tell. *Shakespeare in Love* was advertised as 'funny, sexy . . . everything you *never* expected Shakespeare to be'. Luhrmann's *Romeo and Juliet* boasted that it was 'Not your father's Shakespeare'. A film I did not discuss here, *10 Things I Hate About You*, revised *The Taming of the Shrew* so completely I could not decide whether it was feminist de-construction (*10 Things I Hate About* Shrew?) or simple bowdlerization. In rescuing Shakespeare for popular feminism – in this case, and in the case of the films I have analysed above – what are the costs to Shakespeare? What are the costs to feminism? Does feminism, at its ideological core, need Shakespeare?

If one thing is clear, it is that Shakespeare needs feminism – almost as much as he needs the film industry. Shakespeare needed feminism in 1611, when John Fletcher pleased audiences with the first *Shrew* rebuttal, *The Tamer Tamed*, and Shakespeare needs feminism today. Perhaps directors of period romance will one day catch wind of canon-reform in university English departments and turn – whether out of feminist enlightenment or plain curiosity – to playwrights like Aphra Behn, but until then I see no harm in women's consumption of Shakespearian bodice-busters starring doe-eyed 'babes' like Leonardo DiCaprio. For the two or three feminist critics in the audience, who might be aware, at times, of the tension between Shakespeare's politics and that of the movie, we might view that conflict as part of the fun. A kind of spectator sport – like mud-wrestling, or better yet, bear-baiting. Only we know who wins. And let's face it – he's had it coming to him.

NOTES

1 Even pornography, which seems to depict the biological 'truth' of sex as distinct from eroticism, can only do so at the expense of the body's integrity within the visual field, delivering its revelation of the genitals and the visible 'fact' of male climax by way of dismembering close-ups. On this and other contradictory aspects of mainstream porn, see Linda Williams, *Hard Core: Power, Pleasure, and the 'Frenzy of the Visible'* (Berkeley, 1989), pp. 93–119, and Celia R. Daileader, 'The Uses of Ambivalence: Pornography and Female Heterosexual Identity', *Women's Studies*, 26.1 (January 1997), 73–88.
2 Richard Burt, 'Mass Culture in Love, with Shakespeare: Literary Authorship, Academic (Feminist) Criticism, and the End of the Shakespearean', in *Shakespeare, Film, Fin de Siecle* eds. Mark Thornton Burnett and Ramona Wray (London, 2000), p. 7.
3 Burt, 'Te(e)n Things I Hate About Girlene Shakesploitation Flicks in the Late 1990s, or, Not So Fast Times at Shakespeare High', in *Screening the Bard: Shakespearean Spectacle, Critical Theory, Film Practice* (forthcoming, Madison and Teaneck), p.11.
4 See, for example, Gary Taylor's *Reinventing Shakespeare* (London, 1990) or Kathleen McLuskie's 'Patriarchal Bard', in *Political Shakespeare : New Essays in Cultural Materialism* ed. by Jonathan Dollimore and Alan Sinfield (Manchester, 1985).
5 Burt, *Unspeakable ShaXXXspeares: Queer Theory and American Kiddie Culture* (New York, 1998), p. 6.
6 See Ibid., pp. 159–72, and Peter S. Donaldson, *Shakespearean Films/Shakespearean Directors* (Boston, 1990), pp. 153–88.
7 See, for instance, Laura Mulvey, 'Visual Pleasure and Narrative Cinema', *Screen*, 16.3 (Autumn 1975), 6–18.

8 Another way of framing the distinction between popular and academic feminism is to speak in terms of a readership of consumers versus intellectuals. These glossy magazines, unlike *Ms.* or the kind of journals in which I have published, target young female professionals who are liberal and ambitious but also intensely heterosexual; having money to spend, they are enthusiastic consumers of fashion, cosmetics, health/diet items, and sexual advice literature. Unlike some branches of academic feminism, this group sees sexual relations with men as empowering and healthy, at least when sex is 'done right' – and many of these magazines (*Cosmo* in particular) make it their mission to teach women the best techniques.

9 For the sake of focus I will have to skip the love-scenes in Branagh's *Hamlet*, which are the briefest and, in my opinion, the least textually justified.

10 On Shakespeare's connection to the romance novel, I am indebted to the work of Laurie E. Osborne. See Osborne, 'Sweet, Savage Shakespeare', in *Shakespeare Without Class*, ed. Don Hedrick and Bryan Reynolds (New York, 2000) and 'Romancing the Bard', in *Shakespeare and Appropriation*, ed. Christie Desmet and Robert Sawyer (New York, 1999) pp. 47–64.

11 See Ace G. Pilkington, 'Zeffirelli's Shakespeare', in *Shakespeare and the Moving Image: The Plays on Film and Television*, ed. Anthony Davies and Stanley Wells (Cambridge, 1994), pp. 164–5.

12 Daileader, *Eroticism on the Renaissance Stage: Transcendence, Desire, and the Limits of the Visible* (Cambridge, 1998), p. 51.

13 Roland Barthes, *The Pleasure of the Text*, trans. Richard Miller (New York, 1975), p. 10.

14 See Donaldson's analysis of this scene (pp. 165–71).

15 See Daileader, *Eroticism*, pp. 40–6.

16 Discussion of Luhrmann's film has been lively, to say the least. See, for instance, Leah Guenther, 'Luhrmann's Top 40 Shakespeare and the Crisis of Shakespearean Consumption', *Journal of American Culture* (forthcoming); Stanley Kauffmann, 'Blanking Verse', *New Republic* (2 Dec. 1996), 40; Anthony Lane, 'Tights! Camera! Action! What Does It Mean That the Bard Recently Hit No. 1 at the Box Office?' *New Yorker*, 25 (Nov. 1996), 65–77; and W. B. Worthen, 'Drama, Performativity, and Performance', *PMLA* 113.5 (October 1998), 1093–107.

17 I owe these observations to Jennifer Butts, 'Here Lay Those Whose Names Are Writ in Water: Baz Luhrmann's (William Shakespeare's) *Romeo and Juliet* and Gender Fluidity for the Millennium', unpublished paper, 1997.

18 Here I feel compelled to reply to Burt's clumsy description of Danes as 'extremely flat-chested', a quality which he inexplicably lists as one of the film's 'queer effects' (*ShaXXXspeares*, p. 161). The comment is grating not only for its locker-room style exaggeration. After all, the actress is playing a fourteen-year-old. If she sported a buzz-cut and overalls – and was 'extremely flat-chested' – Burt might have a point. The film has many 'queer effects', but Danes is not one of them.

19 See Donaldson, *Shakespearean Films*, pp. 168–9.

20 Everett declared his homosexuality in 1986 (Dave Karger and Degen Pener, '*Entertainment Weekly* Invites You to Share in the Joy as Rupert Everett Becomes the "Best" Man . . .' *Entertainment Weekly*, 11 July 1997).

21 See Jay Tolson, 'The Return of the Bard: As the World Goes Virtual, We Crave His Earthy Genius', *U. S. News & World Report*, 1 February 1999, and Alan Bisport, 'Downsizing Shakespeare: Pop Culture Loves Him, but Academia is Giving the Bard the Boot', *The Hartford Advocate*, 20 February 1997.

22 Ann Barr Snitow, 'Mass Market Romance: Pornography for Women is Different', in *Powers of Desire*, ed. Snitow *et al.* (New York, 1983), pp. 245–63.

23 Richard Goldstein, 'Pornography and Its Discontents', in *The Erotic Impulse: Honoring the Sensual Self*, ed. David Steinberg (New York, 1992), p. 92.

Index

Abrahams, Roger D., 16, 29 n.6
Adelman, Janet, 3, 29 n.10
Admiral's Men, 61
Africa, 162
Alexander III, Pope, 118, 119–20, 121
Anne of Denmark, 179
Aristophanes, 40
Aristotle, 95
  Physics, 32 n. 26, 108
  Rhetoric, 132
Aristotle's Master Piece, 22, 27, 32 n.27, 34 n.33
Ascham, Roger, *Scholemaster*, 143–4 n.49
Astington, John H., 29 n.10
Austen, Jane, 197
Australia, 39

Baildon, W., 144 n.52
Baker, I. H., 125, 142 n.25, 142 n.26, 143
  n.42
Baker, Sir Richard, 182 n.3
Bakhtin, Mikhail, 18
Baldwin, T. W., 166 n.46
Bamber, Linda, 88 n.3
Barber. C. L., 30 n.15, 73
Barker, Deborah H., 5
Barksted, William, (with John Marston) *The
  Insatiate Countess*, 69 n.7
Barron, Dennis, 165 nn.37–8
Barthes, Roland, 184, 187
Bataille, George, 50 n.27
Batchelar's Banquet, The, 100
Bate, Jonathan, 50 n.26, 89 n.6
Beaumont, Francis, 108
Beer, Gillian, 61
Behn, Aphra, 198
Beijing Opera, 180
Belsey, Catherine, 5, 6, 8, 49 n.7, 49 n.9, 49
  n.15, 50 n.36, 72–91
Benjamin, Jessica, 51 n.37
Bennett, Josephine Waters, 163 n.7
Benson, John 146–9, 153, 162

Benveniste, Emile, 149
Berggren, Paula S., 8
Berkeley, David S., 112 n.23
Berry, Philippa, 5
Bettelheim, Bruno, 77, 111 n.8
Bible, 27
  Galatians, 112 n.32
  Proverbs, 77
Bisport, Alan, 200 n.21
Bloch, R. Howard, 110 n.2
Bloom, Harold, 185, 195
Bly, Mary, 10, 52–71
Boccaccio, Giovanni, 137, 144 n.51
Book of Common Prayer, The, 117, 143 n.38
Boone, Joseph, 5
Boose, Lynda E., 4, 9, 103
Booth, Stephen, 163 n.6, 164 n.16, 164 n.22,
  166 n.49, 167 n.53, 167 n.54
Bordieu, Pierre, 158
Boswell, James, 151–2, 164 n.27
Bradley, A. C., 106
Branagh, Kenneth, 185, 194, 199 n.9
Brathwaite, Richard,
  Loves Labyrinth, 33 n.28
  Strappado for the Divell, A, 32 n.26
Bray, Alan, 6, 154, 161, 179
Brontë, Emily, *Wuthering Heights*, 48
Brook, Peter, 92
Brooke, Arthur, *The, Tragicall Historye of Romeus
  and Juliet*, 35, 43, 46
Brown, James, 54, 70 n.15
Brown, John Russell, 9, 168–82
Brown, R., 165 n.40
Brundage, James A., 141 n.10
Bryant, Mark, 89 n.16
Bullen, A. H., 142 n.33
Bullough, Geoffrey, 50 n.33, 50 n.35, 84
Bulman, James C., 9
Burckhardt, Sigurd, 29 n.4
Burt, Richard, 9, 184, 185, 197, 198 n.6, 199
  n.18

Burton, Robert, *The Anatomy of Melancholy*, 27, 168, 180–1
Bury, Shirley, 142 n.33
Butts, Jennifer, 199 n.17
Buxton Opera House, 110 n.1

Cadden, Michael, 5
Calahorra, Ortuñez de, 108
Calderwood, James L., 34 n.37
Callaghan, Dympna, 46, 49 n.19, 115 n.82
Calvin, Jean, 100, 112 n.37
Carlson, Eric Joseph, 141 nn.6–7
Carroll, William C., 10, 14–34, 71 n.23
Cartari, Vincenzo, 31–2 n.22, 33 n.32, 34 n.34
Castiglione, Baldassare, *The Book of the Courtier*, 32 n.26, 41, 111 n.9 114, n.71
Catullus, 19, 31 n.21, 34 n.33
Chapman, George,
　Hero and Leander, 19, 24–5
　Widow's Tears, 169
Chaucer, Geoffrey,
　Knight's Tale, 83, 86
　Parliament of Fowls, 73–4
Chedgzoy, Kate, 5, 7
Chettle, Henry, 71 n.24
Children of Paul's, 63
Children of the Chapel Royal, 84
Cirlot, J. E., 142 n.33
Clement of Alexandria, 25
Cohen, Walter, 88 n.2
Coke, Sir Edward, 141 n.11
Cole, Howard, 140 n.3, 144 n.51
Cole, J., 144 n.57
Coleridge, Samuel Taylor, 39–40, 43
Comes, Natalis, 34 n.34
Compass Theatre Company, 92–3
Consett, Henry, 131
Cook, Carol, 10
Coriden, James A., 141–2 n.14
Crooke, Helkiah, *Microcosmographia*, 22–3, 26–7, 29–30 n.11
Curren-Aquino, Deborah T., 10

Daileader, Celia R., 5, 9, 183–200
Danes, Claire, 188, 190
Daniel, Samuel, 153
Danson, Lawrence, 89 n.4, 90 n.27
Dash, Irene, 4, 10
Davis, Lloyd, 35–51
Davis, Natalie Zemon, 29 n.2, 105
Day, John, *The Isle of Gulls*, 70 n.16
De Grazia, Margreta, 6, 146–67
Dekker, Thomas,
　Blurt, Master Constable, 52–4, 57, 60, 64–8

Roaring Girl, The (with Thomas Middleton), 8
Shoemaker's Holiday, The, 54
Dennis, C. J., *A Sentimental Bloke*, 39
Dent, R. W., 70 n.17
Derrida, Jacques, 111 n.16
Desmet, Christy, 10
DiCaprio, Leonardo, 198
Dickens, Charles, 48
Dickinson, Emily, 183
Dodd, William, 90 n.23
Dollimore, Jonathan, 7, 8, 40, 153
Donaldson, Peter S., 188, 198 n.6, 199 n.19
Donne, John, 15, 31 n.19, 33 n.31, 38, 96, 97–8, 168
Doran, Madeleine, 141 n.4
Douglas, Mary, 18–9
Drakakis, John, 88 n.2
Drummond, William (of Hawthornden), 19
Dryden, John, *Troilus and Cressida*, 90 n.26
Duby, Georges, 86
Dundas, Alan, 29 n.6
Dusinberre, Juliet, 3, 8

E., T., 145 n.68
Eccles, Audrey, 30 n.11, 32 n.26
Eden, Kathy, 143 n.44
Edwards, Richard, *Damon and Pithias*, 83–4
Eliot, T. S., 106
Elizabeth I, Queen, 19, 26, 86, 108, 114 n.60, 161
Elyot, Sir Thomas,
　Defence of Good Women, 111 n.9
　Governour, The, 83, 84, 90 n.30
Empson, Sir William 97, 166 n.49
Engle, Lars, 88 n.3, 166 n.44
Erasmus, Desiderius, 31 n.19, 158–9
Erickson, Peter, 5, 9
Essex, Earl of, 119
Everett, Rupert, 193

Fallow, T. M., 142 n.21
Fenner, Dudley, 143 n.37
Ferguson, Moira, 114 nn.74–5
Festus, Sextus Pompeius, 25, 33 n.32
Fiennes, Joseph, 196, 197
Fineman, Joel, 49 n.6, 157, 164 n.14
Fitz, Linda T., 4
Fitzgerald, F. Scott, *The Great Gatsby*, 48,
Fletcher, John, 108
　Night Walker, The, 70 n.17
　Tamer Tamed, The, 198
Folger Shakespeare Library, 147
Foucault, Michel, 1, 2, 4, 50 n.21, 95, 97, 104, 110, 112 n.31, 154, 165 n.33
Franklin, Helen, 93

Free, Mary, 8
Freedman, Barbara, 36
Freud, Sigmund, 29 n.5, 30 n.14, 49 n.7, 51
n.44, 80, 88, 89 n.15, 94, 102–4, 108,
110, 111 n.8, 113 n.48
Furnivall, Frederick J., 142 n.18, 142 n.22,
142 n.31, 143 n.36, 143 n.43, 143 n.46
Fyftene Joyes of Maryage, The, 100

Gager, William, 101
Galen, *De Usu Partium*, 26
Garber, Marjorie, 3, 7, 113 n.51
Gay, Penny, 9
Geary, Keith, 6, 88 n.3
Gesta Romanorum, 77
Gibbons, Brian, 49 n.2, 49 n.4, 63
Gilby, Anthony, 143 n.37
Gildon, Charles, 153
Gilman, A., 165 n.40
Goldberg, Jonathan, 7, 50 n.19, 162, 165 n.41,
167 n.57
Golding, Arthur, 25, 41
Goldstein, Richard, 200 n.23
Goolden, P., 17
Gordon, D. J., 25
Gorfain, Phyllis, 17
Greaves, Richard L., 143 n.37
Greenaway, Peter, 185
Greenberg, David F., 91 n.38
Greenblatt, Stephen, 4, 37, 90 n.25, 90 n.34,
115 n.84, 179
Greene, Thomas M., 166 n.48
Guenther, Leah, 199 n.16
Guillemeau, James, 34 n.38
Gurr, Andrew, 69 n.2, 165 n.39

Hacking, Ian, 145 n.69
Hale Hale, W., 145 n.66
Hales, Nancy K., 9
Hali Meidenhad, 31 n.19, 33 n.29
Hall, Kim, 167 n.61
Hall, Sir Peter, 139
Halprin, N. J., 69 n.11
Hastrup, Kirsten, 30 n.13
Hattaway, Michael, 5–6, 92–115
Heale, William, *An Apology for Women*, 101
Healy, Thomas, 115 n.79
Heilbrun, Carolyn, 4
Helmholz, R. H., 141 nn.7–8, 142 n.28
Helms, Lorraine, 8
Henke, James, 69 n.7, 70 n.16
Henslowe, Philip, 61, 69 n.2, 71 n.24
Herbert, George, 48
Heywood, Thomas, *1 The Fair Maid of the West*,
62

Hibbard, G. R., 112 n.35
Hoby, Sir Thomas, 32 n.26
Hoffman, Michael, 185, 187, 192–4
Holderness, Graham, 49 n.18
Houlbrooke, Ralph, 137, 141 n.7, 143 n.34,
144 n.59
Howard, Lady Frances, 119
Howard, G. E., 141 n.9
Howard, Jean E., 5, 8, 89 n.3, 179
Hurstfield, Joel, 140 n.3
Hussey, Olivia, 188, 189, 192
Hutson, Lorna, 144 n.51

Illich, Ivan, 165 n.33
India, 180
Ingram, Martin, 105, 138, 141 nn.7–8,
142 n.28, 144 nn.54–5, 145 n.65

Jackson, Gabriele Bernhard, 34 n.35
James, Henry, 48
Bostonians, The, 114 n.61
Jane Anger's *Protection for Women*, 95, 108
Japan, 180
Jardine, Alice, 5
Jardine, Lisa, 8, 179
Jarman, Derek, 7
Jatra Theatre, 180
John, Saint, 119, 120
Johnson, Samuel, 15
Jones, G. P., 165 n.39
Jong, Erica, *Serenissima*, 72
Jonson, Ben, 19, 97, 163 n.7
Alchemist, The, 25
Hymenaei, 25
New Inn, The, 114 n.72
Poetaster, 67,
Volpone, 168–9
Jordan, Constance, 111 n.9

K., E., 159–60
Kabuki, 180
Kahn, Coppélia, 3, 5, 51 n.40
Kamps, Ivo, 5
Kathakali, 180
Kauffman, Stanley, 199 n.16
Keesee, Donald, 112 n.23
Kelley, Donald, 145 n.69
Kelly-Gadol, Joan, 115 n.78
Kerrigan, John, 146, 164 n.29, 166 n.50
Kingsmill, Andrew, 143 n.37
Kinkead-Weekes, Mark, 111 n.13
Klein, Kevin, 194
Kleinberg, Seymour, 6
Kofman, Sarah, 89 n.15
Kolin, Philip C., 3, 5, 10

Kristeva, Julia, 51 n.43
Kunz, G. F., 142 n.33
Kyd, Thomas, *The Spanish Tragedy*, 35

Lacan, Jacques, 48, 49 n.7, 74–5, 89 n.9, 157
Lactantius, 93
Lamartine, A. de, 69–70 n.11
Lane, Anthony, 199 n.16
Languet, 159
Laplanche, Jean, 49 n.7, 89 n.9
Laqueur, Thomas, 2, 3, 32 n.26, 34 n.38, 98, 111 n.15, 114 n.69, 154–5
Lawrence, D. H., 95
Lawrence, W. W., 141 n.4
Lee, Sir Henry, 23
Lee, Sir Sidney, 163 n.1
Leech, Clifford, 71 n.25
Levenson, Jill, 69 n.10
Lever, J. W., 31 n.19
Levin, Carole, 30 n.16
Levin, Harry, 50 n.30, 70 n.12
Levine, Laura, 8, 9, 89 n.14
Lintott, Bernard, 164 n.20, 164 n.26
Loomba, Ania, 167 n.61
Lucian, 181
Luhrmann, Baz, 185, 186, 187, 188, 189–90, 193, 194, 197
Lupton, Julia Reinhard, 51 n.44
Lyly, John, *Endimion*, 83, 84
Lyly, William, 155–6

MacCary, W. Thomas, 90 n.28
McCown, Gary, 70 n.12
McGill, Donald, 94
McGinn, Donald, 143 n.37
Machiavelli, Niccolò, 135, 144 n.51
Maclean, Ian, 143 n.47, 145 n.69
McLuskie, Kathleen, 3, 8, 198 n.4
Mahood, M. M., 29 n.4, 69 n.10
Malone, Edmond, 148–58, 159, 164 n.27
Mann, Thomas, *Death in Venice*, 72, 75
Marlowe, Christopher, 6, 196
    Hero and Leander, 19, 21
    Tragedy of Dido Queen of Carthage, The, 56
Marotti, Arthur F., 165 n.39
Marston, John
    Insatiate Countess, The (with William Barksted), 68 n.2, 69 n.7
    Jack Drum's Entertainment, 68 n.2
    Scourge of Villainie, The, 69 n.3
Massey, Gerald, 69 n.11
Masten, Jeffrey, 7
Maus, Katharine Eiseman, 111 n.6
Mead, Margaret, 94
Mellor, Aubrey, 49 n.16

Meres, Francis, 159
Middleton, Thomas, 75
    Changeling, The (with William Rowley), 97, 113 n.50
    Roaring Girl, The (with Thomas Dekker), 8
    Women Beware Women, 33 n.31
Milson, S. F. C., 142 n.27
Milton, John, 23, 33 n.31
    Comus, 31 n.19
    Paradise Lost, 48
Moisan, Thomas, 51 n.42, 88 n.2
Montaigne, Michel de,
    Apologie of Raymond Sebond, 42–3
    'Of Friendship', 90 n.30
Montrose, Louis Adrian, 30 n.15, 144 n.57
Mowat, Barbara, 4
Mukherji, Subha, 116–45
Mullaney, Steven, 79
Mulvey, Laura, 198 n.7

Nashe, Thomas, 109, 110
    Unfortunate Traveller, The, 114 n.73, 144 n.49
National Theatre, 183
Neely, Carol Thomas, 4
Nevo, Ruth, 29 n.9
Newman, Karen, 6, 89 n.3
Nietzsche, Friedrich, 95
Nohrnberg, James, 33–4 n.32
Noonan, J. T., 120
Nosworthy, J. M., 70 n.17
Novy, Marianne, 50 n.34, 51 n.38
Nuttall, A. D., 141 n.9

Oldys, William, 154
Orgel, Stephen, 8, 9, 81, 87, 89 n.14, 111 n.8. 166 n.50, 166 n.52, 178–9
Orwell, George, 93–4, 95
Osborne, Laurie E., 199 n.10
Ovid, 56
    Metamorphoses, 25, 41–2, 89 n.6

Palace of Pleasure, The, 129, 137, 142 n.24
Paltrow, Gwyneth, 196
Parey, Ambrose, 27–8, 32 n.25
Parker, Barbara L., 50–1 n.36
Parker, Oliver, 185, 187, 189, 190–2, 197
Parker, Patricia, 9
Parnassus Plays, 52–3, 182 n.2
Partridge, Eric, 10–11, 114 n.63, 114 n.66
Paster, Gail Kern, 9, 112 n.23
Patey, Douglas Lane, 145 n.69
Pequigney, Joseph, 6
Pettie, George, *The Petite Pallace of Pettie his Pleasure*, 44, 46

Pfeiffer, Michelle, 193
Pilkington, Ace G., 199 n.11
Plato, *Symposium*, 40–1
Plutarch, *Moralia*, 100
Polanski, Roman, 185, 186
Pontalis, J.-B., 89 n.9
Porter, Henry, *The Two Angry Women of Abington*, 52–4, 57–64, 66–8
Porter, Joseph A., 6, 50 n.19, 50 n.32
Prest, W. R., 144 n.52
Primaudaye, Pierre de la, *The French Academie*, 113 n.37, 114 n.69
Problems of Aristotle, The, 110 n.2, 112 n.26, 112 nn.28–9
Prospero's Books, 185
Puritan, The, 52, 63–4
Puttenham, George, *The Arte of English Poesie*, 78–80, 81

Quaife, G. R., 144 n.62
Queensland Theatre Company, 49 n.16
Quinze Joyes de Mariage, Les, 100

Rabelais, François, 25, 113 n.55
Rackin, Phyllis, 5, 8
Raine, James, 141 n.12, 142 n.17, 143 n.43
Ramsey, Paul, 167 n.56
Ranald, M. L., 140 n.3
Redfern, Walter, 53
Reinhard, Kenneth, 51 n.44
Ricks, Christopher, 111 n.20
Rimmon-Kenan, Shlomith, 49 n.3
Roesslin, Eucharius, 34 n.38
Rollins, Hyder E., 146–7, 164 n.11, 164 n.23, 166 n.46
Rose, Jacqueline, 4
Rose, Mary Beth, 8, 29 n.1, 90–1 n.36, 113 n.44
Rose Theatre, 61
Rougemont, Denis de, 74
Rowley, William, *The Changeling* (with Thomas Middleton), 97, 113 n.50
Rubinstein, Frankie, 10–11, 70 n.14
Rueff, James, 32 n.25, 32 n.27
Ryan, Kiernan, 88 n.2

Sadler, John, 34 n.38
Saslow, James M., 6
Schafer, Elizabeth, 9
Schleiner, Winfried, 34 n.35
Schwartz, Murray M., 3
Scott, Michael, 68 n.2
Sedgwick, Eve Kosofsky, 6, 87, 165 n.30, 179
Sewell, George, 153

Shakespeare, William,
    All's Well That Ends Well, 10, 17, 20, 24, 53, 95, 97, 107–8, 116–45, 182 n.4
    Antony and Cleopatra, 4, 15, 23, 48, 169, 175–6, 177
    As You Like It, 8–9, 21, 96, 170, 171, 172, 173, 180
    Coriolanus, 104
    Cymbeline, 10, 23
    Hamlet, 4, 9, 15, 21, 28, 30 n.11, 33 n.28, 43, 48, 107, 110, 112 n.23, 169, 171–2, 173, 185, 194, 199 n.9
    Henry IV, 165 n.41, 173
    Henry V, 15, 169, 173
    Henry VI, 175
    1 Henry VI, 23, 169
    2 Henry VI, 21, 175
    3 Henry VI, 23
    King Lear, 3, 4, 9, 18, 29 n.11, 32 n.23, 102–3, 109, 161, 162, 169, 170
    'Lover's Complaint, A', 112 n.24
    Love's Labour's Lost, 10, 15–6, 94, 95, 99–100, 113 n.39
    Macbeth, 23, 48, 79, 80, 169, 172, 185, 186
    Measure for Measure, 3, 4, 10, 17–18, 21, 92–4, 97, 111 n.19, 141 n.9, 144 n.53, 169, 170
    Merchant of Venice, The, 6, 17, 72–91, 173
    Merry Wives of Windsor, The, 15, 16
    Midsummer Night's Dream, A, 15, 22, 28, 44, 92, 103, 172, 174, 185–6, 187, 192–4
    Much Ado About Nothing, 10, 53, 57, 84–5, 94, 103, 170, 172, 173, 180
    Othello, 9, 10, 15, 18, 20, 24, 48, 53, 72, 84, 99, 103–4, 105–7, 169, 172, 185, 187, 189, 190–2, 197
    Pericles, 17, 21, 24, 32 n.24, 115 n.77, 140
    Rape of Lucrece, The, 9–10, 114 n.76
    Richard III, 28, 169
    Romeo and Juliet, 10, 21, 23, 35–51, 52–71, 115 n.78, 168, 169, 183, 185, 186, 187–90, 195–6, 197
    Sonnets, 6, 36, 113 n.50, 146–67
    Sonnet 2, 154, 159
    Sonnet 5, 161
    Sonnet 6, 158, 161
    Sonnet 10, 158
    Sonnet 11, 158
    Sonnet 13, 158
    Sonnet 16, 160
    Sonnet 17, 159
    Sonnet 20, 147, 148, 149–50, 153
    Sonnet 25, 166 n.48
    Sonnet 27, 70 n.19
    Sonnet 53, 153

Sonnet 62, 160
Sonnet 63, 160, 166 n.48
Sonnet 93, 149, 150
Sonnet 101, 147
Sonnet 104, 147
Sonnet 105, 147
Sonnet 106, 147
Sonnet 108, 147
Sonnet 109, 163 n.6
Sonnet 110, 147, 166 n.48
Sonnet 111, 149
Sonnet 122, 149
Sonnet 126, 154, 157, 160
Sonnet 127, 154, 159
Sonnet 128, 162
Sonnet 129, 160–1
Sonnet 131, 160
Sonnet 132, 160
Sonnet 135, 160, 161
Sonnet 136, 160, 161
Sonnet 137, 160, 161
Sonnet 138, 160
Sonnet 144, 154, 160, 161
Sonnet 145, 165 n.42
Sonnet 147, 160, 161
Sonnet 150, 160
Taming of the Shrew, The, 102, 172, 197
Tempest, The, 24, 54, 170, 173
Timon of Athens, 104
Titus Andronicus, 18
Troilus and Cressida, 53, 108, 170–1, 176
Twelfth Night, 8–9, 28, 29, 112 n.27, 172, 173, 174, 175
Two Gentlemen of Verona, The, 23, 84, 171
Two Noble Kinsmen, The, 14, 21, 23–4, 84, 87–8
Venus and Adonis, 42, 114 n.68
Winter's Tale, The, 22, 95, 101–2, 140, 172, 173, 174
Shakespeare in Love, 185–6, 187, 195–6, 197
Shapiro, Michael, 9
Sharpham, Edward,
  Cupid's Whirligig, 68 n.2
  Fleire, The, 71 n.25
Shaw, George Bernard, 10
Shepherd, Simon, 34 n.35
Sidney, Sir Philip, 37, 153
  Arcadia, 159
Sinfield, Alan, 37
Sissons, Neil, 92
Smith, A. J., 95
Smith, Bruce R., 12 n.35, 164 n.19, 166 n.50, 167 n.57
Smith, Paul, 5
Snitow, Ann Barr, 200 n.22

Snow, Edward, 51 n.38, 70 n.20, 113 n.54, 114 n.56, 114 n.64, 115 n.84
Socrates, 40–1
Spark, Muriel, *The Prime of Miss Jean Brodie*, 183
Spenser, Edmund, 108, 149, 153, 166 n.50
  Amoretti, 23
  Faerie Queene, 23, 81, 86, 109–10, 111–12 n.20, 113 n.39, 167 n.60
  Fowre Hymnes, 41
  Shepheardes Calendar, The, 113 n.39, 159
Stallybrass, Peter, 114 n.60, 163–4 n.8, 179
Steevens, George, 148, 150–1, 154, 164 n.20
Stockholder, Kay, 3, 44
Stone, Lawrence, 165 n.33
Stratton, Jon, 181
Strong, Sir Roy, 30 n.15, 32 n.28, 34 n.36
Stubbes, Phillip, 33 n.28
Sundelson, David, 3
Swetnam the Woman Hater, 95
Swinburne, Henry 116–18, 122–3, 127, 128, 131, 132, 133–4, 136, 137, 141, n.8, 141 n.11, 142 n.16, 143 n.34

Tasso, E. and T., *Of Marriage and Wiving*, 112 n.29
Taylor, Barry, 29 n.2
Taylor, Gary, 153–4, 166 n.47, 198 n.4
10 Things I Hate About You, 197
Theyam, 180
Thomas, Sir Keith, 114 n.62
Thompson, Ann, 1–13
Thompson, Stith, 89 n.17, 143 n.33
Thorpe, Thomas, 149
Thorssen, Marilyn J., 6
Tilley, M. P., 113 n.55
Tillyard, E. M. W., 90 n.27
Tofte, Robert, 100
Tolson, Jay, 200 n.21
Tourneur, Cyril, *The Revenger's Tragedy*, 96–7
Traub, Valerie, 3, 4, 7, 9, 179
Trilling, Lionel, 114 n.61
Turner, James Grantham, 112 n.30, 113 n.45
Turner, Victor, 35
Tyler, Margaret, 108

Underdown, D. E., 114 n.60

Varchi, B., *The Blazon of Jealousy*, 98
Vaughan, Henry, 33 n.28
Verstegan, Richard, 166 n.51
Vicary, Thomas, *The Anatomie of the Bodie of Man*, 22, 98
Vickers, Nancy, 9–10, 114 n.76
Virgil, 166 n.50

Warner, Marina, 18, 30 n.12
Webbe, William, 152
Webster, John, *The White Devil*, 112 n.20
Westbrook, David, 92
West Side Story, 39
Wheeler, Richard P., 30 n.15
Whiting, Leonard, 192
Whittier, Gayle, 35, 51 n.39, 69 n.10
Wiesner, Merry E., 114 n.60
Wikander, Matthew H., 8
Wilde, Oscar, 7
Willbern, David, 34 n.37
Williams, Gordon, 11
Williams, Linda, 198 n.1
Williamson, Marilyn, 51 n.40
Wilson, Katharine M., 166 n.46

Wilson, Scott, 89 n.13
Wilson, Thomas, 155, 158
Wind, Edgar, 112 n.33, 113 nn.39–41, 113 n.43
Winterson, Jeanette, *The Passion*, 72, 75
Wittkower, Rudolf, 34 n.32
Woodbridge, Linda, 69 n.4, 111 n.11
Worthen, W. B., 199 n.16
Wright, Celeste Turner, 34 n.35
Wroth, Lady Mary, 114 n.61
Wyatt, Sir Thomas, 90 n.20

Yates, Frances A., 30 n.15

Zeffirelli, Franco, 183, 185, 186, 187–90, 192, 197
Zimmerman, Susan, 71 n.22